BILLING Innovations

New Win-Win Ways to End Hourly Billing

Richard C. Reed

ABA Section of Law Practice Management

Cover design by Gail Patejunas.

Printed in the United States of America.

Library of Congress Catalog Card Number 96-83726

ISBN 1-57073-295-7

00 99 98 97 96 5 4 3 2 1

Dedicated to the memory of HAROLD A. FEDER,
inspiration to all who knew him, valued member
of the Section of Law Practice Management,
beloved by his friends and family.

Contents

PART TWO

How to implement innovative billing; the relationship and importance of client trust and satisfaction; motivating lawyers to change how law is practiced; overcoming lawyer resistance to alternative billing methods; the imperative for change; designing for the future.

Acknowledgments

Thanks go to all who contributed to this third book on alternative billing methods. Specifically, the names of those lawyers who have shared their knowledge and fee agreements with the legal profession are shown in the notes that end each chapter.

I would be remiss if I failed to thank Charles F. Robinson, Clearwater, Florida, who had the foresight as chair of the Law Practice Management Section in 1987–88 to see the need for reexamination of hourly billing and to appoint the Task Force on Alternative Billing Methods. It was Gary A. Munneke who recruited me to edit *Beyond the Billable Hour: An Anthology of Alternative Billing Methods* (1989) and Paula S. Tsurutani who came up with the title of that book. This led to *Win-Win Billing Methods: Alternatives That Satisfy Your Clients and You* (1992), the joint product of task force members Robert J. Arndt, Luther J. Avery, Ezra Tom Clark Jr., William C. Cobb, Demetrios Dimitriou, Richard C. Reed, and Milton W. Zwicker.

While others may rightly claim credit for the success of the earlier books, only I can accept the responsibility for the contents of this third part of what has turned out to be a trilogy. My self-assigned task has been to chronicle what has happened in the legal profession since 1987 and to predict what it will take for lawyers to succeed in providing quality legal services and value to clients in the years to come. Arthur G. Greene of Manchester, New Hampshire, made valuable comments and suggestions on how to best convey my intended message.

Most important, I thank my wife, Darelyn Reed, for tolerating my long hours preparing the draft and for her painstaking review of the text, exercising her sharp eye for typos and punctuation and her poetic ear for the sound and the flow of language. Yes, she had the courage to tell me what was right and what was wrong with my chosen words. Our marriage of forty-eight-plus years has survived another test!

Richard C. Reed
Bellevue, Washington

About the Author

Richard C. Reed practiced law for forty-one years in Seattle, Washington, and was chairman of the board of the Reed McClure law firm. Since 1989 he has been a management consultant to the legal profession in the Bellevue, Washington, office of Altman Weil Pensa. He is a past chair of the American Bar Association's Law Practice Management Section and was chair of the Task Force on Alternative Billing Methods. He was editor-author of two books, *Beyond the Billable Hour: An Anthology of Alternative Billing Methods* and *Win-Win Billing Strategies: Alternatives That Satisfy Your Clients and You* and the author of *Managing a Law Practice: The Human Side*, all published by the American Bar Association. He wrote the chapters on compensation and billing in *The Lawyer's Handbook, 3rd edition*. He was editor-author of *Applying Total Quality Management to the Law Office* published in 1993 by Altman Weil Pensa Publications. He has written extensively for legal periodicals including *Law Practice Management*, the *ABA Journal*, and the *National Law Journal*.

In addition, Mr. Reed has lectured frequently at the Institute on Law Firm Management, the American Bar Association, the Canadian Bar Association, the Law Society of Upper Canada, and the state bar associations of Arizona, Oregon, Kansas, and Washington.

He is currently president and a member of the Board of Trustees of the College of Law Practice Management, an honorary organization that recognizes individuals who have contributed to law practice management for a period of ten years or longer.

Mr. Reed has A.B. and J.D. degrees from the University of Chicago and now lives in Bellevue, Washington.

Foreword

In 1989, the American Bar Association's Section of Law Practice Management published the landmark study, *Beyond the Billable Hour: An Anthology of Alternative Billing Methods.* This best-selling work was produced by the Section's Task Force on Alternative Billing Methods, chaired by Richard C. Reed, to share the task force's research and work product on the question of how to set fees for legal services—fees that are fair to both the clients and the lawyers, in an era where increased use of computers and other technology has made the lawyer's time an unreliable measure of value in many instances.

Beyond the Billable Hour sparked numerous seminars and programs where hundreds of lawyers shared their experiences with alternative methods of valuing legal services. The resulting dialogue between law firms and corporate counsel encouraged development of and debate over many innovative billing methods and the relation of issues such as value, quality, ethics, financial and cost management, and law firm administration. This continuing dialogue resulted in publication by LPM of the best-selling *Win-Win Billing Strategies: Alternatives That Satisfy Your Clients and You.* In their second book, Mr. Reed and the task force provided in-depth discussion of value billing concepts, with practical and detailed steps for implementing alternative billing procedures, including twenty fee agreements in use by lawyers.

Interest in alternative billing arrangements among corporate counsel and other clients and the law firms has skyrocketed. It seems that every legal periodical and even the popular press is examining the subject, from the point of view of the clients who wish to limit the costs of legal services and from the perspective of the lawyers who are motivated to change or are resistant to it. Richard Reed has remained at the forefront of lawyers involved in this revolution in how legal services are valued. In *Billing Innovations: New Win-Win Ways to End Hourly Billing,* Mr. Reed reports from the front on the new billing and pricing methods currently in use among solo, small, medium, and large firms, and what corporate counsel are doing. In addition, he shows how to implement innovative billing procedures in a firm, how to overcome resistance to change, and how to integrate strategic planning, quality control, compensation, marketing, governance, and technology systems to produce an environment where value billing methods can succeed.

LPM Publishing specializes in producing practical materials that expose lawyers to the latest information and tools for responding to the changing nature of the practice of law and assists them in obtaining and maintaining client trust and satisfaction. We believe that this book, like its two predecessors, should be required reading for all law firms, small and large, planning for success in the twenty-first century.

Robert J. Conroy
Judith L. Grubner
Co-Chairs, LPM Publishing

Preface

> The manager administers, the leader innovates. The manager maintains, the leader develops. The manager relies on systems, the leader relies on people. The manager counts on controls, the leader counts on trust. The manager does things right, the leader does the right things.
>
> —*Fortune* magazine

Some of you may have read *Beyond the Billable Hour: An Anthology of Alternative Billing Methods*,[1] which was designed to raise questions about how lawyers charge for their services. Others may be familiar with *Win-Win Billing Strategies: Alternatives That Satisfy Your Clients and You*,[2] a how-to-do-it book describing how billing alternatives could be used in day-to-day law practice. Maybe some have read both books. It is not my intention to duplicate either of the earlier books, although references will be made to some of the concepts and ideas they include.

This book is intended to make sense to readers who have not seen the others. It is also intended to demonstrate how ingenious lawyers have explored and successfully used innovative billing. The ultimate purpose of this book is to give testimonial that billing methods other than straight hourly billing *do* work in the real world of law practice.

Part One consists of seven chapters that describe what the billing methods are and how they are being used. The significant news is that ingenious lawyers are adapting some of the fourteen generic billing methods described in detail in *Win-Win Billing Strategies* (and repeated here in chapter 2 for your convenience), customizing their approaches to billing and pricing of legal services, while, at the same time, changing the way they provide those services. Chapters 1 and 2 provide a brief background of the movement away from straight hourly billing. Chapters 3 and 4 include examples of these new methods with copies of actual representation agreements used by progressive lawyers. To measure the extent of the change that has occurred in the years since *Beyond the Billable Hour* was published in 1989, chapter 5 includes survey results measuring quantitatively the extent of the change. Chapter 6 describes in greater detail the most frequently used alternative method, the fixed fee. Chapter 7 concentrates on litigation, the practice area where alternative methods are most frequently used.

Part Two, comprising chapters 8 through 19, deals with how to implement a changed approach to billing and pricing, including important concepts and techniques in the evolving ways that law firms are meeting the needs of their clients. The theme that runs through these considerations is *the need for client trust,* which results when lawyers identify the objectives of their clients, determine the value to the client of their services, charge based on client value, and deliver quality services. Meeting these objectives will require many changes in the way law is practiced. *Where there is client satisfaction, there will be client trust, and where there is client trust, most often there will be client satisfaction.*

The last chapters relate to how to motivate lawyers to change to meet the demands of the future and how to organize your practice. The final chapter points the way to the future by synthesizing the relevant concepts that will lead to enduring success for lawyers who are willing and able to change, to innovate, and to move to new dimensions in practice management. It is intended to challenge your thinking and to stimulate you to think in terms of new paradigms.

It has become abundantly clear that billing and pricing should not be considered as a single topic isolated from other functions of the legal organization. How you measure value in your billing and pricing is intertwined with the other five component functions of your practice, namely, strategic planning, producing quality services, marketing, instituting a compensation system that motivates and rewards, and firm governance, all of which must be internally consistent and mutually supportive. Although chapters on these functions are separated (in sequence, chapters 11, 14, 12, 16, 15, and 17, respectively), the reader should be constantly aware that what you do in one of your component functions will affect the other functions.

Throughout this trip you should bring your own creative ideas into each discussion. The predicted route is not necessarily the only one. You can develop your own permutations, map your own route to success. In doing so, you will benefit and will help the profession move into new win-win relationships.

Although in preparing the two earlier books the Task Force on Alternative Billing Methods never contended that hourly billing would completely disappear, it is probable that straight hourly billing (billing by hours spent without limit and without regard for the benefits conferred) will virtually disappear in the years ahead.

Without a doubt, quality and value will be the keys to excellence and success in the years to come. Lawyer-client relationships based on mutual trust and satisfaction are prerequisites. The time has come to say goodbye to time as the *sole* criterion for measuring the value of legal services.

NOTES

1. Richard C. Reed, ed., *Beyond the Billable Hour: An Anthology of Alternative Billing Methods* (Chicago: Section of Law Practice Management, American Bar Association, 1989).

2. Richard C. Reed, ed., *Win-Win Billing Strategies: Alternatives That Satisfy Your Clients and You* (Chicago: Section of Law Practice Management, American Bar Association, 1992).

PART 1

New billing and pricing methods—and how they are being used

CHAPTER 1

Evolution and Revolution in the Practice of Law

MAYBE THE LEGAL PROFESSION has reached such a stage of perfection in straight hourly billing that other industries are beginning to copy the legal approach. Enjoy this report from Kevin B. Pratt, a lawyer in Colorado Springs, Colorado.[1]

AIRLINES GOING TO BILLABLE HOURS?

The Denver lawyer stepped up to the airline ticket counter and asked to buy a ticket for a flight to Chicago.

"No problem," said the clerk, "but before I issue the ticket, I should remind you of the new way we charge for tickets. This year we have adopted a 'basic rate' of three dollars a minute for our flights. The clock starts when you check in at the gate and stops when you pick up your luggage. We mail you a bill about two months after the flight."

"Well, I guess that's okay," commented the lawyer.

The clerk continued, "Remember, we call it a 'basic rate' because we sometimes adjust that rate up or down if the flight is very empty or very full. Too, we may multiply that rate if our expert pilot finds a tailwind. We also adjust the rate according to what you will be doing in Chicago. You look like a lawyer, so I'll assume it's very important that you get there by plane, so we quadruple the basic rate. Another thing, how much is your annual income? You see, if you earn a great deal and it turns out the plane crashes, we will have to pay more on your spouse's damage claim, and we have, of course, to consider that increased risk of the airline."

The astounded lawyer choked, "But how much will this trip cost me? How do I know you don't slow down on purpose? How do I know your bill will be correct?"

The clerk stared down over the end of his nose. "I can see you're not familiar with the complexities of airline work. There are so many things we just can't know in advance—the winds, traffic delays, the weather, the routing. Airlines are a business, and we have to make a

> profit to stay in business. Now don't worry, we're very honest and sensitive about all this billing business and I am sure you'll be pleased with our fully itemized bill when you get it. If there's any question just call." Then the clerk whispered, "But just so we understand each other, if you don't pay the bill in full and promptly, you'll never fly on this airline again."
>
> "Oh," grunted the Denver lawyer, "is there anything else I should know?"
>
> The clerk smiled thoughtfully and murmured, "On your flight there is a new copilot in training, and we charge an additional 50 cents a mile. Copilots are really very important, you know, to carry the pilot's charts, to fly on clear calm days, even to land the plane if the pilot is busy with other matters. Too, if you fly with us again, your copilot may have become your pilot. Wouldn't that be great? One other thing, if the copilot uses computerized flight routing there will be an additional $75 charge. But of course computerized flight routing is almost standard charge with technologically advanced airlines."
>
> "But I just wanted to get to my meeting in Chicago and come home. Now I don't even know if I should fly at all," groaned the lawyer.
>
> The clerk smiled again. "Mature passengers come to understand that flying is just a cost of doing business. They never know how much it costs 'til we bill them. But then, there's really no choice, is there?"
>
> "No," conceded the lawyer, "I guess not."
>
> And then the lawyer tried again. "Why can't you just give me a fixed price and I'll decide if I'll go or not?"
>
> The clerk frowned. "But we can't do that. That wouldn't be fair to you. We might overcharge you and then you'd be unhappy. Or we might underestimate and then the airline would lose money and couldn't maintain the planes, and we certainly don't want that."
>
> And so the Denver lawyer came to hate airlines and took his revenge by regaling acquaintances at cocktail parties about the new pitfalls of airline travel.
>
> Fortunately, none of you readers run an airline, so you won't feel defensive.

This is more than a book about dollars. It will deal with changes, threats, and challenges that confront the legal profession. There are implications that many, if not most, legal practitioners choose to ignore, if they are aware of at all, the tremendous problems that must be solved in providing quality legal services at a price clients can afford.

The types of services, the requirements of clients, the organizational structure of law firms, the methods of practice, the pricing framework for legal services, and the competitive pressures are changing with a rapidity never before experienced. Unless lawyers take action to adapt to these new conditions, the fallout from the ever-accelerating evolutionary and revolutionary changes will affect the professional and personal lives of lawyers and ultimately the role of the legal profession in society.

It has been said that if there were no lawyers, it would be necessary for society to invent lawyering, by whatever name, to act as the regulators and protectors of individuals in their relationships with each other and in the society in which they live. Therefore, the premise is that the role of lawyers in society is worthwhile and valid, notwithstanding the current vilification of the processes of the law and of lawyers as a group.

One of the major complaints against lawyers is that they charge too much for their services. With time being a major criterion for billing, the complaints against total cost become criticism that lawyers are not efficient or productive, or, at the very least, have little incentive to minimize time spent because it would diminish the fees to be charged.

That is why the question was asked, "Is billing by the hour the best and fairest way to set the value of legal services?" This was the issue raised back in 1987 by the Task Force on Alternative Billing Methods of the Law Practice Management Section.

In examining the various methods of billing, two major themes predominate. The first, and most obvious, is

Any billing method that does not depend exclusively on time spent *as a measure of value* provides an incentive for efficiency and early resolution of the matter being handled.

The second theme that is becoming increasingly apparent is that you cannot consider billing methods as a separate, compartmentalized part of the practice of law. The value of legal services to the client and the quality of the services, both *as perceived by the client*, are inextricably tied together, if not synonymous. The deeper you get into consideration of billing methods the more apparent it is that how you charge for legal services is tied to what kind of law practice you have, how you provide those services, and whether the services meet the needs and desires of the clients.

From the lawyer's point of view, billing by the hour may seem appropriate and advantageous (although a strong argument to the contrary will be made in a later chapter). From the client's point of view, "time" is not what clients feel they are buying when they consult a lawyer. Clients want favorable solutions, results, and benefits.

Both evolution and revolution involve change. "Evolution" connotes a gradual process of moving from a lower to a higher level. "Revolution" connotes a sudden, radical, or complete change. As these terms relate to the legal profession, more particularly to billing methods, we may still be in an evolutionary stage, but, if the rate of change continues to accelerate in the future at the same or greater speed, legal historians may look back and call it a revolution.

Consider the impact of technology in the past ten years on the legal profession and on society as a whole. Before the computer, law practice was carried on in the way it had been for decades. In the past five years the whole realm of technology and communications has changed at a mind-boggling rate. Telecommunications have increased the pace of living. Lawyers are expected to have facsimile machines. Clients use and require their lawyers to use mobile phones, phones from airplanes, electronic mail, voice mail, and other devices that enable almost instant lawyer-client contact. Computer research to databases is available to all practitioners. Anyone who purchased a personal computer five years ago knows that changes in technology have made that PC obsolete.

The ultimate reason for the utilization of technology in law practice is to reduce the human time required. For lawyers billing only for time spent, the greater the savings in time the lower the income of the firm. The cost of technology is hard to capture when straight hourly billing is predominant. This is called the productivity paradox. To remain financially stable, lawyers must deal with this problem.

Hourly billing is essentially cost-based billing. Determine in some way the cost of producing services, add a profit factor, bill by the hour, and hope for the best. Today firms are in transition from this cost-based system (which is lawyer-focused) to billing in methods that relate to value or benefits conferred (which is client-focused).

It has become apparent that success in moving from hourly billing to alternate methods is strongly influenced by the degree of mutual trust and level of satisfaction in the lawyer-client relationship. Where mutual trust exists, it will be easier to move to alternative methods. In new client relationships, or in existing relationships that lack the desired mutual trust and satisfaction, efforts should be made to improve the quality of the service and the fairness of the fees.

We will appraise the extent to which alternative billing methods are being used to determine whether the principles of alternative billing are valid and the extent to which billing practices have changed in the current evolutionary process. Actual examples by way of testimonials will abound (a snapshot of the profession). Later chapters will deal with total relationships, best practices, threats and challenges, and the very real possibility of revolution, not evolution, in the practice of law (a bit of gazing into the crystal ball).

Many individuals and firms have shared information and ideas that will be incorporated into this book. At the end of each of the following chapters, endnotes will show attribution, contribution, and credit where appropriate.

Since our first book on alternative billing methods was published in 1989, there have been innovators, leaders, pioneers, copiers, procrastinators, skeptics, and naysayers on the subject. Among consultants and others informed about what is taking place in many firms around the country, there is a strong feeling that firms continuing in the old ways, even though now still profitable, may decline in the years ahead unless radical steps are taken. In chapter 3, where copies of innovative fee agreements are set forth, the firms described have done more than just change billing methods. They have set objectives, improved the quality of their work, given thought to optimum size and firm structure, and made other adjustments to make their firms client-focused. In doing so, marketing opportunities have been developed that place those firms in a more competitive position.

NOTE

1. Kevin B. Pratt, Esq., Colorado Springs, Colorado, published in the Denver Bar Association's *Docket*.

CHAPTER 2

The Past—A Bit of History of Alternative Billing Methods

THIS BOOK, *Billing Innovations: New Win-Win Ways to End Hourly Billing*, completes a trilogy, although it was not exactly planned that way back in 1987 when I was asked to head the Task Force on Alternative Billing Methods.

In retrospect, there is a logic to the series. *Beyond the Billable Hour: An Anthology of Alternative Billing Methods*, published in 1989, was intended to provoke thought, promote discussion, and ask questions about the pros and cons of various methods of billing. The collected articles contained differing, often contradictory, views of thirty-two different authors. Various examples and descriptions of billing methods were scattered throughout. It was the question book.

In the seminars that followed, many lawyers indicated a willingness to try alternative methods, but asked how to do it. This led to the second book, *Win-Win Billing Strategies: Alternatives That Satisfy Your Clients and You*, published in 1992. As editor/chapter author, I coordinated the contributions of the six other members of the task force. In trying to provide answers and illustrations, the approach was to make it a how-to-do-it book that would give the reader advice on the total process of billing. Step-by-step instructions were provided. Fourteen generic billing methods were outlined and discussed. William Cobb's Value Curve was explained, along with the distinction between billing method and pricing. Numerous legal representation agreements and examples of win-win billing methods were included. It was the answer book, and it remains the definitive work on the subject of billing methods. With few exceptions, only the concepts and definitions from that book will be included here. The book you are reading now can be read without having read the earlier *Win-Win*, but there will be double benefit if both are studied in detail.

The members of the task force and the Law Practice Management Section can rightfully take credit for starting the colloquy on billing methods. Like forming a small snowball at the top of hill and giving it a push, other events occurred to increase the momentum and scope of the movement. Indeed, the snowball has gained in size and momentum and is still rolling.

The major intervening event was the economic recession that struck in the early nineties (for which the task force accepts neither credit nor blame). In the frantic 1980s, mergers and acquisitions, junk bonds, high finance, high personal and business incomes, indifference to expense—all made for a seller's market for lawyers. Law firms grew exponentially. Law work poured in from corporate clients who seemed indifferent to high legal expense. Hourly billing flourished. The more timekeepers the higher the revenue. Leveraging added to law firm profits. Notwithstanding the flow of law school graduates entering the market year after year, most lawyers had all the work they could handle. As operating expense for salaries, space, and other overhead escalated, the answer was to increase the hourly rate to whatever the traffic would bear. It was paradise. Just keep on increasing the hourly rate, bill by the hour, increase the number of timekeepers, and increase the number of billable hours per lawyer. From the point of view of the lawyers, it was a golden era, and most clients didn't mind since the era was golden for them too. The indifference of clients to legal expense was matched by the indifference of law firms to efficiency. Work more, use more people, increase the number of billable hours, raise hourly rates, expand, branch, do not be concerned whether fees charged fairly reflect the value of the services—those were the rules of the game.

The recession hit the clients first. As corporate profits decreased, management looked for ways to cut corporate costs of operation. Legal expense became a target. In-house legal staff size increased when corporate counsel conceived that legal work could be produced at a lower cost in-house than with outside counsel. Corporate downsizing occurred first. The managers of businesses began to focus on efficiency and cost reduction. They became conscious of the need for quality of performance both inside their businesses and by the law firms serving them. Ultimately, the recession reached the legal profession, and the rules of the game for the 1980s no longer prevailed.

Some members of the legal profession, realizing that it was now a buyer's market, took appropriate steps to adjust to the new situation. Many did not, enunciating that this was but a phase that would pass and that the good old days would return. Long-term high-rent leases, reliance on bank financing to meet overhead or even to pay the draws of partners, and failure to recognize that this was a new ball game brought down prominent, long-established firms.

Initially, many corporate counsel were not attracted to the alternative billing methods advocated by the task force. Having been raised and trained on hourly billing, many lawyers attempting to deal with high outside legal expense felt more comfortable trying to control hourly billing excesses than in considering alternatives to hourly billing. Some attempted to force budgeting on matters being handled on an hourly billing basis. Others resorted to outside audit firms in an attempt to monitor and control legal expense. Many corporate counsel continued to permit hourly billing, but insisted on discounts. That practice continued all of the disincentives to efficiency characteristic of hourly billing and dealt merely with the pricing level. Task-based billing was instituted in an attempt to require statements for legal services to be organized in a way that would permit comparisons and be the basis for the control of total expense.

When confronted with these demands outside lawyers were forced to react and to rethink the way legal services were provided. Some firms reacted to the symptoms, not the cause. When law firm profitability decreased, some firms downsized, cut salaries, weeded out unproductive (pronounced "unprofitable") partners. As the profit squeeze continued, some firms split, dissolved, or merged, often for the wrong reasons. Yet the flood of newly admitted lawyers continued. The ratio of nonlawyers to lawyers in the United States continued to decrease. More lawyers competed for less and less legal business. Competition within the profession became more cutthroat.

Among the early reactions to proposals to use other than hourly billing, litigators were vocal in insisting that hourly billing was the only feasible method considering the variables inherent in litigation.

These are some of the major factors that accelerated the use of alternative billing methods. The task force did not, and could not, foresee that the movement towards billing for value would be given such impetus. Expectations were that the use of alternative billing methods would evolve slowly. It could not have been anticipated that gigantic forces would not only hasten the change but necessitate major changes in the way that law is practiced.

It should be noted here that whatever billing method you use, you should conform to the rules and decisions in your jurisdiction. For example, where there is a nonrefundable retainer (not permitted in some jurisdictions) the agreement should clearly state that the retainer is fully earned upon receipt. The agreement should be signed by the client. It is inconsistent to link hourly billing and a fully earned retainer. Certain contingent fee agreements are being scrutinized, criticized, and regulated.[1]

> *Remember:*
> Any billing method that does not depend exclusively on time spent *as a measure of value* provides an incentive for efficiency and early resolution of the matter being handled.

A SUMMARY OF GENERIC BILLING METHODS

As essential background for the material discussed and illustrated in later chapters, the meat of this chapter is a summary of the fourteen generic billing methods, presented in outline form for easy reference.

1. Fixed or Flat Fee

The fixed or flat fee is the price that will be charged for defined services. It may be the total fee for the engagement or may apply to segments of the total services. It may stand alone or be combined with either an hourly fee or a contingent fee.

Advantages

- Forces agreement between lawyer and client on what services will be required and furnished.
- Requires you to know cost of providing defined services.
- Client knows what the fee will be.
- Can be competitive with the market.
- Useful in marketing services.
- Not dependent on time spent.
- Can be keyed to value of benefits to client.

Disadvantages

- Unprofitable if cost of providing services exceeds estimated cost.
- Unprofitable if services are not performed efficiently.
- Unprofitable if there is no specific definition of what services are included and unforeseen problems arise requiring extra work that is clearly covered by the representation agreement.
- Should not be used when there are foreseeable uncertainties.

When to Use

- For routine services where experience shows what is normally required so that you can foresee and define included services.
- When you can estimate both the time required and the mix of standard billing rates.
- For commodity services in a highly competitive market.
- For volume work on a repetitive basis.
- When you are comfortable accepting the risk of unprofitability if cost of production exceeds the fixed fee.

Predictability of Total Fee

- Excellent—enables clients to know what the fee will be.

Incentive for Efficiency

- Encourages use of systems, appropriate delegation, and technology.

Recognition of Value to Client

- Can be priced to reflect value to client.
- Value to client rather than time expended can be the standard in setting the fee, subject to competitive market conditions.

2. Contingent Fee

The contingent fee is a charge that depends on the results achieved. It requires clear agreement on what the desired results will be. Those results may be positive (direct) in the sense of achieving a desired objective, or negative (reverse) in the sense of avoiding exposure to liability.

A contingent fee may be combined with a fixed or flat fee, or with hourly billing.

Advantages

- Client does not pay unless favorable result is achieved.
- Clients who are otherwise unable to pay can obtain legal representation.
- You assume the risk of providing services without assurance of being paid.
- Can be lucrative if you are careful in accepting the representation and screen cases well before agreeing to proceed.
- Depends on results, not time expended in obtaining results.
- Terms of representation can be clearly defined in fee agreement.

Disadvantages

- You assume risk of providing services without assurance of being paid.
- Carrying costs. The expense of litigation may have to be advanced or carried by the lawyer if the client is unable to do so.
- Some jurisdictions are limiting contingency percentages in prescribed cases.
- Uneven cash flow for the lawyer.
- The time and effort required may exceed estimates.

When to Use

- When it is desirable to represent individuals who are otherwise unable to pay.
- When your expertise and reputation attract good cases.
- When you can skillfully screen the desirability of a representation so that you accept only cases with a likelihood of success.

Predictability of Total Fee

- Clear formula for measuring results that determine the amount of the fee, even though the exact fee is not known at the outset.

Incentive for Efficiency

- Excellent, as your goal will be maximum results with the least expenditure of time and effort. However, if lawyer and client differ on whether the matter should be settled or tried, complications can arise.
- Not tied to time spent.

Recognition of Value to Client

- Tied directly to results achieved so presumably will reflect value.
- If matter is mishandled so that good results are not obtained, client will not receive value, even though no or low fee is paid.

3. Straight Hourly Billing

In the past quarter century hourly billing (sometimes referred to as time/rate billing) has predominated. It is predicated on the keeping of accurate, contemporaneous records of time expended by lawyers, legal assistants, and other staff members. The hourly rate for each fee charger is intended to cover the cost of production plus a profit factor. Therefore, knowing the cost of production is important, although many lawyers do not have reliable cost data. To some extent, hourly rates are market driven, particularly at the commodity level, and can reflect lawyer expertise and anticipated value at the high end of the Value Curve (described in Chapter 11).

Hourly billing has developed some non-time-related entries such as minimum time charged for particular services, for example, minimum time entries of a quarter hour or minimum entries for each letter or phone call.

Many lawyers or firms will have different rates for different fee chargers, and different rates for a specific lawyer depending on the type of service, the client, the subject matter, or other variables. These variations recognize that the value to the client will differ and that time spent, per se, does not accurately measure the fee to be charged.

Can be combined with contingent fee or fixed or flat fee billing.

Advantages

- Both lawyers and clients have become accustomed to the hourly method of billing and are, therefore, comfortable with this method and how it operates.
- Rate schedules can be set, quoted, and used by the lawyer and checked, monitored, and compared by clients.
- Billing can be somewhat automatic, particularly with computerized billing systems that multiply time recorded by pre-established rates per hour to produce statements.
- Subjective judgments in billing are not required.
- Detailed itemized statements based on contemporaneous time entries are a chronology of work done and can be a means of communication between lawyer and client.
- Detailed itemized statements when regarded as tangible evidence of work done create the appearance of objectivity and evidence of the services provided to justify the charge being made.
- All risks (except the risk of nonpayment of the fee) are placed on the client.

Disadvantages

- Client is unable to know what the total charges will be.
- Discourages efficiency, incentive to reach an early conclusion and to provide cost-effective services.
- Clients are resisting the high cost of legal services.
- Clients must accept all of the risks, including lawyer inefficiency.

- The fee charged may have little relationship to the value of the benefits received by the client.
- Time spent does not recognize the benefits of the use of systems and technology, nor does it compensate adequately for the cost of development of such methods.
- The lawyer is not adequately compensated in high-value and high-responsibility matters.
- Does not recognize extraordinary, priority, or emergency services.
- There are finite limits for billable hours per year and for hourly billing rates, so there is a cap on maximum gross income.
- Does not promote finding better ways to provide legal services at a reasonable cost to the client.

When to Use

- When the client demands hourly billing and will not consider alternative methods.
- When there are variables that cannot be foreseen with reasonable accuracy.
- When no reasonably fair alternative method can be used.
- When the lawyer is willing to accept the representation but not willing to accept any risk.
- In situations requiring court approval of fees, where the court only recognizes hourly billing in approving fees.

Predictability of Total Fee

- Difficult unless there is a guaranteed maximum.
- Sophisticated clients having past experience with similar matters and/or with prior use of the same lawyer may be able to anticipate the range of the fee that will be charged.
- Limited even with case control by the client.
- Dependent on willingness of lawyer to write down fee for client based on retrospective review.

Incentive for Efficiency

- Not inherent except to generally please the client and to preserve the lawyer-client relationship.
- Generally perceived to promote inefficiency and disregard for relating fee for services to the value to the client of those services.

Recognition of Value to Client

- Generally unrelated to value to the client. The lack of relationship between the amount of the fee and the value to the client may penalize either the lawyer or the client.

4. Blended Hourly

The blended hourly rate is a hybrid of the hourly rate. Instead of specific hourly rates for individual fee chargers, one rate applies to all hours billed on a matter.

Advantages

- Generally the same advantages as for the hourly method.
- Is thought to be more simple to negotiate and administer than the method of having specific rates for each fee charger.
- Can be advantageous to the lawyer if work can be performed by individuals with lower normal hourly billing rates. This is dependent on capabilities of those individuals and the retained right of the lawyer, not the client, to direct who will do the work.
- May encourage delegation.

Disadvantages

- Generally the same disadvantages as for the hourly method.
- Appears to be simple, but is still dependent on knowing cost of production.
- May endanger the quality of the work product unless quality controls are in place.
- Will be unprofitable unless the blend in practice is at the high end.

When to Use

- When the type of work involves a typical pattern and the fee-charger mix to do the work is reasonably foreseeable.
- Should not be used uniformly if the matters subject to the agreement vary in required level of expertise and specialization or in responsibility assumed.

Predictability of Total Fee

- Same as for hourly billing.

Incentive for Efficiency

- By providing incentive to delegate, there may be more efficient use of individual skills. Care must be taken to ensure quality of product and to avoid increased cost to the client if low-end personnel are markedly less efficient than high-end individuals.

Recognition of Value to Client

- Generally unrelated to value to the client. The lack of relationship between the amount of the fee charged and the value to the client may penalize either the lawyer or the client.

5. Fixed or Flat Fee plus Hourly

In this hybrid method, the portions of the services that can be defined as to scope are charged on a fixed or flat fee basis; the portions of the services that cannot be defined because of variables or uncertainties are charged on a time-rate or hourly basis. This method can be used in both litigation and transactional matters. Numerous variations can occur, and the sequence of steps in the method of charging may vary.

To illustrate the use of this method in a transactional matter, in an estate-planning assignment during the initial phase when the objectives of the client are being determined, asset information is being gathered, and tax ramifications are being determined, the services can be charged on an hourly basis. When the route has been determined and what will be required can be defined, the preparation of documents and services necessary to complete the assignment can be charged on a fixed or flat fee basis.

To illustrate the use of this method in litigation, a flat fee can be charged for handling what appears to be routine litigation with some agreement on what services are included for that fee. If it is necessary to do extra work, there can be an hourly charge for services beyond the original defined scope.

Advantages

- There is a compromise or balancing in risk-sharing and predictability of the fee by use of this blend.
- The advantages of the hourly and the fixed or flat fee methods are accordingly modified.
- If the fixed or flat fee is quoted after some of the variables or unknowns have been cleared, the client will have an economic basis upon which to decide to proceed.

Disadvantages

- There is a compromise or balancing in risk-sharing and predictability of the fee by use of this blend.
- The disadvantages of the hourly and the fixed or flat fee methods are accordingly modified.

When to Use

- When some but not all of the contemplated services can be defined so that a fixed or flat fee can be quoted. At the outset the general approach to charging can be specified even though the precise fixed or flat fee cannot be specified until some of the variables or unknowns have been cleared.

Predictability of Total Fee

- The method of charging will be agreed upon, though the exact total cannot be predicted because of the portion not included in the fixed or flat fee.

Incentive for Efficiency

- A combination of the incentives described above for the fixed or flat fee and hourly methods.

Recognition of Value to Client

- Compromise between the two methods.

6. Hourly plus a Contingency

By combining hourly billing and a contingency factor, client and lawyer are sharing risks within the limitations of the representation agreement. Since a portion of the fee will be hourly, the lawyer is guaranteed a minimum amount. This is true whether the hourly fee is based on regular hourly rates or the agreed hourly rates are lower than the regular rates. That will guarantee some payment to the lawyer but leave some risk with the client.

As in straight contingency agreements, both the client and the lawyer are motivated to obtain the maximum results since both will benefit.

It is important to define clearly the way the contingent fee will be measured. If the achieved result justifying the contingent fee is not directly expressed in dollars, there must be some agreement spelled out on the amount of the contingent fee and how it will be measured. For example, the basis for the contingent fee might be obtaining a rezoning, acquiring a business, or obtaining a restraining order, any of which needs to be assigned a value or tied to the fee amount that will be paid.

Advantages

- Lawyer and client share some of the risks and the benefits.
- The hourly fee offsets the cost of carrying the matter.
- The client will not pay the full hourly rate if the objective is not achieved, and will share proportionately only if there are benefits.
- May enable a client not able to pay fully to achieve a result for which the client will be able to pay because of the benefit received.

Disadvantages

- As with any contingent fee agreement, the lawyer must determine the chances of success and exercise care in accepting the representation.
- Disagreement can result if the fee agreement does not clearly define how the contingent fee will be computed.
- Except to the extent of the compromise, has the same disadvantages as both the hourly and the contingent fee methods.

When to Use

- With carefully selected clients.
- After careful appraisal of chances of success.
- Where significant potential dollar value exists (the contingent fee potential must offset the reduced hourly fee).

Predictability of Total Fee

- Limited.

Incentive for Efficiency

- Generally the same as with any continent fee representation.

Recognition of Value to Client

- Close relationship to value because of contingency factor and how success will be measured.

7. Percentage

Typically, percentage fees have been based on a schedule of fees related to the amount involved in the matter being handled. The amount may be predetermined or may, in some instances, be related to the amount ultimately determined. Examples include a percentage of the value of estates being probated, the amount of a real estate transaction, and the amount of a bond issue. The percentage rate may be constant or may be graduated.

Advantages

- Relatively easy to state the terms in the representation agreement.
- Reflects the amount involved and the exposure of the lawyer to liability.
- Is not dependent on time spent.
- If percentage and amount of transaction are predetermined, same advantages as fixed or flat fee.
- If percentage is known but amount of transaction is not known, same advantages as contingent fee.

Disadvantages

- If set too high, may not be competitive.
- If set too low, may be unprofitable.
- If complications arise and extra services are required, risk is on the lawyer, unless representation agreement closely defines what services are included.
- If percentage and amount of transaction are predetermined, same disadvantages as fixed or flat fee.
- If percentage is known but amount of transaction is not known, same disadvantages as contingent fee.

When to Use

- In situations as shown in the above examples.
- There appears to be a growing tendency to use a percentage fee in court awards in common fund fee approvals, in lieu of lodestar or hourly methods.

Predictability of Total Fee

- Method is known even if the amount of the fee cannot be calculated until the amount of the transaction is determined.

Incentive for Efficiency

- Good, because not tied to hours spent or duration of the transaction.
- Provides incentive to use most effective and most economical personnel to complete the assignment and maximize results.

Recognition of Value to Client

- To the extent that the amount involved represents value, this method recognizes value to client.

8. Retrospective Based on Value

This method differs in approach from most of the alternative billing methods in that the exact amount of the fee is not known to either lawyer or client until the matter is concluded. However, the factors that are to be considered in setting the final fee can be set forth in the representation agreement. Often these are the factors set forth in the Model Rules of Professional Conduct. It is possible to establish either a maximum or minimum fee that will be charged. May be combined with an hourly fee in setting a minimum by agreeing at the outset that the fee will be no less than a prescribed amount. The amount of the fee should be determined by the lawyer, not the client.

Advantages

- Allows a retrospective determination of the amount of the fee at a time when all uncertainties and unknowns no longer exist. An effort is made to equate the amount of the fee to the value to the client of the services performed.
- Dependent on benefits conferred rather than solely on time spent.
- Because determining the amount of the fee is subjective, can be more equitable than if some mechanical system is used.

Disadvantages

- Client does not know in advance what the fee will be.
- Is dependent on close and trusting lawyer-client relationship; not frequently used today.
- Sophisticated purchasers of legal services are wary of potential abuses and inability to budget or monitor legal expense.
- Should cut two ways with reduction of fee below normal hourly rates where value is not achieved despite efforts to do so or higher than normal rates if results are exceptional.
- Lawyer's determination of value may differ from client's perception of value received.
- If no payment is made until conclusion of the matter, the lawyer will have the cost of carry with limited cash flow, unless agreement is made for partial payment of fees as the matter progresses, subject to final adjustment.

When to Use

- When lawyer and client have a trusting relationship characterized by good communication and awareness by the client of the work that was done and the true value of the results.
- Use selectively depending on client and nature of the matter being handled.
- When both lawyer and client have confidence that the other will act fairly.

Predictability of Total Fee

- Difficult, unless a maximum or minimum range is set with clearly defined criteria for setting the fee.

Incentive for Efficiency

- Generally good, because time spent is not necessarily a major criterion.

Recognition of Value to Client

- By definition, the best way to relate fee charged to value to the client, conditioned on being applied fairly and equitably.

9. Availability-Only Retainer

The availability-only retainer, sometimes referred to as a "pure retainer" or "right-to-call retainer," is characterized by payment to the lawyer of a fee for which no direct services (or limited services as specified) will be performed, in exchange for the lawyer's commitment to be available when requested and to refrain within a specified time period from representing either parties adverse to the client or competitors of the client. This method is not widely used. It normally will be used when the lawyer has high-level expertise or prestige. The funds when received belong to the lawyer and need not be deposited into the client's trust account.

Advantages

- Lawyer is not expected to do any work for the fee.
- Client is assured of representation by the lawyer of client's choice.
- Client is assured that lawyer will not represent any party adverse to client or competitor of the client.
- Client may deem lawyer's prestige will add to the prestige of the client.

Disadvantages

- Lawyer will be unable to accept desirable work from other clients.
- Client may decide that amount paid does not bring expected benefits.
- Lawyer's loss of business opportunities may exceed amount of the retainer.

When to Use

- When the mutual benefits exceed the disadvantages.
- When the monetary amount is significant enough to justify being unable to take work from other clients.

Predictability of Total Fee

- Entirely predictable.

Incentive for Efficiency

- Not relevant, since no services are provided.

Recognition of Value to Client

- Should be reflected by the negotiated amount of the availability-only retainer.

The Washington State Formal Opinion 186 recognizes the distinction between "advance fee deposits," which are client funds and must be put into a trust account, and "retainers," which are funds paid by a client to secure a lawyer's availability over a given period of time. The funds are considered earned at the time of payment and must NOT be put into the client's trust account. This opinion cites *Baranowski v. State Bar,* 154 Cal. Rptr. 752,593 P.2d 613, 618, and Rule 1.14(a), Model Rules of Professional Conduct. Some jurisdictions prohibit nonrefundable retainers; others permit them, if reasonable in amount.

10. Retainer as a Deposit against Future Services

By way of definition, the retainer as a deposit against future services is distinguished from the payment of an annual retainer. The annual retainer is a subspecies of the fixed or flat fee, in which the client pays an agreed-upon annual or monthly amount for specified services such as informal counseling or telephone advice.

The retainer as a deposit against future services is not per se a billing method, but a technique to ensure that the client will pay for services to be rendered or for disbursements to be made on behalf of the client. The funds when received by the lawyer must be placed into the client's trust account, subject to withdrawal only when services have been performed or disbursements made on behalf of the client. At the conclusion of the representation, any balance must be returned to the client.

This technique can be used with a variety of billing methods, as it is a deposit against future charges however computed.

Advantages

- Requires financial commitment by the client at the start of the representation.
- Minimizes fee collection problems if retainer balance is kept at an agreed level throughout the representation.

- Enables lawyer to know throughout the representation that the lawyer will be paid.

Disadvantages

- Client must come up with up-front funds.
- If balance at the end of representation is insufficient to cover the final charges, there could be a collection problem.
- There may be a timing problem as to when client can take a tax deduction for legal expense.

When to Use

- From the standpoint of the lawyer, whenever possible for cash flow purposes.
- If there is doubt about when the lawyer has been hired and is obligated to the representation, a representation agreement specifying that the representation will start only when funds have been deposited will protect against certain malpractice claims.

Predictability of Total Fee

- Not relevant.

Incentive for Efficiency

- Not relevant.

Recognition of Value to Client

- Dependent on method of billing chosen.

11. Unit

The unit fee is a subspecies of the fixed or flat fee in that a fixed charge is made for a specific service irrespective of the actual time spent in providing that service. Illustrative are fixed charges for each letter, phone call, deposition, etc. This approach normally is combined with hourly billing for services not included in the unit billing. Some representation agreements provide that for a specified service either the unit fee or the hourly rate fee will be charged, whichever is greater.

Advantages

- Simplifies time recording somewhat.
- Reduces lost time from inadequate record-keeping.
- Can add a premium over straight hourly billing.

Disadvantages

- Distorts time records if records are used for purposes other than billing.
- May be deceptive if client believes fee will be charged on hourly basis.
- Requires clear explanation in representation agreement of what the unit charges will be.

When to Use

- When lawyer has accurate knowledge of typical time required to provide a specific service.
- When client will agree to this method.

Predictability of Total Fee

- Same as for hourly billing.

Incentive for Efficiency

- Encourages efficiency in providing the services covered by the unit fee portion of the representation agreement.
- Encourages minimum time expenditure for a specific service.

Recognition of Value to Client

- Not keyed to value unless unit price is below hourly rate.

12. Lodestar

The lodestar method of setting fees had its origin in the federal court system in *Lindy Brothers Builders, Inc. v. American Radiator & Standard Sanitary Corp.*, 487 F.2d 161 (3d Cir. 1973), and has been adopted in some states. To have an objective system that could be applied by the courts with some consistency, the method involves multiplying the hours spent by a reasonable billing rate per hour to determine the "lodestar." Then that amount is multiplied by a factor, e.g., 1.4, 1.7, 3.0, or 0.8, to recognize factors other than time spent.

Court decisions have restricted the factors that can be considered as a multiplier, contending that those factors are subsumed in the hourly billing rate. For example, "expertise" originally was a factor in determining the amount of the multiplier, but now is generally considered to be reflected in the hourly billing rate. Uncertainty of payment remains a factor for the multiplier.

Courts often set billing rates that are below the market and sometimes will disallow a portion of the hours expended if the court deems the hours unnecessarily spent.

One objection to the lodestar method is that approving fees based on the method takes up too much court time.

Advantages

- In theory, the hourly rate method can be modified upward or downward based on criteria other than time spent.

Disadvantages

- Same as those for the hourly billing method, plus the tendency of courts to disallow a portion of the hours expended.
- Many contend that this method encourages inefficiency, discourages early settlement, and is too complicated.

- As in any court approval process, permits second guessing of what was required.
- Awards may not reflect market value of the services.

When to Use

- When required by the court to do so.

Predictability of Total Fee

- Little predictability.

Incentive for Efficiency

- Very limited; padding may be encouraged if lawyer believes the court will most likely not allow all hours recorded.

Recognition of Value to Client

- None.

13. Relative Value

The relative value method of billing involves the creation of schedules that break down the services performed by a lawyer by subject matter and by task and assign a "relative value" or multiplier to each. Each fee charger can be assigned a different basic rate or charge that is then factored into the equation. There are variations in this method as used by individual practitioners who have developed their own schedules. Proprietary systems also exist.

Inherent in this approach is a determination or judgment in the first instance of the value of each component service or task. The predicate is that tasks performed by a lawyer differ in value, whereas straight hourly billing assumes that all time spent in performing various tasks has equal value.

Once the relative value schedules have been established, the base rate factor can be changed, thereby producing a changed fee.

The relative value method combines elements of hourly, fixed or flat fee, and value billing.

Advantages

- If uniformly used within a law firm, will tend to provide more uniform or consistent statements.
- Addresses value in the development of the schedules.
- May permit fine-tuning in fee determination.

Disadvantages

- Time-consuming to prepare and maintain schedules of relative value.
- Thought to be cumbersome to use.
- Client's perception of value may or may not coincide with values assigned in the schedules.

- May ignore such factors as results achieved or responsibility assumed unless final charges are reviewed.

When to Use

- When the tasks to be performed can be classified and are reasonably predictable.

Predictability of Total Fee

- Limited, except in routine matters that fall into a billing pattern.

Incentive for Efficiency

- Dependent on whether system is task-oriented rather than time oriented.

Recognition of Value to Client

- Inherent in this method is a determination of value in the production of legal services, which may or may not coincide with the client's perception of value.

14. Statutory or Other Scheduled Fee System

The amount to be paid for legal services is spelled out in some statutory enactments, in schedules for prepaid legal service plans, or by purchasers of legal services on a volume basis. Some are imposed, some are negotiated. Some may be fixed or flat fee; some prescribe methodology; some are in fee-shifting situations; some reflect government-imposed social policies.

Advantages

- Lawyers know in advance what the fee will be or how it will be computed.
- Client or the plan can negotiate fee amounts.
- From client point-of-view may aid in cost containment.

Disadvantages

- Often rigid and/or arbitrary.
- May not recognize the cost of production.
- May be out-of-date if not revised frequently.

When to Use

- When compelled to do so.
- When fee will fairly pay for services provided.

Predictability of Total Fee

- Reasonably predictable.

Incentive for Efficiency

- Can be incentive if fee is fixed and not dependent on time spent.

Recognition of Value to Client

- Typically not much correlation.

Moving from the past to the present, the most interesting development that has occurred is the extent to which innovation has been displayed by ingenious lawyers in adapting the generic billing methods to specific client situations. As we shall see in the chapters that follow, counsel have used caps; minimums; bonus provisions; royalty payments when relief obtained is ongoing (as when a copyright is established); credit against future or different legal work based on volume of work; guarantees of satisfaction; combinations of the generic methods; and other neat twists that reflect a departure from traditional billing methods.[2]

We no longer should think in terms of "alternative billing methods." The more accurate description is "innovative billing methods."

No matter what method of billing you use, there are three important caveats:

1 ▪ **The fee of lawyers must be reasonable.** Be sure to meet the ethical standards of your jurisdiction. In doing so, remember that time spent is but one of the criteria for determining reasonableness. Some jurisdictions prohibit certain types of agreements, by either statute, rule, or case decision.

2 ▪ **Discuss with your client the method of billing that you propose to use.** Recognize that a fiduciary relationship exists and that you must avoid any conflict of interest. This is especially true if you change from one billing method to another during the course of a representation, where it might be contended that the change was prompted by your superior knowledge of the probable outcome of the representation and was made for your benefit.

3 ▪ **Have a written fee or representation agreement that describes the method of billing.** Some jurisdictions require written fee agreements for certain types of representation; even without such a requirement it is sound business to always reduce the fee agreement to writing.

An example of the ethical questions raised when there is a change from one billing method to another during the course of a representation is the decision of the 2d U.S. Circuit Court of Appeals decision of September 28, 1994, in *Levine v. Angus*. It was reported that the lawyer initially agreed to charge $100 an hour for fifty hours, a total of $5,000. Three months later he proposed that his fee be 10 percent of any royalties obtained by his client. It was contended that this fee agreement constituted a business transaction requiring independent counsel. This alleged breach of fiduciary duty was not accepted by the court, which awarded the lawyer a fee of $316,627 based on the contingent fee agreement, but points out the need to act within ethical precepts.[3]

Now let us see what is happening in the use of innovative methods by some real-life examples, presented in chapter 3.

NOTES

1. *National Law Journal*, January 30, 1995, p. A7.

2. Robert L. Haig and Steven R. Caley, "What's a Fair Bill for Winning a Big Case?" *Federal Litigation Guide* (May 1993); Robert L. Haig and Steven R. Caley, "What Is a Fair Fee for a Litigator?" *Litigation* (Fall 1993). These two articles describe the advantages and disadvantages of various billing methods, including the contention that hourly billing is not necessarily all bad. They conclude that with any method with mutual trust a satisfactory relationship can exist.

3. *National Law Journal*, October 17, 1994, p. A6.

CHAPTER 3

The Present—Solo, Small, Medium, and Large Firms Are Doing It

I HAD JUST FINISHED SPEAKING at a seminar on billing methods in Tucson, Arizona, when I was approached by a person from the audience that I had never seen before. Her first words to me were, "Mr. Reed, you changed my life." When I asked how this had happened, she replied, "I read *Win-Win Billing Strategies*, then changed my billing methods in my solo estate planning and elder law practice. Now I am earning more, but working less." Since then I have had ongoing contact with her. She is Geraldine Champion from San Luis Obispo, California, one of whose representation agreements for Medicaid planning (known as Medi-Cal in California) is reprinted on pages 31–34 as Exhibit 3-1. Ms. Champion first describes the four-stage process she uses.

ILLUSTRATION 1: GERALDINE E. CHAMPION

The Four-Stage Process

Stage One: Opinion Letter—The strategy of the case (flat fee)

Stage Two: Repositioning of assets to qualify (flat fee)

Stage Three: Actual Medi-Cal application with face-to-face office interviews and follow-up to produce asset verification (hourly)

Stage Four: Update estate planning documents to coincide with Medi-Cal planning (flat fee)

Stage One: Opinion Letter— The strategy of the case

Spells out the client's facts and applies current law. Stage One articulates procedures to qualify for Medi-Cal and takes the form of an "opinion letter." The amount of time required is predictable, so we flat fee based upon value billing, i.e., value to the client. To determine value to the client, ask for estimated life expectancy of nursing home resident. If resident has Alzheimer's disease and a five-year life expectancy, value is greater than if resident has renal failure and a short life expectancy.

Stage Two: Repositioning assets

Following the creation of the opinion letter we invite the client and sometimes family members for a line-by-line reading and explanation. The letter explains the required steps to reposition assets. We obtain the client's written consent and often the children's consent, particularly if children have been named as agents under a Durable Power of Attorney or beneficiaries of the client's estate. Repositioning assets amounts to several predictable time units. Thus, we also flat fee Stage Two.

Stage Three: Interaction with Medi-Cal office

Most aspects of interaction with the Medi-Cal office are uncertain with respect to time. In California Medi-Cal applicants are required to attend a minimum of two conferences at the Medi-Cal office. The first conference is brief. After a wait of thirty minutes to a hour, the conference lasts five minutes. The second conference requires watching a thirty-minute video, which attempts to explain Medi-Cal, and thereafter a minimum two-hour face-to-face interview with the eligibility worker. Thereafter, the Medi-Cal office follows with a stream of asset verification requests. Herein exists the potential for large unreimbursed time expenditures for the unwary. As an example of what not to do, in an early Medi-Cal case, we used one flat fee for all four stages of the work. We spent four times as long as expected on Stage Three. We absorbed the loss, but we learned the lesson to always bill *hourly* for Stage Three.

Stage Four: Update estate planning documents

Easy to flat fee because of predictable time units to complete.

Timing of Fee Payments—We require four separate payments in advance of each stage. The client commits one stage at a time. Thus, if the nursing home resident passes on or circumstances change, the work can easily cease at that stage.

The Medi-Cal Legal Services Agreement (Exhibit 3-1) attempts to satisfy the client's need for predictability regarding fees and the firm's need to avoid committing itself to an indefinite amount of service at one flat fee. To accomplish these goals, there is a flat fee for the stages where the time required is known and hourly billing for the balance.

EXHIBIT 3-1: Legal Services Agreement

THE LAW OFFICES
OF

GERALDINE E. CHAMPION

(Send All Correspondence to
San Luis Obispo Office)

1345 BROAD STREET
SAN LUIS OBISPO, CALIFORNIA 93401
(805) 541-1515
FAX (805) 544-2135

937 E. Main, Suite 206
Santa Maria, CA 93454
(805) 928-5996

MEDI-CAL

LEGAL SERVICES AGREEMENT

This document (the "agreement") is the written fee contract that California law requires attorneys to have with their clients.

1. IDENTIFICATION OF PARTIES. This agreement is made between The Law Offices of Geraldine E. Champion, hereafter referred to as "Attorney," and ______________ ______________________________, hereafter referred to collectively as "Client." Attorney will provide legal services to ____ , on behalf of ____ .

2. LEGAL SERVICES TO BE PROVIDED. The legal services to be provided by Attorney to Client are as follows: Personal interview with Client to provide evaluation regarding the disposition of assets consistent with Client's intentions. Analysis of assets owned by Client; provision of legal services to qualify ______________________ for Medi-Cal benefits. ______ ____ .

3. LEGAL SERVICES SPECIFICALLY EXCLUDED. Under no circumstances will Attorney offer advice regarding investments and financial planning, or litigation services. If Client wants Attorney to provide any legal services not stated under this agreement, a separate written agreement between Attorney and Client will be required.

4. RESPONSIBILITIES OF ATTORNEY AND CLIENT. Attorney will perform the legal services called for under this agreement and will attempt to respond to Client's inquiries and communications within 24 hours. Nevertheless, Client recognizes that Attorney sometimes receives crisis calls which require emergency response by Attorney. Thus, Attorney will respond as soon thereafter as possible. Client will be truthful and cooperative with Attorney and timely make any payments required by this agreement.

(continued on next page)

EXHIBIT 3-1 (continued)

5. ATTORNEY'S FEES.

STAGE ONE: Client will pay to Attorney the non-refundable fixed fee of $____________________, payable upon signing this agreement, for the preparation of an **opinion letter**.

STAGE TWO: Further, Attorney will **reposition assets** to qualify for Medi-Cal for a non-refundable fixed fee of $________________________ .

____

____

STAGE THREE: In addition, services are available at an **hourly** rate. (Minimum billing unit is .2 of an hour or 12 minutes.) Services available "hourly" upon request: completion of MC210, interviews at Medi-Cal office, Medi-Cal verification, documents to prevent recovery from state and federal claims and liens, Fair Hearing, appeals beyond Fair Hearing, and guardian ad litem proceedings (even if these arise in the delivery of services under Stage One or Two of this agreement). Current hourly rates for legal personnel are: Attorney $150 per hour; paralegals $75 per hour. The estimated costs of this stage range from $2,500 to $4,500. Attorney reserves the right to demand a deposit to be held in a trust account. Client hereby authorizes Attorney to use that fund to pay the fees and other charges incurred on Client's behalf. Client agrees to pay all deposits within thirty days of Attorney's demand. Except for the minimum fee, any unused deposit at the conclusion of Attorney's services will be refunded.

STAGE FOUR: New estate planning documents to coincide with Medi-Cal planning. The estimated costs of this stage range from $900 to $1,500.

____ .

Attorney will charge Client for the time Attorney or Attorney's legal personnel spend on telephone calls relating to Client's matter, including calls with Client, County Department of Social Services personnel, opposing counsel and court personnel. Legal personnel assigned to Client's matter will confer among themselves about the matter, as required. When they do confer, each person will charge for the time expended. Likewise, if more than one of Attorney's legal personnel attends a meeting, court hearing or other proceeding, each will charge for the time spent. Attorney will charge for waiting time in court and elsewhere and for travel time, both local and out of town.

All non-refundable fixed fees are considered earned upon deposit, unless the fee retained would be unconscionable. Client is aware that a refund will not be made once substantial services have been performed even if, for example, Client's spouse should pass away, Client should abandon the desire to pursue Medi-Cal planning, or for any other reason—including a change in the law.

(continued on next page)

EXHIBIT 3-1 (continued)

Balance is due and payable in full upon receipt of the statement and becomes delinquent thirty (30) days after the statement date. A carrying charge will be assessed at the rate of 1½ percent per month (18 percent per annum) on the unpaid balance from the date of the statement.

6. BILLING STATEMENTS. Attorney will send Client periodic statements for fees and costs incurred. Each statement will be due within thirty (30) days of its date.

7. MULTIPLE CLIENTS: CONFIDENTIALITY AND CONFLICT. Any communications and information may be fully disclosed by Attorney to both clients. Clients are informed that California state law requires that an attorney not disclose confidential communications or secrets of a client. Each client hereby expressly consents to such disclosure to the other client. Nothing in this provision is intended to authorize, under any circumstances, Attorney's disclosure of confidential communications or secrets of either client to any individual or entity other than the other client.

Clients are further informed that the Rules of Professional Conduct of the State Bar of California require the clients' informed written consent before an attorney may concurrently represent two or more clients interested in the same subject matter. Attorney has explained to Clients the possibility of conflict that is raised by such multiple representation. Specifically, potential conflicts in this case include, but are not limited to, the following: (a) how property should be held (e.g., in one name, in both names as community property, in both names as joint tenancy property); and (b) how property should be disposed of and what persons should serve in fiduciary capacities (e.g., executor, trustee, conservator). Clients may have different interests, goals, or perspectives regarding these or other matters. Each client hereby expressly consents to multiple representation despite the possibility of conflict.

Attorney may withdraw from representing one or both clients if there is an actual conflict between the interests of the clients, provided the withdrawal is permitted under the Rules of Professional Conduct of the State Bar of California.

8. DISCHARGE AND WITHDRAWAL. Client may discharge attorney at any time whereupon all unpaid charges are immediately due and payable. Attorney reserves the right to withdraw from representation at any time. Normally, Attorney will not withdraw from representation unless (i) Attorney's fees remain unpaid for 30 days; (ii) Client breaches this agreement in some other substantial way; (iii) Client fails to take Attorney's advice on a material matter; or (iv) Attorney is required to withdraw by the California State Bar Act, The Rules of Professional Conduct of the State Bar of California, or any other applicable laws or regulations. In the event of such withdrawal, Client agrees to pay Attorney, in accordance with this agreement, for services performed and expenses incurred prior to the date of withdrawal and for any expenses incurred in reproducing Client's files.

9. WORK PRODUCT. All of Attorney's work product will be owned by Attorney. Client will retain title to Client's original documents. Client will pay for any expenses incurred in reproducing Client's file(s).

(continued on next page)

EXHIBIT 3-1 (continued)

10. DISCLAIMER OR GUARANTEE. Nothing in this agreement and nothing in Attorney's statements to Client will be construed as a promise or guarantee about the outcome of Client's matter. Attorney makes no such promises or guarantees. Attorney's comments about the outcome of Client's matter are expressions of opinion only.

11. DUAL REPRESENTATION/CONFLICT WAIVER. It is understood that providing advice to Client's children, ______________________________ ______________________________, on Client's behalf, may cause a conflict of interest to arise. An example of such a conflict could exist if Client's children, who are beneficiaries of Client's estate, want to place Client in a nursing home, paid for by Medi-Cal, to preserve *Client's* assets for *their* benefit. By signing this agreement, Client waives any such conflict of interest.

12. EFFECTIVE DATE OF AGREEMENT. The effective date of this agreement will be the date when, having been executed by Client, one copy of the agreement is received by Attorney and Attorney receives the initial payment required by Paragraph 5 of this agreement, provided the copy and the payment are received on or before ________________, 1994, or Attorney accepts late receipt. The effective date will be retroactive to the date attorney first performed services.

The foregoing is agreed to by:

Dated: ______________________, 1994 ______________________________

Dated: ______________________, 1994 ______________________________

Dated: ______________________, 1994 ______________________________

Dated: ______________________, 1994 ______________________________

THE LAW OFFICES OF
GERALDINE E. CHAMPION

Dated: ______________________, 1994 By: ______________________________
GERALDINE E. CHAMPION

ILLUSTRATION 2: JEFFREY M. ARESTY

Jeffrey M. Aresty is a solo practitioner in Boston, Massachusetts. Mr. Aresty stated, "Value billing has been instrumental to me in the development of my international law practice." His approach is to set two priorities. One is client satisfaction as it relates to value; the other is the value to his practice as it relates to long-term client retention and economic viability. He makes a point of discussing the prospective client's concept of "value" at a face-to-face meeting.

Here are his own words:

> One example of my firm's approach to the concept of value billing was with an international corporate client, with limited funding, which wanted to establish and expand its business in the United States. With this client, I discussed my willingness to work with them and assist with their funding, even though they were only a start-up company. I explained to them that I would provide quality legal services for their company and related corporate and business services. In addition, I would introduce them to my contacts in the business world, including financiers who would be willing to work with them on a low-cost, deferred basis. In exchange for those services, the value my firm would receive initially would include a long-term relationship with the client and some equity in the client's corporation. Once the client was through the initial funding stage, the client would agree to sign a retainer agreement with my office, listing myself as "general counsel" to their company. This retainer agreement would call for "premium billing" to compensate my office for working with the client during its early stages, prior to the initial funding stage.

Mr. Aresty believes that where the lawyer is willing to sacrifice immediate payment for long-term gain, close, long-enduring relationships can be developed. With client satisfaction come long-term mutual benefits.

DISCUSSION: INNOVATION APPLIES TO SMALL AND MEDIUM FIRMS

While speaking around the country on the subject of billing methods, I encountered many solo and small-firm practitioners who have quietly gone about adopting innovative billing methods. For example, in a Seattle program fellow panelists reported their use of flat or fixed fees for adoptions; a schedule of flat or fixed fees for eight different processes in an immigration practice; a flat or fixed fee for the original drafting of an international franchising agreement, followed by a fixed fee for adapting the basic agreement to meet the requirements of each country where the franchise was used.

Quite often it is the large national law firms or the corporate counsel from a large corporation whose billing methods are reported in the news media. This does not mean that the billing revolution is not being forwarded by smaller firms, only that the headlines go to the big organizations.

More important, small-firm practitioners should not delude themselves that the use of innovative methods is not applicable to them. Many small firms do work for insurance companies, banks, and other corporations. Those same companies often are proponents of alternative methods. Further, corporate counsel are following two disparate policies. On the one hand, many are reducing the number of outside firms to consolidate their efforts and to obtain volume discounts. On the other, many in-house lawyers are making a greater effort to assign cases based on the skill or resource level required for a particular matter, which has the effect of bringing law business previously assigned to large firms in metropolitan areas to smaller firms, many of which are practicing in nonmetropolitan areas.

Solo or small-firm practitioners often do not realize the advantage that they have in competing with the large firms, especially in crafting innovative billing methods. There is less inertia in small practice groups, less bureaucracy to deal with in getting permission to try something different. In addition, the use of technology has been a great leveler, enabling proficient solos or small-firm lawyers to compete well against larger firms. Many sense a trend towards the boutique firms or individual practitioners who have a high skill level in a specific field of practice.

The point of all this is that the contents of this chapter regarding national firms and the following chapter 4 describing what corporate counsel are doing about alternative billing methods apply to small-firm lawyers.

To illustrate, a midsize firm known to me had a managing partner who felt that his firm would benefit from learning more about alternative billing methods by having a firm retreat on that topic. The members of his management committee initially did not accept his recommendation despite his frequent urging. One morning a member of the management committee received a letter from in-house counsel of a national corporation for whom the firm had done work for years. The letter announced a new corporate policy requiring all outside firms used by that company to submit proposals for alternative billing methods as a condition for continuing to receive legal work in the future. You can guess which member of that management committee suddenly began to press for a firm retreat to learn more about innovative methods.

Perceptive readers will note the evolution of the adjective used to describe "billing methods." In *Win-Win Billing Strategies* nonhourly billing methods were described as "alternative billing methods." Generic methods were described in that book in detail. Since that book was published, counsel have created many hybrid methods that have been described as "innovative." Now another adjective may seem appropriate, namely, "customized."

Each of the illustrations in this chapter reflects a tailoring of approaches to fit the specific representation. The customizing process produces some beneficial side effects. The process necessarily requires consideration of the wishes and objectives of the client, the cost to the law firm of doing the work, an evaluation of the risks, the financial impact on both client and lawyer, and a determination to accept a change in how business is conducted. The implication is that clients and the representation will be treated differently based on different situations. Firms that traditionally billed only on an hourly basis did not have to deal with these considerations, with the possible exception of negotiating the hourly rates to be charged.

There is another reason why solo or small firms should pay attention to what is going on. Some practitioners might be inclined to say, "We don't do any insurance defense work or work for corporate clients, so this billing methods talk doesn't apply to us." Wrong! Those same lawyers may now compete with small firms that are involved with insurance companies or corporations. Those firms that are forced by insurance or corporate clients to streamline and systemize their work methods, reduce operating costs, improve efficiency, and focus on client needs will become stronger, making them better able to compete with their complacent local competitors because of the discipline that has been forced upon them. This secondary effect makes it important for all practitioners to give attention to what is going on, for in the long run they will be affected.

This chapter and the chapters that follow illustrate the many ways that alternative or innovative billing methods have been used successfully by lawyers individually or by law firms in tailoring their billing methods to fit the new economic and competitive conditions in the legal profession.

Innovation occurs in different settings. Among them are the following:

- One individual practitioner, whether working as a solo or as one member of a firm, has a flair for innovation and is willing to experiment with some new approach to billing.
- The whole firm, or a practice group within a firm, recognizes that hourly billing in general is not the best way to measure the value of legal services and commits to a different approach to billing.
- A client requests or demands that an alternative method be adopted, sometimes in a request for proposal, making it imperative for the lawyer to respond.
- A lawyer, or the firm as a whole, while continuing to use hourly billing as the predominant billing method, seizes the opportunity to innovate to fit a specific situation.
- Competitors force the issue by offering an innovative billing method that is attractive to clients.

ILLUSTRATION 3: BICKEL & BREWER, A MIDSIZE FIRM

Bickel & Brewer, with offices in Dallas, Chicago, New York City, and Washington, D.C., has been extremely innovative. Some years ago the firm determined that the incentives and the efficiencies achieved by a variety of alternative billing methods could not be realized as effectively by billing on an hourly basis. The nine representation agreements used by the firm are summarized starting below as Exhibit 3-2. The boldtype summary preceding each agreement stresses its innovative features. All representation agreements are in letter form; "Firm" means Bickel & Brewer; "Client" means the specific client being represented. Introductory paragraphs and descriptions of disbursements that will be billed separately are omitted in some instances for sake of brevity.[1]

EXHIBIT 3-2: Nine Summarized Representation Agreements from Bickel & Brewer

1. One-time payment; bonus based on a percentage recovered in excess of a specified amount.

Client and Bickel & Brewer (the "Firm") have agreed that Client will make a one-time payment to the Firm in the sum of $______ to cover all attorneys' fees incurred in prosecuting this matter to conclusion, whether by settlement, verdict, or otherwise, including any appeals as may be necessary. As Client and the Firm have further agreed, the Firm will be entitled to receive ______% of all sums recovered in this matter, over and above the amount of $______, whether such sums are recovered by settlement, verdict or otherwise.

Client payment of $______ will extend to and cover the fees set forth in the Firm's most recent bill, dated ______, and such payment shall be due immediately upon Client's acceptance of this letter. However, the one-time payment of $______ will not cover, or be applied to, any future disbursements in this matter, including experts' fees and expenses. As in the past, the firm will continue to render monthly bills showing attorneys' fees and disbursements incurred during the prior month. Client will continue to pay all amounts billed for disbursements in the Firm's monthly bills, as well as all other disbursements forwarded to Client for payment.

This agreement with respect to future attorneys' fees shall not apply to any fees or disbursements incurred in connection with any new matters or representation undertaken in behalf of Client.

To signify Client's agreement to the foregoing terms, please execute this letter in the space provided below, and return the fully executed original to me at your earliest convenience. The enclosed copy of this letter is for your files.

2. Hourly charges before complaint is filed; during pretrial stage hourly charges with a cap; additional maximum fee for trial stage; percentage fee for settlement or trial based on recovery above a specified sum including a percentage of royalties obtained for a period of three years; percentage fee if treble damages are recovered; maximum fee if no treble damages are recovered; maximum fee if treble damages are recovered.

1. As previously discussed, Bickel & Brewer will render legal services on behalf of Client in this matter on an hourly basis through the date of filing the complaint against (adverse party). Our services during that period will include review and analysis of the facts, development of legal strategy, research and analysis of applicable law and the preparation and filing of all papers necessary to commence an action against (adverse party). The Firm will charge hourly rates for services rendered by its professionals at rates ranging from $______ to $______ per hour.

(continued on next page)

EXHIBIT 3-2 (continued)

2. Client will pay all costs, expenses, and disbursements associated with the Firm's representation, including but not limited to court costs, copying, travel, meals, computer-aided research, communications costs, supplies, expert fees, and related customary out-of-pocket expenses.

3. Following the filing of suit, the Firm will render and perform all legal services, as directed or agreed to by Client, in the pretrial phase of the litigation (including preparing and responding to written discovery requests, taking and defending depositions, conducting fact investigations and legal research, interviewing fact witnesses, retaining expert witnesses, and formulating and developing claims, positions and strategies) for a maximum fee of $______. During this period, the Firm will continue to prepare and send monthly fee statements to Client. If the fees billed for the period between the filing of suit and the conclusion of discovery total an amount less than $______, Client will pay only the fees actually billed. If such amount exceeds $______, Client will pay only $______.

4. If the litigation does not settle by the conclusion of discovery, the Firm will perform all services, as directed or agreed to by Client, necessary to prepare for trial and try the action (including witness preparation, preparation of trial briefs and submissions, the actual conduct of trial, and posttrial motion practice and appeals for an additional maximum fee of $______. During this period, the Firm will continue to prepare and send monthly fee statements to Client. If the fees billed for the period between the close of discovery and the date the judgment becomes final and non-appealable (or the date the case is settled) total an amount less than $______, Client will pay only the fees actually billed. If such amount exceeds $______, Client will pay only $______.

5. Of course, Client will continue to pay all approved disbursements associated with this Firm's representation during the pretrial, trial, and posttrial phases of the litigation, including those items set forth in paragraph 2 above.

6. If the Firm succeeds in obtaining a settlement with (adverse party), the Firm will receive an additional fee equal to ______% of the difference between the settlement amount actually collected by Client (including royalties on past sales and services) and all fees and expenses paid by Client. In addition, the Firm will receive ______% of all royalties actually collected by Client on future sales or services for a period of three years. The payments to the Firm shall be made in arrears on a quarterly basis.

7. If, however, the litigation proceeds to trial and judgment, the Firm will receive an additional fee equal to ______% of the difference between the actual damages awarded and collected by Client (including royalties on past sales or services for a period of three years). The payments to the Firm shall be made in arrears on a quarterly basis.

8. If the judgment provides for increased damages (treble damages), the Firm shall also receive an amount equal to ______% of the difference between the total increased (trebled) damages awarded to and collected by Client and the actual compensatory damages awarded to Client.

9. Notwithstanding any provisions herein to the contrary, in the event the litigation is settled or a judgment is entered providing only for compensatory damages (and no award of treble or increased damages), the Firm shall be entitled to receive no more than a maximum of $______ in fees pursuant to the provisions and limitations set forth in the preceding paragraphs.

(continued on next page)

EXHIBIT 3-2 (continued)

10. Notwithstanding any provision herein to the contrary, in the event a judgment is entered which awards treble or increased damages, the Firm shall be entitled to receive no more than a maximum of $______ in fees pursuant to the provisions and limitations set forth in the preceding paragraphs.

11. Our invoices for fees and expenses are forwarded monthly and are payable within thirty days after receipt.

3. Maximum fee, provided the trial is not later than a specified date; continuance of trial to be opposed; proposal represents a discount; excludes certain items from fee cap; incentive bonus based on a schedule as set forth.

The purpose of this letter is to outline a fee proposal for this litigation that may be mutually beneficial to Client and Bickel & Brewer.

Based on our estimate of the pretrial, trial and posttrial work that is likely to be required for this case, we propose a total cap of $______ for professional fees and services beginning (date), through the conclusion of this matter. This amount contemplates appeals and related posttrial work. It specifically does not include an amount for retrial should one be necessary. This estimate is based on the assumption that trial will begin anytime within fifteen days of (date), provided, however, the Firm will, unless otherwise agreed by Client, oppose and seek to convince all co-defendants to oppose any continuance of the trial date. Obviously, it will need to be revised if trial does not begin in this time frame.

The proposal represents, at a minimum, a ______% discount on professional fees to Client, from an estimated $______ to $______ with a ceiling of $______. This discount does not take into account the $______ we estimate will be required should this case result in an appeal posttrial. The Firm will invoice client for professional fees as they are incurred each month, and will be paid monthly up to a total cap of $______. There will be no cap on monthly fees until the total cap of $______ is reached. In the event that the cap is reached prior to the completion of the representation described above, the Firm will absorb the incremental fees and there will be no additional charges for the Firm's professional fees to Client.

Out-of-pocket expenses will be paid to the Firm or the provider of services as incurred. Unusual disbursements in excess of $500.00 must have the prior approval of Client. The following types of expense are not included in the total cap, and therefore will be billed to Client separately:

- All expert or consulting services such as technical, damage, jury/judge psychology and presentation graphics.
- Paralegal services outsourced for this litigation.
- The Firm's in-house case documentation management services.
- Copy, telephone, fax, overnight mail, travel and other disbursement expenses.

(continued on next page)

EXHIBIT 3-2 (continued)

In consideration for capping its professional fees to Client in this matter, the Firm will receive a bonus incentive in addition to all hourly fees and disbursements. The bonus will be payable to the Firm upon Client's execution of any settlement agreement or upon receipt by Client of any judgment proceeds, whichever comes first. All amounts received by Client will include both cash and cash equivalents.

Amount of Cash or Cash Equivalents	Bonus to Firm Percent of Cash or Cash Equivalents
(a) -0- to $______	-0-%
(b) Over $______ up to $______	10% of the amount over $______ up to $______
(c) Over $______	20% of the amount over $______plus (b) above

The above contemplates a resolution of this dispute by trial or settlement which results in the above amounts in cash or equivalents thereof being available to Client. In the event that Client settles for an amount less than $______, Client agrees to pay all hourly professional fees worked and billed by the Firm in this matter.

The Firm will seek to obtain, via a good faith effort, contributions for fees, costs and/or expenses, on a pro rata basis, from any co-defendant and any amounts so received shall be credited and/or paid to Client, as appropriate. The Client will be represented at all court proceedings, settlement negotiations and other significant proceedings, as determined by Client, by (Lawyer A, Lawyer B, or Lawyer C) unless otherwise agreed to by Client in advance.

4. Hourly charges through trial; maximum fee actual billings with a cap; an additional fee for a percentage of settlement amount, or an additional fee for a percentage of amount of trial award.

This letter is intended to set forth the terms of our engagement.

1. Beginning on (date) Bickel & Brewer will render legal services on behalf of Client in this matter on an hourly fee basis for all litigation services up to and including, if necessary, the preparation for and actual trial of the action. Our services during that period may include review and analysis of the facts, development of legal strategy, research and analysis of applicable law, preparation and filing of all papers necessary to commence an action, preparing and responding to written discovery requests, taking and defending depositions, conducting fact investigations and legal research, interviewing fact witnesses, retaining expert witnesses, formulating and developing claims, positions and strategies, preparation of trial briefs and submissions, the actual conduct of trial, and posttrial motion practice and appeals. The Firm will charge hourly rates for services rendered by professionals at rates ranging from $______ to $______ per hour.

(continued on next page)

EXHIBIT 3-2 (continued)

2. The Firm will provide all of the necessary services referenced in paragraph 1 above for a maximum fee of $______. Throughout the term of the litigation of this matter, the Firm will prepare and send monthly statements to Client. If the fees billed for the period between the date the Firm begins and ends providing the litigation services referenced in paragraph 1 (or the date the case is settled) total an amount less than $______, Client will pay only the fees actually billed. If such an amount exceeds $______ Client will pay only $______.

3. Client will pay all costs, expenses, and disbursements associated with the Firm's representation, including but not limited to court costs, copying, travel, means, computer-aided research, communication costs, supplies, expert fees and related customer out-of-pocket expenses, not to exceed $______.

4. If the Firm succeeds in obtaining a settlement with (adverse party), the Firm will receive an additional fee equal to ______% of the difference between the settlement amount actually collected by Client and all expenses and fees paid by Client.

5. If, however, the litigation proceeds to trial and judgment, the Firm will receive an additional fee equal to ______% of the difference between the actual amounts awarded and collected by Client and the expenses and fees paid by Client.

5. Hourly charges with cap; defense contingency with premium for results.

The Firm will render and perform legal services incident to the above-referenced litigation on an hourly fee basis. However, the total amount of hourly fees in this representation will not exceed $______. Furthermore, if the Firm negotiates an advantageous settlement of $______ or less or obtains a favorable result on the merits of $______ or less, the Firm will be entitled to a premium.

(Standard provision regarding disbursements and monthly billings follows at this point.)

6. Fixed one-time fee; bonus for court award in excess of specified amount.

We recognize that legal representation on matters such as these can be an expensive undertaking. The Firm will endeavor to reach an advantageous result for you in as cost-efficient a manner as possible. The Firm currently charges from $______ to $______ per hour for its support staff and attorneys.

You agree to reimburse the Firm for all expenses directly relating to your matters which, in the discretion of the Firm, are appropriate. Disbursements will include, but are not limited to: (Insert list of pertinent disbursements.)

All disbursement fees over one hundred dollars will be sent directly to you. In return, you agree to make payment directly to the vendor. The Firm reserves the right to have the client billed directly.

We require that you pay a one-time fee of $______ in order to engage Bickel & Brewer to represent you in this matter. You also agree to pay the Firm ______% of any amount over $______ awarded to you by the Court in this matter.

(continued on next page)

EXHIBIT 3-2 (continued)

In conformity with the standards of our profession, the Firm is undertaking to zealously represent you with all due care. The Firm has not and will not guarantee that any certain result will be obtained. It is agreed that you are not relying on any statements concerning potential results as a basis for retaining the Firm or for entering into this agreement.

7. Hourly rates with cap for services to a fixed date; includes main litigation and any related litigation; fee bonus to be paid if Client extends the agreement; negotiations for future representation are contingent on payment of the fee bonus.

Bickel & Brewer currently charges from $______ to $______ per hour for its paralegals, consultants and lawyers. My hourly rate is currently $______ per hour, as is Lawyer B's. Lawyer C's hourly rate is currently $______ per hour. Lawyer D and Lawyer E, who will also assist in our representation, have hourly rates of $______ and $______ respectively. We reserve the right to adjust our hourly rates periodically.

The Firm will place a ceiling of $______ on our hourly fees for paralegals, consultants and lawyers, for the period ending (date). In exchange the Firm will represent Client in the above-referenced matter and any other pending pieces of litigation, should they become inherently interrelated to the above-referenced matter. Please note, however, that this ceiling does not include disbursements, as set forth below.

On (same date) Client shall, of course, have the option to end its association with the Firm. However, should Client choose to extend the Firm's representation beyond (same date), Client shall pay within twenty days a fee bonus of $______. Similarly, on (same date) the Firm may end its representation of Client. Should the parties agree to continue their attorney-client relationship beyond (same date), and should Client tender the above-mentioned fee bonus of $______, the parties may then negotiate and enter into a new agreement concerning the remainder of their attorney-client association.

We require payment of all disbursements, etc.

Monthly billing for legal services from (date) shall not exceed $______ for each month. The final bill will adjust the outstanding balance.

Our invoices for fees and expenses are forwarded monthly and payable on receipt.

We will be formally retained as soon as we receive the executed return of this letter.

8. Hourly rates with a fee cap; if normal hourly rates exceed the fee cap and a copyright is acknowledged by settlement or judicial determination, normal hourly fees as charged will be paid up to a maximum of an additional specified amount; if cash sum is obtained by settlement or trial, a percentage bonus is to be paid.

First we and Client have agreed to a fee cap of $______ for attorney fees incurred in this case from and after October 1, 19___. The fee cap applies to the above-captioned suit, as well as an additional suit that may be filed by Client against (adverse party) charging various forms of unfair competition. The Firm will charge its usual hourly rates, up to the fee cap.

(continued on next page)

EXHIBIT 3-2 (continued)

You agree that this fee cap does not include other miscellaneous charges and/or disbursements such as document processing costs, imaging costs (if used), computerized research charges, expert witness costs, and other costs. We estimate that such additional charges will run approximately $______.

Second, Client agrees that if the Firm, as calculated on the basis of its normal hourly fees, has exceeded the fee cap of $______, and if a settlement or judgment results in either an acknowledgment of copyright by (adverse party) or a judicial declaration to the effect, Client will pay the Firm its actual fees, up to a maximum of an additional $______.

Third, if there is a judgment or settlement resulting in a cash payment from (adverse party) to Client whether in the form of a lump sum payment or a licensing fee, and such payment exceeds the amount of the Firm's fees from and after (date), Client shall pay the Firm a sum equal to ______% of the judgment or settlement payment, after deducting the Firm's fees and expenses incurred in the litigation after (date).

9. Fixed fee agreement for representing multiple plaintiffs in litigation and arbitration, payable in four equal monthly payments; right to collect attorney's fees in excess of the fixed fee amount; percentage of damages obtained by settlement, trial or appeal.

This letter is written to set forth the agreement between the Plaintiffs in the above-captioned matters and the firm of Bickel & Brewer concerning representation of the Plaintiffs and their officers, directors, shareholders, agents and employees in the above-referenced litigation and arbitration, and the appeals of either of these two matters (collectively, the "Litigation").

For and in consideration of the Firm's representation of Plaintiffs in the Litigation, the Firm agrees as follows:

1. Plaintiffs shall pay the Firm $______ as and for all the legal fees and costs arising from the Litigation. Such amount shall be paid in four equal monthly installments beginning (date), or upon the settlement and resolution of the Litigation.

2. In addition, the Firm shall receive any and all attorneys' fees and costs awarded to Plaintiffs by any court or jury in the Litigation in excess of the amount of all attorneys' fees and costs (exclusive of amounts paid in paragraph 3 below) paid directly to the Firm by Plaintiffs.

3. In addition, the Firm shall be entitled to ______% of any amount of damages collected from Defendants or otherwise paid to Plaintiffs as a result of settlement, trial or appeal of the above referenced Litigation.

William A. Brewer III (co-founding partner of Bickel & Brewer) and Dennis J. DuBois wrote an interesting article on creative methods of billing that appeared in *The National Law Journal* in December 1994.[2] Here are two quotes from that article:

> Long the sacred cow of the legal industry, the billable hour is fast reaching the end of its life cycle. Billing by the hour creates unhealthy competition between lawyer and client by rewarding inefficiency. Lawyers profit by spending more time on a matter, whether productive or not.
>
> • • •
>
> What is needed is a "win-win" solution by which clients pay for results, and law firms are paid for the value they have produced in return.

ILLUSTRATION 4: A LARGE NATIONAL FIRM

In talking with a litigation partner in a large national firm, I learned that various approaches to billing had been successfully used on a very current basis. This firm had learned the competitive advantages of innovative methods. While willing to share with me on a confidential basis, they specifically declined to be identified. Suffice it to say that if the firm name were disclosed, every reader would instantly recognize the preeminent position that the firm has long enjoyed. With the consent of the firm, the summary of five different approaches follows, using the words of the partner as he shared them with me.[3]

1. **A fee arrangement covering complete outsourcing of legal work by a company previously having a legal staff of five to seven lawyers.**

> This is a situation in which a client with a number of recurring legal problems determined that it would eliminate its in-house legal department, with the possible exception of a single attorney who would then be the general counsel. The company provided us with a description by category of the types of litigation in which it found itself involved over the past several years. There was then an indication of the number of hours devoted to each particular category by each of the attorneys in-house in prior years. We were given a two-year history. We were asked to bid on the basis that our firm would get all of the work previously done in-house.
>
> Using the two-year history of types of services as a description of the "scope of services" that we would perform, we were asked to submit a fixed fee proposal. We did so indicating that the agreement would extend for a two-year period. We specifically excluded (and left open for determination—case by case) matters that would be considered major, basically under the standard of "We'll know it when we see it." This particular client had not experienced a significant amount of major litigation in the prior two-year period, at least not "major" in the sense that it needed to be performed by outside counsel. We submitted a

proposal agreeing to perform the indicated services for a flat fee that exceeded $3 million a year, which was to be payable on a pro rata basis monthly in advance. We agreed that the annual fee we quoted would apply without adjustment, unless there were a truly aberrational experience, and, in such case, we indicated a willingness to negotiate on a basis that would be fair to our firm and the client. We also suggested, in light of the fact that this was a two-year term, that there would be a review at the end of the first year to evaluate whether the arrangement had been inequitable to either the firm or the client, and whether or not such inequity was likely to continue into the second year.

We had to deal with the issue of "conflicts." That is, since we were agreeing to handle all of the company's work for a flat fee, we needed to make clear whose obligation it would be to pay another law firm in the event we were conflicted out of a particular representation of this client. We proposed that at such time as the conflict became apparent, we would arrive at a proration of fees with the client at that time.

The ultimate resolution of this matter was that the client determined to retain the services of the highest-ranking attorney as the general counsel, and that a panel of three firms was approved, including ours, for the work to be done. We are presently in the course of discussing which segment of the work and at what fixed price that work would be performed with the client. This is, of course, a critical discussion, since some segments of the work would appear to be more "profitable" for a law firm to perform than others. While this ultimate decision is pending, the legal staff of the company has been reduced to the single general counsel, and we are receiving work on a fee-for-service basis in the interim.

2. **A proposal to a major corporation with a very significant legal budget and nationwide operations.**

We were advised by a major corporation with a sizable legal staff of its own, which it would continue to maintain, that it desired to drastically reduce the number of outside law firms representing it. It was represented that this would result in a significant volume of work to be performed by those outside firms that were ultimately selected to represent the client. We were given data on the total numbers of dollars spent for legal services in various geographic areas of the United States by this client in the years preceding the time of the request for proposal. It was clearly understood that, because of the geographic distribution of the work, there would be more than one firm that would ultimately be engaged by this client.

We submitted a proposal under which we would extend discounts from our standard rates, which discounts would increase as the volume of legal fees payable to our firm increased. The discussions within the firm were, of course, interesting. It became necessary for us to calculate a break-even point with respect to the size of the discount that could be given before we would not cover our expenses and overhead. Obviously, this is a flexible concept because it all depends on who would do the additional work. For example, if you simply did another million dollars' worth of work for this client on top of whatever else you were doing, and that work could be performed by the existing staff working longer hours, the amount of the discount that could be given on that additional work would be greater than if you had to hire new people to perform it. At any rate, we made a proposal along the following lines. For the first $1 million of work, that is, from $1 to $1 million, we would extend a 5 percent discount off our normal hourly rates, which were provided to the client. (There was also a provision for annual revision in consultation with the client.) From $1,000,001 to $2,000,000, we proposed a 10 percent discount from our normal rates, and $2,000,001 to $3,000,000, we agreed to a 15 percent discount. There was considerable discussion in our firm about whether or not we should include a retroactive feature after the work exceeded $3 million per year. It was ultimately decided that if the work exceeded $3.5 million, we would apply retroactively the 15 percent discount to the fees from $1 to $2,000,000. This means that we would credit the client for the first $1 million of work performed in the year with an additional 10 percent discount, and with respect to the second million, we would credit the client with an additional 5 percent. This means we would have extended, as an incentive, an additional $150,000 credit once the billings exceeded $3.5 million. Thereafter, the 15 percent rate would apply as the top discounted rate. We are presently receiving work from the client on this basis.

3. **A corporate plaintiff's case with a sizable amount paid up front to cover fees up to that amount, plus a percentage of the recovery.**

This was a case involving a significant commercial dispute in which there was a real possibility of punitive damages against a very well heeled and solvent defendant. We agreed to handle the case with the client depositing in our trust account $500,000. This $500,000 was to cover our fees at our normal hourly rates. All out-of-pocket costs and expenses were to be paid by the client directly, or reimbursed to us within ten days after the submission of the bill to the client. If the matter was concluded prior to the time that our fee for services would have reached $500,000, the remaining portion of the $500,000 would be repaid by us to the client. As our services were rendered, we were authorized to withdraw the money from our trust account to apply against our fees. In addition, regardless of whether or not our time devoted to the matter would have resulted in fees of more or less than $500,000, we were to receive 20 percent of any net recovery in excess of $500,000. This allowed the client to recoup the amount paid to us under the fee-for-service arrangement, before any percentage of recovery would inure to our benefit. (This, of course, assumes that the recovery was equal to or in excess of $500,000.)

This matter was happily concluded for all concerned, but not until the eve of trial. We had expended substantially more than the $500,000 up-front money, but substantially less that the total fee we received as a result of the sizable recovery. The 20 percent contingency obviously is less than what a straight contingent fee would normally have been, but it was arrived at after allowing for the fact that the client had also committed to spending a substantial amount of up-front money for the fee-for-service billings.

4. **A variation of number 3, being a corporate client's plaintiff's matter in which we were paid a reduced hourly fee plus a smaller than usual percentage of any net recovery.**

In this particular case, a corporate client wished to bring a plaintiff's action that appeared to have merit and we agreed with the client that we would accept a blended rate of $100 per hour for all of our time devoted to the matter. Of course, out-of-pocket costs and expenses were to be paid by the client. In addition to any fees charged under the $100 per hour arrangement, we were to receive 20 percent from dollar one of any net recovery. This matter remains in litigation, so we cannot be certain of the ultimate financial wisdom of the deal from our firm's point of view. However, while we have had to spend a considerable amount of time on the case, settlement discussions to date indicate that the matter will be resolved at what would appear to be slightly better than a break-even arrangement for us if we calculated the total recovery under this arrangement versus what we would have charged pursuant to our normal hourly rates.

5. **A very substantial volume of work being done for a corporate client of a repetitive nature involving a large number of cases.**

In this scenario, the client has a pipeline filled with cases of the same general variety that need to be brought in a number of geographical locations. Because the cases are repetitive, they can be staffed with lower hourly rated personnel than usual. However, partners' or senior associates' time is frequently required for the more significant court appearances. The volume of cases could be expected to last for a number of years. In this case, we agreed to charge the normal billing rates for paralegals and attorneys and junior associate attorneys. Senior associates' and partners' time is to be billed at 90 percent of the standard hourly rate of each particular lawyer in the year preceding the date on which we entered into the arrangement. This gave the client a substantial discount on senior attorney time involved not only because there was a 10 percent discount applied, but because the discount was applied to the attorney's rate in a prior year. It was agreed that these partner rates would continue for a two-year period, at which time it was contemplated that the rates would be updated so that the time would be charged at 90 percent of that lawyer's normal hourly rate for the year preceding the revision of the arrangement. For example, when the contract was originally entered into in 1993, senior associates' and partners' rates to be charged on these cases was to be 90 percent of the hourly rate charged in 1992. This continued for the years 1993 and 1994. In 1995, the rate was changed to 90 percent of the particular attorney's 1994 rate. And this again will continue for a two-year period subject to revision in 1997.

ILLUSTRATION 5: A LARGE OUTSIDE FIRM

Here is another approach that was entered into after long negotiations:

A major insurance company used several outside law firms to handle complex and large-exposure litigation. One of the outside firms that did a substantial amount of work for the insurance company entered into negotiations for a different approach to handling these matters. Ultimately, these negotiations led to the representation agreement set forth in Exhibit 3-3. Neither the insurance company (called "Carrier") nor this outside law firm (called "Firm"), which does business both nationally and internationally, wished to be identified specifically. The specific matters are not disclosed in the letter agreement, which has been edited for publication. This agreement shows innovation and customizing.[4]

EXHIBIT 3-3: Representation Agreement Involving Large Outside Firm

Dear ______,

I am writing to confirm our fee agreement for work done for cases during 1995.

A. *THE TARGET FEE ARRANGEMENT*

The Firm agrees to provide all legal services during 1995 for cases, as defined below, based on a target fee of $19 million. The target fee arrangement is as follows:

If the target fee is exceeded, we agree to reduce our fees as follows:

Firm Billings	Amount Paid by Carrier
$19.0 million	$19.0 million
$19.0–21.0 million	$ 1.5 million (75% billings)
$21.0–23.0 million	$ 1.0 million (50% billings)
$23.0–27.0 million	$ 1.0 million (25% billings)
$27.0 million +	$ 0
Total not to exceed fee	$22.5 million

If our fees are less than the target fee, Carrier agrees to pay an incentive bonus as follows:

25% bonus for fees in the $17.0 to $19.0 million range;
50% bonus for fees in the $15.0 to $17.0 range.

Finally, Carrier agrees to pay an incentive bonus of 50% of savings concerning settlements in cases to be selected by Carrier on a quarterly basis. The first three cases and target settlements are:

Case No. 1: $10.5 million
Case No. 2: $20.0 million
Case No. 3: $22.0 million

Our agreement assumes that some of the matters covered by the target fee will be settled in 1995, but will be replaced by other matters of similar size. If Carrier decides to transfer ongoing matters covered by our target fee during 1995, other than those referred to in the following paragraph, we will readjust our target fee in light of the legal work avoided by the transfer of such additional matters. We will meet with you at the end of each quarter to review the level of our work.

(continued on next page)

EXHIBIT 3-3 (continued)

This agreement does not include the cases transferred to in-house counsel or to outside counsel listed in your memoranda dated ______. This agreement also does not include the following particularly active cases set for trial during 1995: (specific cases are listed at this point).

We agree to meet with you or your staff to review, on a quarterly basis, the cases identified above in order to agree on specific tasks, results and costs for the near term. We agree that the fees and costs in these cases need to be carefully monitored and controlled so that pretrial and trial efforts are carried in the most efficient manner possible.

B. BILLING PROCEDURES

1. *Particularly Active Cases Set for Trial During 1995*

Detailed statements covering each of the Particularly Active cases will be sent monthly.

2. *Other Matters with Monthly Bills Exceeding $10,000.00*

Detailed statements will be sent to Carrier each month for each case where unbilled fees and expenses exceed $10,000.00.

3. *Monthly Billing Summaries*

Each month, we will send two sets of the below-listed materials. One set will cover the specified Particularly Active Cases and the other set will cover the other matters with monthly bills exceeding $10,000.00.

(a) A Billing Summary showing, for each case, the amounts incurred during the month, credits and adjustments for the previous month, and net billing for the month. An Example of the Billing Summary is attached as Exhibit 1.

(b) A Billing Sub-Company Summary. This will show the fees and expenses allocated to each Carrier company. An example of this report is attached as Exhibit 2.

(c) A Billing Sub-Company Matter Summary. This will show each matter and the allocation to each Carrier company. An Example of this report is attached as Exhibit 3.

(d) A single page invoice for each case. An Example of this invoice is attached as Exhibit 4.

4. *Detailed Bills for Cases with Less than $10,000.00 in Unbilled Time and Expenses*

For those cases which do not appear on the monthly Billing Summary because less than $10,000.00 in fees and expenses has been incurred, you will be sent detailed billing statements semiannually, showing all work on each matter by individual attorney and paralegal, and all expenses. These statements will be sent in July covering fees and expenses through the end of June, and in January covering the period July through December 1995. In summary, the July and January Billing Summaries will include all matters. Finally, upon request, we will prepare a detailed monthly statement for any matter regardless of whether it meets the $10,000.00 threshold.

(continued on next page)

EXHIBIT 3-3 (continued)

C. OTHER PROCEDURES

Copies of all expense reports will be provided and we will attach receipts for all expenses over $25.00. You will continue to receive all receipts for airline and train tickets.

We will instruct local counsel to send statements directly to the appropriate representative for approval and payment. Of course, if requested, we will be glad to consult with the representative concerning the appropriateness of any charges submitted by local counsel. We will not pay any local counsel's bill.

Each month, a copy of the Billing Summary will be sent to you and (insert names of individuals).

Separate monthly statements will be rendered for any additional work concerning cases transferred from the Firm to other law firms, including your firms located in ______ and ______.

We understand that each month, we will receive payment of the amounts shown on the two Billing Summaries by check within 45 days of receipt. All adjustments agreed upon as a result of review of the detailed bills by insurer representatives will be promptly credited on the next monthly Billing Summaries.

Sincerely yours,

ILLUSTRATION 6: BLACKWELL SANDERS, A MIDSIZE FIRM

Blackwell Sanders Matheny Weary and Sanders, with principal offices in Kansas City, Missouri, and their client, UtiliCorp United, a major utility company, entered into the agreement described below wherein UtiliCorp United outsourced all of their legal work to Blackwell Sanders.[5] The arrangement, as summarized by the firm, and published with the consent of both the firm and the client, omits specific dollar figures. The agreement was based on what had been the total cost to UtiliCorp United of operating its legal department of approximately fourteen lawyers and the total outside counsel expense. The basic arrangement is as follows:

1. The special fee arrangement is for a two-year period initially.
2. Under the agreement, Blackwell Sanders will oversee all of the legal work performed for UtiliCorp.

3. As the result of the agreement, UtiliCorp eliminated all of their in-house legal staff.
4. The fee arrangement calls for Blackwell Sanders to be paid a flat fee in 1995 to cover all fees, including outside counsel, up to an agreed-upon maximum dollar figure, with shared risks and rewards. Under the terms of the agreement, in the event actual fees are less than the fixed amount during the first year, the savings, up to a set amount, will be split 50-50 with UtiliCorp. UtiliCorp's share of the savings will be applied against the flat fee during the second year of the agreement. If there are savings in the second year, these would be split 50-50. Savings in excess of this amount would be retained by UtiliCorp. In the event fees exceed the flat amount during the first year, Blackwell Sanders will absorb overages, up to a specified limit. Fees above this limit will be paid by UtiliCorp at the prevailing Blackwell Sanders rates. Disbursements are reimbursed by UtiliCorp and are not included in the flat annual fee.
5. By mutual agreement, two practice areas are exempt from the flat fee agreement and will be covered by other outside counsel. However, these firms will be engaged by Blackwell Sanders and their work will be supervised by Blackwell Sanders. Expenses incurred by Blackwell Sanders in retaining such outside counsel will be reimbursed by UtiliCorp.
6. Blackwell Sanders, as the result of the agreement, opened a full-service office in Omaha, Nebraska, and a small office in San Antonio, Texas, to service UtiliCorp's needs.

ILLUSTRATION 7: SUSMAN GODFREY, A MIDSIZE FIRM

Stephen D. Susman and the firm Susman Godfrey, L.L.P., in Houston, Texas, have used innovative billing methods in numerous different practice circumstances with a variety of risk-sharing approaches. Twenty-one different fee agreements were sent for use in preparing this book.[6] Space limitations will not permit full reproduction of all of these agreements. Some will be reproduced in whole, others will be summarized with emphasis on unique features. In all instances the names of clients and other identifying information have been omitted to preserve confidentiality.

We will start with a relatively straightforward letter agreement. It includes many of the standard provisions appearing in most, if not all, of the Susman Godfrey agreements that were reviewed.

1. **Exhibit 3-4 is a representation agreement with the following characteristics: defense contingency agreement with $350,000 nonrefundable retainer; bonus if settlement occurs before December 31; billing at 50 percent of normal hourly rates after December 31, with bonus if case is disposed of by settlement or judgment for $35 million or less.**

EXHIBIT 3-4: Susman Godfrey Agreement #1

SUSMAN GODFREY, L.L.P.
A REGISTERED LIMITED LIABILITY PARTNERSHIP
ATTORNEYS AT LAW
5100 FIRST INTERSTATE BANK PLAZA
1000 LOUISIANA
HOUSTON, TEXAS 77002-5096
(713) 651-9366
TELECOPY (713) 653-7897

1400 ALLIANZ FINANCIAL CENTRE
2323 BRYAN STREET
DALLAS, TEXAS 75201-2663
(214) 754-1900

WRITER'S DIRECT DIAL NUMBER:

__________, ______

PRIVILEGED—
ATTORNEY-CLIENT COMMUNICATION

VIA HAND DELIVERY

____
____
____
____

Re: Cause No. ________________________________
____

Dear ______________:

This letter agreement sets forth the terms and conditions on which Susman Godfrey L.L.P. ("SG") will undertake to represent ______________________ ("Client"), in defense of all claims ________________________ or ________________________ have against Client (all such claims are collectively referred to as "cause of action"). We must receive an executed copy of this letter agreement *before* we can agree to this representation. The terms and conditions of our engagement are as follows:

1. *Retainer*
   Upon execution of this agreement, Client will pay SG a non-refundable retainer of $350,000.00, which SG will keep regardless of the outcome of the case to compensate it for its agreement to provide services in defense of the cause of action and for any loss of opportunity to accept other matters.

THIS CONTRACT IS SUBJECT TO ARBITRATION
UNDER THE TEXAS GENERAL ARBITRATION STATUTE.

(continued on next page)

EXHIBIT 3-4 (continued)

2. If the case settles on or before December 31, 1993, for a net present value equal to or less than $33 million, SG would receive an additional bonus of $1 million plus fifty percent (50%) of the savings below $33 million.

   If the case does not settle by December 31, 1993, SG would begin to bill at fifty percent (50%) of its regular hourly rates. SG and I would agree to take an active role in the case. I would agree, at your option, to replace _______________ as lead trial counsel in the case. If the case were disposed of by settlement or judgment for $35 million or less, SG would receive an additional bonus of $1 million plus fifty percent (50%) of the savings below $35 million.

3. *Noncash Settlements*
   If the cause of action is settled in whole or in part by Client's payment of anything of value other than cash, SG shall be entitled to demand and receive at its option (a) payment for all time at its normal hourly rates in effect at the time of settlement (to the extent the total fees exceed the $350,000 paid pursuant to paragraph 1 above), or (b) payment in cash of the bonus set forth under paragraph 2 above, based on (i) the present value of any noncash consideration plus (ii) any cash paid upon settlement.

4. SG agrees that it will not make an appearance as counsel in any litigation asserting the cause of action nor have any discussions with _______________ without Client's prior consent. SG agrees that it will utilize its best efforts and cooperate with Client and its other counsel to achieve an acceptable resolution of any such litigation.

5. *Expenses*
   Client agrees to pay all reasonable litigation costs, expenses, and fees (when applicable) monthly. SG will promptly send to Client, for direct payment by Client, invoices received by SG from third parties such as court reporters, expert witnesses and reproduction centers for services rendered on Client's behalf. Client agrees to pay these third-party invoices when due.

6. *Billing for Independent Vendors' Services*
   When your case requires the services of a court reporter, experts, or other outside vendors, those vendors typically send us the bill. We will promptly forward these invoices to you for payment directly to the vendor. Please be sure to pay these bills promptly, because slow payment can interfere with our ability to arrange for these necessary services on your behalf.

7. *Nonpayment*
   By your execution of this engagement letter, you agree that we are relieved from the responsibility of performing any further work should you fail to pay any monthly statement for fees and expenses (including bills for expenses received from third parties), within fifteen (15) days of receipt of such statements, normally by the first of the month following receipt. In such event, you agree that we may move to withdraw as your counsel in any case where we have made an appearance on your behalf, and that you will promptly execute any withdrawal motions required to accomplish this.

(continued on next page)

EXHIBIT 3-4 (continued)

8. *Estimates*
Client understands that any estimates provided by SG of the magnitude of the expenses that will be required at certain stages of any litigation asserting the cause of action are not precise, and that the kinds and amounts of expenses required are ultimately a function of many conditions over which SG has little or no control, particularly the extent to which the opposition files pretrial motions and engages in its own discovery. SG understands that any estimates made by Client regarding the timing, intensity and potential outcome of the litigation may be affected by numerous factors over which Client has little or no control.

9. *SG's Right to Terminate; Client's Right to Settle*

   A. In the event of a change of ownership of Client (or the filing of a bankruptcy proceeding involving Client) or should Client breach this agreement, then SG shall have the right to terminate this agreement and to demand and receive payment for all unreimbursed expenses advanced on behalf of Client and for all time expended to such date at its hourly rates in effect when the time was expended (to the extent the total fees exceed the $350,000 paid pursuant to paragraph 1 above).

   B. Client shall have the sole and exclusive right to accept or reject any offers for settlement of the cause of action.

10. *No Guarantees*
The Client hereby acknowledges that SG has made no guarantees regarding the successful outcome of this matter and all expressions about the outcome are only opinions. SG hereby acknowledges that any expressions made by client or its counsel as to the timing or likelihood of settlement, the range of settlement value or the potential outcome of the litigation are only opinions.

11. *Association of Co-counsel*
Client understands that SG may, at its expense, but only with the consent of Client, contract with other attorneys for the performance of certain work for the Client and that SG may pay part of the fees it receives under this agreement to such attorneys for the services rendered by them.

12. *Acknowledgment of Fairness*
SG acknowledges that it has had significant experience with contingent fee arrangements, and Client acknowledges that Client has been encouraged by SG to consult other counsel concerning the negotiation of this fee agreement. SG and Client have made sufficient investigation and inquiry to determine that this agreement is fair and reasonable, and that this agreement was the product of arm's length negotiation.

13. *Dispute Resolution*
Any disputes arising under this letter agreement will be submitted to arbitration and the arbitrator's decision shall be binding, conclusive and nonappealable.

(continued on next page)

EXHIBIT 3-4 (continued)

14. *Severability*
If any part of this letter agreement shall for any reason be found unenforceable, the parties agree that all other portions shall nevertheless remain valid and enforceable.

15. *Integration*
This Agreement represents the final and mutual understanding of the parties. It replaces and supersedes any prior agreements or understandings, whether written or oral. This Agreement may not be modified, amended, or replaced except by another signed written agreement.

If this Agreement is satisfactory, you should sign the lower left corner and return the original to this office. The copy is for your files.

Sincerely yours,

SUSMAN GODFREY L.L.P.

____

____

Attachments: Sample Monthly Bill
Hourly Rates

AGREED TO AND ACCEPTED:

____

By: _____________________________________

Date: ____________________________________

2. The Susman Godfrey agreement in Exhibit 3-5 includes the following provisions: sliding contingency with 20 percent of gross sum recovered if settled before trial; after start of trial, 25 percent of first $7 million, 33 1/3 percent if over $7 million; "gross sum recovered" does not include awarded attorneys' fees for computing fee if amount paid to client exceeds $3 million; mediation clause.

EXHIBIT 3-5: Susman Godfrey Agreement #2

__________, _____

PRIVILEGED—
ATTORNEY-CLIENT COMMUNICATION

____
____
____
____

____
____
____
____

Re: ____
____
____

Dear ______________:

This letter agreement sets forth the terms and conditions on which Susman Godfrey L.L.P. ("SG") (which includes any successor to the partnership of SG) will undertake to represent ____ in pursuit of all claims Client has against _______ (all such claims are collectively referred to as "cause of action"). The terms and conditions of our engagement are as follows:

1. *Ownership and Partial Assignment of the Cause of Action*
   Client hereby warrants that it is the sole owner of the cause of action. Client hereby transfers and assigns to SG an undivided interest in the cause of action, such interest being equivalent to the amount or percentage that Client, by this agreement, promises to pay for the services of SG.

2. *Contingent Fee*
   A. SG will receive twenty percent (20%) of the gross sum recovered by settlement before commencement of trial (defined as the commencement of jury selection in the case of a jury trial, or the first introduction of evidence in the case of a trial to the court).
   B. After commencement of trial, SG will receive the following percentages of the gross sum recovered by settlement or judgment:
      1. Twenty-five percent (25%) of the first $7 million, plus
      2. Thirty-three and one-third percent (33-1/3%) of amounts recovered which exceed $7 million.

THIS CONTRACT IS SUBJECT TO ARBITRATION UNDER THE TEXAS GENERAL ARBITRATION STATUTE.

(continued on next page)

EXHIBIT 3-5 (continued)

C. The "gross sum recovered" means all money or other things of value, including the value of any noncash settlement paid to and/or received by Client, and also including any attorney's fees awarded in a judgment and paid by the Defendant. However, the amount of attorney's fees awarded in a judgment shall not be included in the "gross sum recovered" for purposes of calculating SG's fees if the amount of damages awarded and paid to Client exceeds $3 million. (For example, if the damages awarded to the Client are $4 million, and the amount of attorney's fee awarded is $750,000, SG's fee will be the appropriate percentage of $4 million, and Client shall be entitled to receive the $750,000 award for attorney's fee.)

Furthermore, for purposes of calculating SG's contingent fee, there will be no deduction from the "gross sum recovered" for those legal fees paid by Client for bills through April 30, 1993 (in the amount of $93,399.00). All costs and expenses that SG requests Client pay, or which Client has already paid prior to the signing of this agreement, however, shall be deducted from the "gross sum recovered" before calculating SG's fee.

3. *Noncash Settlements*
If the cause of action is settled in whole or in part by the Client's receipt of anything of value other than cash, SG must elect to receive either
   (a) payment in cash, under Paragraph 2 above, of the applicable SG contingent percentages of (i) the present value of any noncash consideration plus (ii) any cash received upon settlement, or
   (b) payment in cash for all time spent by SG in prosecution of Client's cause of action, at twice the normal hourly rates in effect at the time of settlement.

Furthermore, and notwithstanding anything to the contrary herein, in the event the case is resolved whereby Client receives cash of $3.5 million or more, and a noncash settlement whereby the business relationship between _______ and Client is terminated (e.g., _______ or its nominee acquires Client's business[es]), in such event, for the purpose of calculating SG's contingent fee, there shall be a deduction from the "gross sum recovered" in an amount equal to $3 million, provided, however, that the "gross sum recovered" after taking such deduction shall not be less than $3.5 million. If Client receives cash of $3.5 million or less, there shall be no deduction from the "gross sum recovered," and SG's contingent fee will be calculated on the $3.5 million or less amount.

4. *Settlement Payments*
Client authorizes SG to require that any settlement check be made payable jointly to Client and SG, and agrees that after endorsing the check, it will allow SG to cash the same and make payment to the Client of Client's portion of the recovery.

5. *Estimates*
Client understands that any estimates provided by SG of the magnitude of the expenses that will be required at certain stages of any litigation are not precise and that the kinds and amounts of expenses required are ultimately a function of many conditions over which SG has little or no control, particularly the extent to which the opposition files pretrial motions and engages in its own discovery.

(continued on next page)

EXHIBIT 3-5 (continued)

6. *No Other Assignment or Lien*
   Client agrees that they shall not assign in whole or in part or otherwise grant any lien against this cause of action or the proceeds from it, other than the assignment granted to SG herein, without the prior written consent of SG.

7. *Expenses*
   Client agrees to monthly pay all costs and expenses of litigation. SG acknowledges receipt of $32,156.25, which Client has paid SG for May 1993 legal services. Such amount shall be converted from payment for legal services rendered and shall hereafter be held in trust by SG and shall be applied against costs and expenses as they are incurred and until such amount is exhausted. Thereafter, SG will periodically send to Client, for direct payment by Client, invoices received by SG from third parties such as court reporters, expert witnesses and reproduction centers for services rendered on Client's behalf. Client agrees to pay these third-party invoices when due. All such costs and expenses shall be deducted from gross sum recovered before calculating SG's fees.
   In the event Client fails or refuses to timely pay such costs and expenses, SG shall have the option to
   (a) cease performing any further work until such costs and expenses are paid, or
   (b) pay such costs and expenses itself and receive reimbursement from initial "gross sum recovered" plus 10% interest on the amount of such unpaid costs and expenses from time of payment by SG until date of reimbursement, or
   (c) move to withdraw as counsel of record and terminate this letter agreement under the provisions of Paragraph 8A(7) hereafter, whereby upon request, Client agrees to sign any withdrawal motion required to accomplish this.

8. *SG's Right to Terminate*
   A. SG shall have the right to terminate this engagement upon the occurrence of any of the following:
   (1) Should Client elect to abandon any cause of action which in the opinion of SG materially jeopardizes the prospects of successful prosecution of Client's claims;
   (2) Should the conduct of Client materially prejudice the prospects of successful prosecution of Client's claims;
   (3) Change of ownership of Client, if such action materially jeopardizes the prospects of successful prosecution of Client's claims;
   (4) Should the Client fail to disclose material facts or falsely describe material facts, and as such materially jeopardizes the prospects of successful prosecution of Client's claims;
   (5) Should Client unreasonably withhold consent to a settlement proposal which in the judgment of SG is a fair and reasonable basis for disposition of the cause, realizing, however, that Client has the sole and exclusive right to accept or reject any proposal for settlement;
   (6) Filing of a bankruptcy proceeding by or against any Client; or
   (7) Should Client materially breach this agreement in some other manner.

(continued on next page)

EXHIBIT 3-5 (continued)

B. If any such event occurs, and if SG elects to terminate this engagement, SG shall disclaim any further rights to its assignment of the contingent fee interest, and in lieu thereof shall be entitled to receive payment for all unreimbursed expenses and costs advanced for Client, and for all time expended to such date for performance of legal services at this normal hourly rate in effect at the time legal services were performed. Client shall receive credit for any payments made for costs, expenses and legal services rendered prior to the date of this agreement.

C. Should it become the opinion of SG at any time that Client's cause of action lacks merit (for example, because of inability to verify Client's claims through witnesses, because of adverse developments in the law or because of a materially adverse change in the financial condition of the defendant), then SG shall have the option to terminate this agreement and be relieved of any obligation to participate in any pending litigation involving the cause of action. In such event, Client shall be liable to SG only for unreimbursed costs and expenses SG has advanced on behalf of Client, and SG shall disclaim any further rights to its assignment of the contingent fee interest.

9. *Client's Right to Terminate*
   A. Client shall have the right to terminate the engagement of SG at any time, with or without good cause.
   B. If Client terminates SG without good cause, SG shall have the option:
      (1) to receive unreimbursed costs and expenses advanced for Client and the contingent fee provided for herein, or
      (2) to receive payment for all unreimbursed expenses and costs advanced for Client and for time expended to date of termination for performance of legal services, at its normal hourly rates in effect at the time legal services were performed. Client shall receive credit for any payments made for costs, expenses and legal services rendered prior to the date of this agreement.
   C. If Client terminates SG with good cause, SG shall only be entitled to receive payment as provided in Paragraph 9B(2) above.
   D. "Good cause" shall include, without limitation, any event or act as follows:
      (1) If ___________ is withdrawn by SG as the partner in charge of Client's case and some other partner or firm member other than ___________ or ___________ is designated in charge; or
      (2) If ___________ for some other business or personal reason is unable or refuses to continue as lead counsel for Client, unless ___________ or ___________ accepts the role of lead counsel.

10. *No Guarantees*
    The Client hereby acknowledges that SG has made no guarantees regarding the successful outcome of this matter and all expressions about the outcome are only opinions.

11. *Association of Co-counsel*
    Client understands that SG may, at its sole expense, contract with other attorneys for the performance of certain work for the Client and that SG may pay part of the fees it receives under this agreement to such attorneys for the services rendered by them.

(continued on next page)

EXHIBIT 3-5 (continued)

12. *Indemnity*
    Client agrees to indemnify and hold SG harmless for:
    (a) any claims and defense of any claims asserted against any portion of Client's cause of action by anyone other than an attorney or attorneys who may represent Client following termination of SG as provided above or
    (b) any fines, costs or fees asserted against SG as a result of action that SG was directed to take by Client, which in the opinion of SG should not have been taken and about which written notice of such opinion had been given by SG to Client prior to such action being taken.

13. *Joint and Several Obligation*
    It is expressly agreed that each Client is jointly and severally liable for any obligation of any and all other Clients.

14. *Client's Acknowledgment*
    Client acknowledges that Client has been encouraged by SG to consult other counsel concerning the negotiation of this fee agreement, that Client has done so and has made sufficient investigation and inquiry to determine that this agreement is fair and reasonable to Client, and that this agreement was the product of arm's length negotiation with SG.

15. *Dispute Resolution*
    A. **Agreement to Use Procedure.** If any dispute arises relating to this agreement (the "Dispute"), the parties agree to utilize the procedures described herein before commencing any legal action.
    B. **Initiation of Procedure.** The initiating party shall give written notice to the other party, describing the nature of the Dispute, its claim for relief and identifying one or more individuals with authority to resolve the Dispute on such party's behalf. The other party shall have five (5) business days within which to designate in writing one or more individuals with authority to resolve the Dispute on such party's behalf.
    C. **Selection of Mediator.** Within ten (10) business days from the date of designation, the parties shall make a good faith effort to select a person to mediate the Dispute. If no mediator has been selected under this procedure, the parties shall jointly request a State or Federal District Judge of their choosing (of if they cannot agree, the President of the Houston Bar Association) to supply within ten (10) business days a list of potential qualified attorney-mediators. Within five (5) business days of receipt of the list, the parties shall rank the proposed mediators in numerical order of preference, simultaneously exchange such list, and select as the mediator the individual receiving the highest combined ranking. If such mediator is not available to serve, they shall proceed to contact the mediator who was next highest in ranking until they select a mediator.
    D. **Time and Place for Mediation; Parties Represented.** In consultation with the mediator selected, the parties shall promptly designate a mutually convenient time and place for the mediation, such time to be no later than thirty (30) days after selection of the mediator. In the mediation, each party shall be represented by persons with authority and discretion to negotiate a resolution of the Dispute, and may be represented by counsel.

(continued on next page)

EXHIBIT 3-5 (continued)

E. **Conduct of Mediation.** The mediator shall determine the format for the meetings, and the mediation session shall be private. The mediator will keep confidential all information learned in private caucus with any party unless specifically authorized by such party to make disclosure of the information to the other party. The parties agree that the mediation shall be governed by the provisions of Chapter 154 of the Texas Remedies and Practice Code and such other rules as the mediator shall prescribe.

F. **Fees of Mediator; Disqualification.** The fees and expenses of the mediator shall be shared equally by the parties. The mediator shall be disqualified as a witness, consultant, expert or counsel for any party with respect to the Dispute and any related matters.

G. **Confidentiality**. Mediation is a compromise negotiation for purposes of Federal and State Rules of Evidence and constitutes privileged communication under Texas law. The entire mediation process is confidential, and such conduct, statements, promises, offers, views and opinions shall not be discoverable or admissible in any legal proceeding for any purpose.

16. *Severability*

If any part of this letter agreement shall for any reason be found unenforceable, the parties agree that all other portions shall nevertheless remain valid and enforceable.

17. *Integration*

This Agreement represents the final and mutual understanding of the parties. It replaces and supersedes any prior agreements or understandings, whether written or oral. This Agreement may not be modified, amended, or replaced except by another signed written agreement.

If this Agreement is satisfactory, you should sign the lower left corner and return the original to this office. The copy is for your files.

Sincerely yours,

SUSMAN GODFREY L.L.P.

____
____
____
____

AGREED TO AND ACCEPTED:

____

By: ____________________________________

Date: ____________________________________

Social Security or EIN Number:

____

(Please provide this number for bank use in establishing trust account)

3. **Exhibit 3-6 is a Susman Godfrey representation agreement with the following provisions: nonrefundable retainer payable in four periodic installments of $100,000; sliding contingent fee of 16.67 percent before trial, 20 percent during trial and 22.5 percent at conclusion of trial; Gross sum recovered includes any attorneys' fee award. Litigation in non-Texas forum; fee calculation in event of noncash settlement; agreement not to accept cases from other clients relating to specified bankruptcy.**

EXHIBIT 3-6: Susman Godfrey Agreement #3

__________, ______

PRIVILEGED—
ATTORNEY-CLIENT COMMUNICATION

____
____
____
____
____

Re: ____

Dear ______________:

This letter agreement sets forth the terms and conditions on which Susman Godfrey, L.L.P. ("SG") (which includes any successor to the partnership of SG) will undertake to represent ________________ ("Client"), in pursuit of all claims Client has against ________________ relating to the bankruptcy of ______________________________________ (all such claims are collectively referred to as "cause of action"). We must receive an executed copy of this letter agreement before we can go forward. The terms and conditions of our engagement are as follows:

1. *Retainer(s)*
   Upon execution of this agreement, Client will pay SG a non-refundable (except as provided in paragraph 11.C. below) retainer of $100,000, which SG will keep regardless of the outcome of the case to compensate it for its agreement to provide services in pursuit of Client's claims and for any loss of opportunity to accept other matters. As set forth in your June 22, 1992 letter to Steve Susman, ______________ will make three additional payments of $100,000 each to Susman Godfrey on October 1, 1992, January 2, 1993, and April 1, 1993.

THIS CONTRACT IS SUBJECT TO ARBITRATION
UNDER THE TEXAS GENERAL ARBITRATION STATUTE.

(continued on next page)

EXHIBIT 3-6 (continued)

2. *Contingent Fee*
In addition to the payments totaling $400,000 described in Paragraph 1 above, SG will receive 16.67 percent of the gross sum recovered by settlement before commencement of trial (defined as the commencement of jury selection in the case of a jury trial, or the first introduction of evidence in the case of a trial to the court). SG will receive 20 percent of the gross sum recovered by settlement after commencement of trial but before the return of the jury's verdict, in the case of a jury trial, or the conclusion of the submission of evidence, in the case of a bench trial. SG will receive 22.5 percent of the gross sum recovered by settlement or judgment after the return of the jury's verdict in a jury trial and after the conclusion of the submission of evidence in a bench trial. The "gross sum recovered" means all money or other things of value, including the value of any business accommodation recovered by you, including any attorney's fees awarded by the court but net of all litigation costs and expenses (including expert fees) from June 1, 1992 forward. Client authorizes SG to require that any settlement check be made payable jointly to Client and SG, and agrees that after endorsing the check, it will allows SG to cash the same and make payment to the Client of Client's portion of the recovery.

3. *Non-Cash Settlements*
If the cause of action is settled in whole or in part by the Client's receipt of anything of value other than cash, SG shall be entitled to demand and receive at its option (a) payment for all time at its normal hourly rates in effect at the time of settlement, (b) payment in cash, under paragraph 2 above, of the applicable SG contingent percentage of (i) the present value of any noncash consideration plus (ii) any cash received upon settlement, or (c) an undivided interest in any property received by Client, equal to the applicable SG contingent percentage as identified in paragraph 2, plus payment of the applicable SG contingent percentage of any cash received as a result of settlement.

4. *Expenses*
Client agrees to pay all costs and expenses of litigation monthly. SG will periodically send to Client, for direct payment by Client, invoices received by SG from third parties such as court reporters, expert witnesses and reproduction centers for services rendered on Client's behalf. Client agrees to pay these third-party invoices when due.

5. *Cost Deposit*
SG will bill Client for expenses incurred in its investigation of the case prior to the execution of this retention agreement; but SG will not bill Client for its previously incurred fees, notwithstanding any prior understandings.

6. *Litigation in Non-Texas Forum*
SG and Client expect that Client's claims will be filed in Texas. In the event that a Texas court, pursuant to a forum non-conveniens motion or otherwise, dismisses Client's claims without prejudice to Client refiling them in another jurisdiction, Client, at its sole option, may choose to: (a) have SG continue to represent it on these claims in another jurisdiction, pursuant to the terms of this Agreement; or (b) terminate SG and pay SG the amount, if any, by which the value of SG's time (at its normal hourly rates as of the time of termination) exceeds the payments already made to SG pursuant to paragraph 1 above.

(continued on next page)

EXHIBIT 3-6 (continued)

7. *Non-Payment*
By your execution of this engagement letter, you agree that we are relieved from the responsibility of performing any further work should you fail to pay any of the payments described in Paragraph 1 above, or any monthly statement for expenses (including bills for expenses received from third parties), within twenty (20) days of receipt of such statements, normally by the first of the month following receipt. In such event, you agree that we may move to withdraw as your counsel in any case where we have made an appearance on your behalf, and that you will promptly execute any withdrawal motions required to accomplish this.

8. *Estimates*
Client understands that any estimates provided by SG of the magnitude of the expenses that will be required at certain stages of any litigation asserting the cause of action are not precise, and that the kinds and amounts of expenses required are ultimately a function of many conditions over which SG has little or no control, particularly the extent to which the opposition files pretrial motions and engages in its own discovery.

9. *Ownership of the Cause of Action*
Client hereby warrants that it is the sole owner of the cause of action and grants and assigns to SG a lien on said cause of action, including any proceeds obtained from the settlement thereof and any judgment obtained thereon, to the extent of the fees and costs due hereunder.

10. *Assignment*
Client agrees that he shall not assign in whole or in part or otherwise grant any lien against this cause of action or the proceeds from it, other than the lien granted by the preceding paragraph, without the prior written consent of SG.

10a. *Other Plaintiffs*
SG agrees that it will not accept cases from any other plaintiffs with respect to causes of action against ___________ relating to the bankruptcy of _________________________, without consent of Client.

11. *SG's Right to Terminate*
   A. Should Client elect to abandon any litigation asserting the cause of action, should the conduct of Client seriously prejudice the prospects of successful prosecution of such litigation (including but not limited to a change of ownership of Client or the filing of a bankruptcy proceeding involving Client), should Client's failure either to disclose material facts or accurately to describe such facts seriously prejudice the continued prosecution of such litigation, or should Client breach this agreement, then SG shall have the right to terminate this agreement and to demand and receive payment for all unreimbursed expenses advanced on behalf of Client and for all time expended to such date at its hourly rates in effect when the time was expended.
   B. Client shall have the sole and exclusive right to accept or reject any offers for settlement of the cause of action. However, Client shall have an obligation to weigh fully the opinions and recommendations of SG and shall not unreasonably withhold consent to a settlement proposal which in the judgment of SG is a fair and reasonable

(continued on next page)

EXHIBIT 3-6 (continued)

basis for the disposition of the cause of action. Should the Client unreasonably withhold its consent to fair and reasonable settlement, SG shall have the right to terminate this agreement, and to demand and receive payment for all unreimbursed expenses advanced on behalf of Client and for all time to such date at its hourly rates in effect when the time was expended. Hourly rates are reviewed annually and adjusted January 1 if appropriate.

C. Should it become the opinion of SG at any time that Client's cause of action lacks merit (for example, because of inability to verify Client's claims through witnesses, because of adverse developments in the law or because of a materially adverse change in the financial condition of the defendant), then SG shall have the option to terminate this agreement and be relieved of any obligation to participate in any pending litigation involving the cause of action. If that happens, Client shall be liable to SG only for unreimbursed expenses SG has advanced on behalf of Client; and SG agrees to refund to Client any amounts paid to SG in excess of SG's hourly rates for the time expended as of the date of termination.

12. *No Guarantees*
The Client hereby acknowledges that SG has made no guarantees regarding the successful outcome of this matter and all expressions about the outcome are only opinions.

13. *Association of Co-counsel*
Client understands that SG may, at its expense and after consulting with Client, contract with other attorneys for the performance of certain work for the Client and that SG may pay part of the fees it receives under this agreement to such attorneys for the services rendered by them.

14. *Excluded Claims*
Filing of litigation on Client's behalf may subject Client to cross-claims, counterclaims, or claims filed in another action. Client understands that this agreement shall not cover the defense of any claims, counterclaims or cross-claims asserted against Client in any litigation involving the cause of action or in any other case. Should any such claims be filed, the parties hereto shall discuss and attempt to negotiate a separate or supplemental agreement concerning representations of Client with regard to those claims.

15. *Client's Indemnity*
Client agrees to indemnify and hold SG harmless for (a) any claims asserted by others to any portion of the cause of action and (b) any fines, costs or fees asserted against SG as a result of action that SG was directed to take by Client or which SG took after discussion with Client and in the good faith belief that such action was in the best interest of Client.

16. *Joint and Several Obligation*
It is expressly agreed that each Client is jointly and severally liable for any obligation of any and all other Clients.

17. *Client's Acknowledgment*
Client acknowledges that Client has been encouraged by SG to consult other counsel concerning the negotiation of this fee agreement, that Client has made sufficient investigation and inquiry to determine that this agreement is fair and reasonable to Client, and that this agreement was the product of arm's length negotiation with SG.

(continued on next page)

EXHIBIT 3-6 (continued)

18. *Dispute Resolution*
    Any disputes arising under this letter agreement will be submitted to arbitration by the Dean of the University of Texas School of Law or a person appointed by him, and the arbitrator's decision shall be binding, conclusive and nonappealable.

19. *Severability*
    If any part of this letter agreement shall for any reason be found unenforceable, the parties agree that all other portions shall nevertheless remain valid and enforceable.

20. *Integration*
    This Agreement represents the final and mutual understanding of the parties. It replaces and supersedes any prior agreements or understandings, whether written or oral. This Agreement may not be modified, amended, or replaced except by another signed written agreement.

If this Agreement is satisfactory, you should sign the lower left corner and return the original to this office. The copy is for your files.

Sincerely yours,

SUSMAN GODFREY, L.L.P.

____

____

____

____

AGREED TO AND ACCEPTED:

____

By:_________________________
VICE PRESIDENT

Date:_______________________

Social Security or EIN Number:

____

(Please provide this number for bank use in establishing trust account)

4. **Exhibit 3-7 is a Susman Godfrey representation agreement with the following provisions: phased agreement first providing straight hourly billing for investigation by Susman Godfrey in behalf of investors in $35 million note; $500,000 retainer, from which the hourly charges for investigation will be paid. After the investigation, if clients elect not to pursue these claims, the balance of the retainer in the trust account to be returned to clients; contingent fee arising ninety days after suit is filed.**

EXHIBIT 3-7: Susman Godfrey Agreement #4

__________, _____

PRIVILEGED—
ATTORNEY-CLIENT COMMUNICATION

Re: ____
____

Gentlemen:

This letter Agreement sets forth the terms under which Susman Godfrey ("SG") (which includes any successor to the partnership of SG) has agreed to represent ________________ ____ and ____________________________ (collectively the "Clients") in pursuit of all claims Clients have against ________________ ("__________") (other than claims against Clients' own attorneys and advisors) arising out of or related to Clients' investment in a $35 million note offering, with associated stock warrants, by ____________________________ in 1988.

When all Clients have executed and returned this Agreement to SG (which may be done in multiple counterparts), SG has agreed to represent Clients.

1. *Fee*
   A. *Initial Payment.* Upon signing of this Agreement, Clients will pay SG $500,000, such amount to be funded by Clients in proportion to their respective investments in the $35 million note offering of ____________. Immediately after execution of this Agreement, SG shall conduct an investigation of Clients' causes of action against ________. Clients wish this investigation to be completed as soon as possible and agree to cooperate fully in making documents and knowledgeable persons available to SG for the investigation. As provided for in paragraphs 1B and 1C below, Clients shall compensate SG at its regular hourly rates for the investigation out of this $500,000 payment, and shall pay all expenses of the investigation. SG has estimated that this investigation will be completed within two weeks from the date of execution of this Agreement and will cost approximately $25,000 for fees and expenses.

THIS CONTRACT IS SUBJECT TO ARBITRATION UNDER THE TEXAS GENERAL ARBITRATION STATUTE.

(continued on next page)

EXHIBIT 3-7 (continued)

B. *Decision Not to Proceed After SG's Investigation.* If for any reason after this investigation Clients decide not to pursue the causes of action, or if SG decides based on the investigation that it does not wish to pursue the causes of action on a contingent basis in this Agreement, then the $500,000 payment as provided for in paragraph 1A above shall be returned to Clients, less the amount necessary to compensate SG for its reasonable fees (at its regular hourly rates) and expenses of conducting the investigation. In this event, SG will, on request, return to Clients all of SG's files regarding this matter, including the results of all investigations conducted by SG, for Clients' use as they see fit.

C. *Decision to Proceed After SG's Investigation.* If, after the investigation referred to in paragraph 1A above, the decision is made by Clients and SG to continue to pursue the causes of action, SG shall bill Clients for the expenses of the investigation (not including fees), which shall be promptly paid by Clients. In this event, the $500,000 initial fee payment made pursuant to paragraph 1A above shall be handled as follows: (i) If the causes of action are finally disposed of on or before ninety (90) calendar days from the date suit is filed, SG shall refund to Clients the balance of the said $500,000 after deducting an amount equal to twice the fee owing to SG at its regular hourly rates for reasonable services rendered by SG after the date of filing suit, plus SG's reasonable expenses and costs. In such event, SG shall not be entitled to receive, in addition to the amounts at two times hourly rates, the contingent fee under paragraph 1D below. (ii) After ninety calendar days from the date suit is filed, if the causes of action have not been finally disposed of, then SG will keep the $500,000, regardless of the outcome of the causes of action, to compensate it for services rendered and for its commitment to provide services to Clients and for loss of opportunity to accept other matters.

D. *Contingent Fee Arising 90 Days After Suit Is Filed.* In addition to retaining the $500,000 under paragraph 1C above, SG shall receive the following contingent fees in the event that a decision has been made to proceed after the investigation, but the causes of action have not been finally disposed of within ninety (90) calendar days from the date suit is filed: thirteen percent (13%) of gross sums recovered up to $25 million; and fifteen percent (15%) of all gross sums recovered over $25 million. "Gross sums recovered" means all money directly recovered by Clients, including any attorney's fees awarded by the Court, but not including any court costs or other expenses awarded by the Court.

E. *Mechanism for Payment of Contingent Fee.* In the event that SG becomes entitled to a contingent fee under paragraph 1D above, Clients authorize SG to require that SG's contingent fee be paid directly to SG by ________ (by check or wire transfer) out of any cash settlement proceeds, with the balance of such cash settlement proceeds to be paid directly to Clients (by separate checks or wire transfer) in proportion to their respective investments in the $35 million _________ note offering.

F. *Cap on Hourly Fees.* Except as provided below in paragraphs 2, 8, 9A, 9B, and 10, Clients' obligations to SG for payment of fees on an hourly-rate basis shall never exceed the $500,000 initial payment made pursuant to paragraph 1A above.

(continued on next page)

EXHIBIT 3-7 (continued)

2. *Contingent Fee on Non-Cash Settlement*
If, more than ninety (90) calendar days after suit is filed, the cause of action is settled in whole or in part by the Clients' direct receipt of anything of value other than cash, SG shall be entitled to payment in cash, under paragraph 1D above, of the applicable SG contingent percentage of the present value of any non-cash consideration plus any cash received upon settlement. If all or some part of the settlement consideration is not directly received by the Clients, but the Clients are indirectly benefited by acts undertaken or payments made by _______ to entities other than Clients (for example, to ___________ as part of an agreed restructuring of _________ debts), then SG shall not be entitled to a contingent fee based on such indirect benefits to the Clients, but shall instead be entitled to the following: SG shall be entitled to retroactive compensation for all service rendered at twice its normal hourly rates up to $1.5 million, and at its regular hourly rates for fees in excess of $1.5 million, if any; however, SG shall give Clients a credit against such fees for the $500,000 initial payment that SG has kept as provided in paragraph 1C(ii) above.

3. *Expenses and Monthly Reports*
Clients agree to pay all of SG's reasonable costs and expenses of litigation monthly. If Clients decide to pursue the causes of action after SG has completed its investigation, Clients agree that they will promptly deposit the sum of $50,000 in an interest-bearing account out of which account SG shall pay all reasonable expenses. Clients agree promptly, upon request by SG, to replenish said $50,000 cost deposit as expenses are paid. SG agrees that before committing itself to any expenditure in excess of $10,000 on Clients' behalf, SG will seek advance approval of all Clients. Any amounts remaining in this account after payment of reasonable costs and expenses at the conclusion of SG's services shall be returned to Clients. In order that Clients may monitor SG's services, and the costs and expenses SG incurs on Clients' behalf, SG will provide each Client with a monthly statement describing those services and expenses in the general format of the sample statement attached as Exhibit A to this Agreement.

4. *Nonpayment*
By their execution of this engagement letter, Clients agree that SG is relieved from the responsibility of performing any further work should Clients fail to pay any monthly statement for expenses (including bills for expenses received from third parties), within thirty (30) days of receipt of such statements. In such event, Clients agree that SG may move to withdraw as Clients' counsel in any case where SG has made an appearance on behalf of any Client, and that Clients will promptly execute any withdrawal motions required to accomplish this; provided, however, that SG shall give all Clients fifteen (15) days written notice of SG's intent to invoke its rights under this paragraph so that Clients may have an opportunity to cure their default.

5. *Estimates*
Clients understand that any estimates provided by SG of the magnitude of the expenses that will be required at certain stages of any litigation asserting the cause of action are not precise, and that the kinds and amounts of expenses required are ultimately a function of many conditions over which SG has little or no control, particularly the extent to which the opposition files pretrial motions and engages in its own discovery.

(continued on next page)

EXHIBIT 3-7 (continued)

6. *Ownership of the Cause of Action*
   Each Client hereby warrants that it is the sole owner of its causes of action and grants and assigns to SG a lien on said cause of action, including any proceeds obtained from the settlement thereof and any judgment obtained thereon, to the extent of the fees and costs due under this Agreement.

7. *Assignment*
   The rights and obligations of the parties under this Agreement are not assignable in whole or in part, without the prior written consent of the other parties.

8. *SG's Right to Terminate*
   Should Clients engage in conduct which seriously prejudices the prospects of successful prosecution of the Causes of Action (including but not limited to the filing of bankruptcy proceedings in which one or more Clients is the debtor), or should Clients' failure either to disclose material facts or accurately to describe such facts seriously prejudice the continued prosecution of such litigation, or should Clients breach this Agreement, then SG shall have the right to terminate this Agreement and to demand and receive payment for all unreimbursed expenses advanced on behalf of Clients and for all time expended to such date at its hourly rates in effect when the time was expended, to the extent such time exceeds $500,000.

9. *Clients' Right to Terminate*
   A. *Termination of SG by All Clients.* Should all Clients desire to terminate the services of SG for cause, then SG shall receive payment for all time expended to such date at its regular hourly rates in effect when the time was expended, to the extent such time exceeds $500,000. For purposes of paragraphs 9A and 9B of this Agreement, "cause" is defined as either (a) failure of SG to provide legal services in accordance with applicable professional standards, or (b) failure of SG to obey reasonable directions of Clients regarding the causes of action, if, in the good-faith judgment of all Clients, the conduct of SG threatens or materially impairs Clients' prosecution of the causes of action. If Clients unanimously vote to terminate the services of SG, the Clients must notify SG in writing of their decision and provide a statement of the reason or reasons constituting cause for termination. Within 15 days of SG's receipt of such notice, SG may elect to contest the termination (pursuant to the dispute resolution provision in paragraph 17 below) by serving notice in writing upon Clients. The burden of proof shall be upon Clients to prove that termination is for cause as defined herein.
   B. *Termination of SG by Less Than All Clients.* Should less than all Clients desire to terminate the services of SG for cause, then such Clients may engage separate counsel to replace SG without releasing SG from its obligation to continue its representation of the Clients who do not wish to terminate the services of SG. In that event, SG and the Clients who continue to be represented by SG will continue to operate under the fee arrangement specified in this Agreement, as to hourly rates, contingent fees, and expenses. However, any Client who has terminated the services of SG for cause shall immediately pay to SG an hourly fee equal to twice SG's normal hourly rates for its work done to date on behalf of all Clients, up to a total fee equal to the percentage of that Client's ownership of the $35 million __________ note offering. (Each such Client shall be entitled to a credit for its proportionate share of the initial $500,000 payment made pursuant to paragraph 1A above.)

(continued on next page)

EXHIBIT 3-7 (continued)

10. *Settlement*

A. Clients shall each have the sole and exclusive right to accept or reject any offers for settlement of their respective causes of action. However, Clients shall have an obligation to weigh fully the opinions and recommendations of SG and shall not unreasonably withhold consent to a settlement proposal which is a fair and reasonable basis for the disposition of the cause of action. In any dispute between SG and any Client regarding the fairness and reasonableness of a settlement proposal which SG has recommended that the Client accept, the burden shall be on SG to establish that the settlement proposal was indeed fair and reasonable for that Client. Should one or more the Clients unreasonably withhold their consent to fair and reasonable settlement, SG shall have the right to terminate this Agreement as to each such Client, and to demand and receive payment for all unreimbursed expenses advanced on behalf of each such Client and for all time to such date at its regular hourly rates in effect when the time was expended, up to a fee equal to the percentage of that Client's ownership of the $35 million ____________ note offering times the total fee owing. (Each such Client shall be entitled to a credit for its proportionate share of the initial $500,000 payment made pursuant to paragraph 1A above.) Hourly rates shall initially be those set forth on Exhibit B to this Agreement; however, Clients understand that SG's hourly rates are reviewed annually and adjusted January 1 if appropriate.

B. *Partial Settlements During Period Prior to 90 Days After Suit Is Filed.*
If Clients owning twenty-five percent (25%) or more of the aggregate claims arising out of the $35 million __________ note offering settle their claims prior to ninety (90) days after suit is filed, then, as set forth in the following examples, the contingent fees under paragraph 1D to be paid by the remaining Clients who have not settled shall be increased, and the "breakpoints" on the sliding contingent fee scale shall be decreased, by amounts proportionate to the percentage of the aggregate claims that have settled. *Example 1:* If twenty-five percent (25%) of the aggregate claims have been settled within the first 90 days after suit was filed, then, as to the remaining Clients, the contingent fees under paragraph 1D will be 16.25%[1] of all gross sums recovered up to $18.75 million;[2] and 18.75%[3] of all gross sums recovered above $18.75 million. *Example 2:* If, instead, 75% of the aggregate claims have been settled within the first 90 days after suit was filed, then, as to the remaining Clients, the contingent fees under paragraph 1D will be 22.75% of all gross sums recovered up to $6.25 million; and 26.25% of all gross sums recovered above $6.25 million.

11. *Return of Clients' Files*
If this Agreement is terminated as to any Client for any reason and new counsel is selected by all of the Clients or by any one or more of them, SG shall, at the direction of such Client or Clients, promptly turn over its files relating to the causes of action to such new counsel.

[1] 16.25% being the original 13% contingent fee on the first tier of gross amounts recovered, plus (.25 × 13%).
[2] $18.75 million being the original $25 million breakpoint between the first and second tiers of gross sums recovered, less (.25 × $25 million).
[3] 18.75% being the original 15% contingent fee on the second tier of gross amounts recovered, plus (.25 × 15%).

(continued on next page)

EXHIBIT 3-7 (continued)

12. *No Guarantees*
The Clients hereby acknowledge that SG has made no guarantees regarding the successful outcome of this matter and all expressions about the outcome are only opinions.

13. *Association of Co-Counsel*
Clients understand that SG may, at its expense, and with the approval of all of the Clients, contract with other attorneys for the performance of certain work for the Clients and that SG may pay part of the fees it receives under this Agreement to such attorneys for the services rendered by them.

14. *Clients' Indemnity*
Clients agree to indemnify and hold SG harmless for (a) any claims asserted by others to any portion of the causes of action which Clients have warranted that they own (in paragraph 6 above) and (b) any fines, costs or fees assessed against SG as a result of action that SG was directed to take by Clients, which action SG previously advised the Clients in writing to be inappropriate.

15. *Several Obligation*
It is expressly agreed that each Client is severally liable for any obligation of the Clients in proportion to its respective investment in the $35 million __________ note offering.

16. *Clients' Acknowledgment*
Clients acknowledge that Clients have been encouraged by SG to consult other counsel concerning the negotiation of this fee agreement, that Clients have made sufficient investigation and inquiry to determine that this Agreement is fair and reasonable to Clients, and that this Agreement was the product of arms-length negotiation with SG.

17. *Dispute Resolution*
Any disputes arising under this letter Agreement will be submitted to arbitration by the Dean of the University of Texas School of Law, Austin, Texas, or such other arbitrator(s) as may be mutually agreeable to SG and all Clients, and the arbitrator's decision shall be binding, conclusive and non-appealable. If for any reason the Dean is unable or unwilling to serve, he shall be replaced by an arbitrator selected in accordance with the rules of the American Arbitration Association.

18. *Severability*
If any part of this letter Agreement shall for any reason be found unenforceable, the parties agree that all other portions shall nevertheless remain valid and enforceable.

19. *Integration*
This Agreement represents the final and mutual understanding of the parties. It replaces and supersedes any prior agreements or understandings, whether written or oral. This Agreement may not be modified, amended, or replaced except by another signed written agreement.

(continued on next page)

EXHIBIT 3-7 (continued)

If this Agreement is satisfactory, you should sign in the spaces below and return the original to this office. The copy is for your files.

Sincerely yours,

SUSMAN GODFREY

By:____

____

____

Attachments (2)

AGREED TO AND ACCEPTED:

By: ____

Date: ____

____

By: ____

Date: ____

5. **Susman Godfrey Agreement #5: Agreement to pursue claims against officers and directors of Debtor's corporation on normal hourly fee basis, with option of Susman Godfrey to convert the fee agreement by a specified date to 80 percent of normal hourly rates not to exceed $2.5 million, plus 20 percent of recovery reduced by 50 percent of fees actually paid to Susman Godfrey, plus sliding contingent fee as to amounts recovered from designated corporation. A supplemental agreement three years later when it appeared that bonds might be issued to settle the lawsuit set up a sliding contingent fee that would be applicable in the event of settlement and the case did not go to trial.**

COMMENT: The interesting aspect of this agreement is that the right to change the billing method was contained in the original fee agreement. Thereafter, timely notice of election to convert the fee agreement was given. It was preferable to provide for this election in the original agreement rather than to change billing methods mid-representation to avoid contention that the change in billing method was made because of the superior knowledge of the law firm.

• • •

6. **Susman Godfrey Agreement #6: In an action involving claims against companies involved with asbestos abatement at client's buildings, there were hourly charges until disposition of a summary judgment or six months, whichever came sooner, after which Susman Godfrey could elect to convert to a one-third contingency. If SG did not so elect, client had the option to have continuing representation on a normal hourly basis, later negotiated to a 40 percent contingent fee.**

This representation involved a 50-50 split of the fee with co-counsel.

7. **The Susman Godfrey representation agreement shown in Exhibit 3-8 includes the following provisions: short-term hourly fee converting to contingent fee (33 1/3 percent before trial, 40 percent during trial, 45 percent after judgment); provides method for calculating contingent fee in the event of noncash distribution from a trust, with a cap on fees from noncash recovery.**

EXHIBIT 3-8: Susman Godfrey Agreement #7

__________, _____

PRIVILEGED—
ATTORNEY-CLIENT COMMUNICATION

____
____
____

Re: ____
____

Dear ____________________

This letter agreement sets forth the terms and conditions which Susman, Godfrey ("SG") (which includes any successor to the partnership of SG) will convert to a contingency fee arrangement as of November 9, 1989, the existing hourly fee arrangement between SG and ____________________ ("clients"), in pursuit of all claims clients have against __________ ____ (claims are collectively referred to as "cause of action"). We must receive an executed copy of this letter

THIS CONTRACT IS SUBJECT TO ARBITRATION
UNDER THE TEXAS GENERAL ARBITRATION STATUTE.

(continued on next page)

EXHIBIT 3-8 (continued)

agreement *before* we can agree to represent the clients on a contingency fee basis. Then, unless (1) an enforceable agreement under Rule 11 is entered on the record on November 9, 1989 by all parties to the above-referenced suit, and (2) all deeds, checks and other necessary documents (including but not limited to a signed settlement agreement) are delivered to the clients on or before November 27, 1989, SG's fee arrangement shall convert as of November 9, 1989, to the contingent fee terms contained here. The terms and conditions of our contingent fee engagement are as follows:

1. *Contingent Fee*

   SG shall receive thirty-three percent (33-1/3%) of the gross sum recovered by settlement prior to commencement of trial (defined as the commencement of jury selection in the case of a jury trial, or the first introduction of evidence in the case of a trial to the court). SG shall receive forty percent (40%) of the gross sum recovered by settlement after the commencement of trial but prior to the return of the fact-finder's verdict. SG shall receive forty-five percent (45%) of the gross sum recovered by settlement or judgment after the return of the fact-finder's verdict. The "gross sum recovered" means all money recovered free of trust by clients, including any attorney's fees awarded by the court or in settlement, but excluding any sums that represent current trust income or accumulated income and capital gains. "Gross sum recovered" also means the clients' shares, as determined by settlement or judgment, of any sums of money paid into trust by ______________________, in addition to cash already in trust at the date of this agreement. Clients authorize SG to require that any settlement check be made payable jointly to clients and SG, and agrees that after endorsing the check, they will allow SG to cash the same and make payment to the clients of clients' portion of the recovery.

2. *Non-Cash Recovery*

   SG and clients expect that as part of a settlement or judgment, one or both clients will receive distributions free of trust of something of value other than cash; in that event, SG shall be entitled to demand and receive an undivided one-third (1/3) interest in any property received by clients, less the mineral interests, plus payment of the applicable SG contingent percentage as identified in paragraph 1, of any cash received as a result of settlement. SG understands and clients agree that clients intend to use their best efforts to market and sell any non-cash distributions of property they receive as soon as prudently practical and to promptly pay SG's fee under this paragraph out of the gross proceeds of any such sale. If for any reason such property does not sell within a year after clients' receipt of a non-cash distribution, SG shall be entitled to demand and receive, at its option, (a) payment in cash at its hourly rates then in effect for all time worked from the effective date of this agreement, and SG will credit __________________ cash SG receives in paragraph #1 and in paragraph #2 or (b) payment in cash of thirty-three and one-third percent (33-1/3%) of the present value of any non-cash consideration plus the applicable SG percentage, under paragraph 1 above, of any cash received upon settlement or judgment. ____________ will execute and deliver to SG a deed of trust on her undistributed, undivided one-sixteenth (1/16) interest in the corpus of the trust established under the Will of ________________ as security for the payments described in this paragraph. SG agrees not to unreasonably withhold its consent to subordinate its deed of trust on one or more of the parcels of ______________ trust property, up to one-half of such property, should it become necessary for clients to borrow money to pay litigation expenses, and should a lender to one or both clients require a first lien to secure such a loan.

(continued on next page)

EXHIBIT 3-8 (continued)

SG and clients agree that ________________ and SG on her behalf shall use their best efforts to obtain distributions to her, free of trust, of her share of the trust established for the children of ___________________ under the Will of _____________________ and her share of the trust established for the children of __________________ under the Will of ____________________. Upon distribution to ______________ any property free of trust, it shall be subject to the contingent fees stated herein. Any property remaining in an existing trust after final resolution of this dispute, by settlement or judgment, shall not be subject to the contingent fee stated herein. Should trial or settlement result in the clients' obtaining an order or agreement splitting out either or both of their shares of the trust for the children of __________________ under the will of _________________ and/or either or both of their shares of the trust for the children of _________________ under the will of _____________ into one or more separate trusts for either or both of their benefit, under the control of trustees appointed by ______________ and/or ______________ the property (including cash and other liquid assets) in such trust(s) shall be subject to the contingent fee stated in this paragraph. Also, any distribution free of trust of cash assets representing accumulated trust income or capital gains shall be subject to the contingent fee stated in this paragraph, and not paragraph one, above.

3. *Cap on Fees from Non-Cash Recovery*
   In no event shall SG be entitled to demand more than the sums specified in paragraph 1, plus $200,000 based on receipt free of trust or a split of property into individual trusts, unless this case is appealed, in which event the cap shall be $250,000 plus the sums specified in paragraph 1.

4. *Expenses*
   Clients agree to pay all costs and expenses of litigation monthly. SG will periodically send to clients, for direct payment by client, invoices received by SG from third parties such as court reporters, expert witnesses and reproduction centers for services rendered on clients' behalf. Clients agree to pay these third-party invoices when due.

5. *Cost Deposit*
   A. Clients also agree to maintain their present cost deposit of $10,000 to cover other necessary expenses of litigation, such as travel, telephone, messenger service and photocopying, that SG may advance on client's behalf, plus any hourly attorney's fees clients may be required by this agreement to pay. Susman Godfrey has placed these funds in an interest-bearing trust account. Each month, as SG submits its bills to client, the expenses due will be deducted from the cost deposit. Client is obligated to replenish the cost deposit on receipt of the monthly bills and to maintain the cost deposit at its initial amount. Upon the termination of our services, we will promptly refund the cost deposit to you, less any balance for fees and expenses unpaid as of the date of our final bill.
   B. Our agreement to provide legal representation in this matter is conditioned upon maintenance of the requested cost deposit.
   C. This firm retains the discretion to request a supplemental cost deposit, over and above the cost deposit required prior to our commencement of the engagement, in the event of an increase in our anticipated fees and expenses during the course of litigation.

(continued on next page)

EXHIBIT 3-8 (continued)

6. *Nonpayment*
By your execution of this engagement letter, you agree that we are relieved from the responsibility of performing any further work should you fail to pay any monthly statement for fees and expenses (including bills for expenses received from third parties), or for supplemental cost deposits, within fifteen (15) days of receipt of such statements, normally by the first of the month following receipt. In such event, you agree that we may move to withdraw as your counsel in any case where we have made an appearance on your behalf, and that you will promptly execute any withdrawal motions required to accomplish this.

7. *Estimates*
Clients understand that any estimates provided by SG of the magnitude of the expenses that will be required at certain stages of any litigation asserting the cause of action are not precise, and that the kinds and amounts of expenses required are ultimately a function of many conditions over which SG has little or no control, particularly the extent to which the opposition files pretrial motions and engages in its own discovery.

8. *Ownership of the Cause of Action*
Clients hereby warrant that they are the sole owners of their causes of action and grant and assign to SG a lien on said cause of action, including any proceeds obtained from the settlement thereof and any judgment obtained thereon, to the extent of the fees and costs due hereunder.

9. *Assignment*
Clients agree that they shall not assign in whole or in part or otherwise grant any lien against this cause of action or the proceeds from it, other than the lien granted by the preceding paragraph, without the prior written consent of SG.

10. *SG's Right to Terminate*
    A. Should clients elect to abandon any litigation asserting the causes of action, should the conduct of clients seriously prejudice the prospects of successful prosecution of such litigation (including but not limited to a bankruptcy proceeding involving clients), should clients' failure either to disclose material facts or accurately to describe such facts seriously prejudice the continued prosecution of such litigation, or should client breach this agreement, then SG shall have the right to terminate this agreement and to demand and receive payment for all unreimbursed expenses advanced on behalf of client and for all time expended to such date at its hourly rates in effect when the time was expended.
    B. Clients shall have the sole and exclusive right to accept or reject any offers for settlement of the cause of action. However, clients shall have an obligation to weigh fully the opinions and recommendations of SG and shall not unreasonably withhold consent to a settlement proposal which in the judgment of SG is a fair and reasonable basis for the disposition of the cause of action. Should the clients unreasonably withhold their consent to fair and reasonable settlement, SG shall have the right to terminate this agreement, and to demand and receive payment for all unreimbursed expenses advanced on behalf of clients and for all time to such date at its hourly rates in effect when the time was expended. Hourly rates are reviewed annually and adjusted January 1 if appropriate.

(continued on next page)

EXHIBIT 3-8 (continued)

C. Should it become the opinion of SG at any time subsequent to the date of this agreement, that clients' cause of action lacks merit (for example, because of inability to verify clients' claims through witnesses, because of adverse developments in the law or because of a materially adverse change in the financial condition of the defendant), then SG shall have the option to terminate this agreement and be relieved of any obligation to participate in any pending litigation involving the cause of action. If that happens, clients shall be liable to SG only for unreimbursed expenses SG has advanced on behalf of clients.

11. *No Guarantees*
The clients hereby acknowledge that SG has made no guarantees regarding the successful outcome of this matter and all expressions about the outcome are only opinions.

12. *Association of Co-Counsel*
Clients understand that SG may, at its expense, contract with other attorneys for the performance of certain work for the clients and that SG may pay part of the fees it receives under this agreement to such attorneys for the services rendered by them.

13. *Excluded Claims*
Filing of litigation on clients' behalf may subject clients to cross-claims, counterclaims, or claims filed in another action. Except for pending claims, cross-claims and counterclaims, clients understand that this agreement shall not cover the defense of any claims, counterclaims or cross-claims asserted against clients in any litigation involving the cause of action or in any other case. Should any such claims be filed, the parties hereto shall discuss and attempt to negotiate a separate or supplemental agreement concerning representations of client with regard to those claims.

14. *Clients' Indemnity*
Clients agree to indemnify and hold SG harmless for (a) any claims asserted by others to any portion of the cause of action and (b) any fines, costs or fees asserted against SG as a result of action that SG was directed to take by client or which SG took in the good faith belief that such action was in the best interest of clients.

15. *Joint and Several Obligation*
It is expressly agreed that each client is jointly and severally liable for any obligation of the other client named in the first paragraph of this agreement. However, ___________ acknowledges that, because of her age and the operation of the trust instruments, it is likely that she will bear the initial brunt of SG's fees under this agreement, and agrees that she will not involve SG in her agreement with ______________ as to how, between them, they intend to apportion the fees paid under this agreement.

16. *Clients' Acknowledgment*
Clients acknowledge that clients have been encouraged by SG to consult other counsel concerning the negotiation of this fee agreement, that clients have made sufficient investigation and inquiry to determine that this agreement is fair and reasonable to clients, and that this agreement was the product of arms-length negotiation with SG.

(continued on next page)

EXHIBIT 3-8 (continued)

17. *Dispute Resolution*
Any disputes arising under this letter agreement will be submitted to arbitration by the Dean of the University of Texas School of Law or a person appointed by him, and the arbitrator's decision shall be binding, conclusive and non-appealable.

18. *Severability*
If any part of this letter agreement shall for any reason be found unenforceable, the parties agree that all other portions shall nevertheless remain valid and enforceable.

19. *Integration*
This Agreement represents the final and mutual understanding of the parties. It replaces and supersedes any prior agreements or understandings, whether written or oral. This Agreement may not be modified, amended, or replaced except by another signed written agreement.

If this Agreement is satisfactory, you should sign the lower left corner and return the original to this office. The copy is for your files.

Sincerely yours,

SUSMAN GODFREY

____
____
____

____

Attachments

AGREED TO AND ACCEPTED:

By: ___________________________________

Date: ___________________________________

By: ___________________________________

Date: ___________________________________

Social Security or EIN Number: ______________________________
(Please provide this number for
bank use in establishing trust account)

8. **Susman Godfrey Agreement #8: Fifty percent contingency for recovery for city of unpaid franchise fees or street use fees by a utility company; involves audit and collection of sums due; right of SG to engage co-counsel at the expense of SG.**

COMMENT: This agreement contains detailed provisions for payment of SG fees if payment to the client in satisfaction of its claims is in the form of non-cash assets or rights.

9. **Susman Godfrey Agreement #9: Contingent fee agreement in action to acquire permits necessary to operate a hazardous waste disposal facility in a salt dome.**

COMMENT: This is one of the more complicated of the Susman Godfrey contingent fee agreements in that it contemplated payment in the form of equity securities resulting after a possible corporate merger, a third-party subscriber, compliance with securities law, co-counsel engaged by SG, payment of permitting expenses, the allocation of those permitting expenses, an appeal of an adverse denial of the requested permits, and other issues.

The contingencies involved issuance of permits, exhaustion of all appeals, and the consummation of a corporate merger.

SG had the right to terminate the agreement after it had paid or incurred payments to third parties for permitting costs of $2 million.

This is a gross oversimplification of a complex transaction, but serves to illustrate that innovative arrangements and risk-taking can take place in nonroutine, large-dollar situations.

Susman Godfrey's other approaches to billing methods in four different representations include the following:

- A retainer of $1 million to be replenished when hourly billing at 50 percent premium rates exhausts the initial retainer, at which time additional retainer deposits shall be made based on quarterly budgets; nonbankrupt clients and bankrupt clients are jointly liable for the payment of fees; $50,000 deposit for costs, to be replenished.
- A retainer of $25,000 to be kept by the firm, if the recovery is less than $100,000. If the recovery is more than $100,000, the firm keeps the retainer and 25 percent of gross sum recovered. Services include from pre-complaint investigation through any appeals, with right to employ co-counsel at the expense of the firm.
- Thirty percent contingency with detailed arrangements for payment of fee in the event of noncash portion of settlement or judgment, including creation of a trust to ensure payment. If settlement is reached within ninety days after the action is started, the maximum cash fee shall not exceed $6 million; if settled within one year, the cap is $50 million; maximum fee will be $100 million.
- Nonrefundable retainer waived; SG to receive 1 percent of settlement proceeds for each month after commencement of representation to a maximum of 5 percent; 10 percent contingency after commencement of trial.

CLOSING COMMENT

When examples are used that refer to large sums of money or extremely complex issues, some practitioners conclude that the illustration does not apply to their practice, that they do not command fees in that range or their practice does not include matters of similar complexity. We are talking about principles and approaches that are applicable to all practice settings and to firms of all sizes. In this chapter the unidentified law firms have hundreds of lawyers. Bickel & Brewer and Susman Godfrey, however, might be termed "midsize" firms, with fewer than forty lawyers. Small firms can learn from the larger firms, just as the large firm can learn from innovative small-firm lawyers.

Now it is time to see, in chapter 4, what corporate counsel have been doing about billing methods, since it is in this arena that the most direct pressure for change is taking place. In a buyer's market, the customer controls.

NOTES

1. Bickel & Brewer has generously consented to the publication of the nine fee agreements, which appear in redacted form. In some instances introductory or recurring standard provisions have been omitted for sake of brevity. The essential innovative features of each agreement have been included. Special thanks go to Robert P. Cummings, Esq., for his cooperation and to the other members of Bickel & Brewer.

2. *National Law Journal*, Dec. 19, 1994, p. C4.

3. Thanks to those who shared these approaches to innovative billing, although their request for confidentiality precludes my identifying the firm and the partners who cooperated.

4. Because of their requests for confidentiality, I can only say thanks without mentioning names to those who consented to the publication of this innovative fee agreement.

5. Thanks to Blackwell Sanders Matheny Weary and Sanders and to UtiliCorp United for permitting the use of this summary of their innovative representation agreement.

6. Thanks to Steve Susman and to John G. George, Firm Administrator of Susman Godfrey, for furnishing copies of actual fee agreements used by that firm and consenting to the use of these materials.

CHAPTER 4

The Present—Corporate Counsel Are Doing It

IN THE LATE 1980s, when alternative billing methods were being discussed by some lawyers, many corporate counsel reacted negatively against change away from straight hourly billing, contending that they could monitor and manage outside counsel. It is difficult to know exactly why this stand was taken. One assertion was that matters assigned to outside counsel often involved litigation with so many uncertainties and uncontrollable aspects that any other billing method simply would not work. Another suggestion was that many general counsel had grown up professionally in an era dominated by hourly billing and hence were accustomed to that method almost to the exclusion of other methods. A surmise was that some of the negative reaction was simply inertia against change.

As mentioned in chapter 2, while early discussions were going on regarding changed billing methods, the general economic recession took place, accompanied by the cumulative effect of an overabundance of lawyers. As the profits of many businesses declined, companies were forced to examine their own expenses and cut their costs wherever possible. Simultaneously, a sizable number of companies had become involved with the total quality management (TQM) movement. TQM forced inward thinking by the companies about quality of product and the need for efficiency to remain competitive. At a relatively early stage, some law departments began to analyze whether certain law work traditionally assigned to outside counsel could be done more effectively and at a lower cost by keeping that work in-house. The size of law departments grew, which meant less work for outside law firms.

Companies that had gone through the TQM process with respect to their manufacturing side ultimately required their own law departments to submit to the TQM discipline. As the companies sought to reduce cost of operations generally, one target that came under scrutiny was the expense of legal services, both inside and outside. It was not just the fees and disbursements that were scrutinized, but the total cost of legal services, including the payment of claims against the company. Thus, there were pressures to reduce legal cost while maintaining or increasing the quality level of services. To many—at least, to the unenlightened—it appeared that the effort to reduce legal expense was primarily price-shopping, with less regard for quality of service.

As part of this process, long-term relationships with outside firms were reexamined to the point that it no longer was automatic for matters to be referred to the same firms that the company had used for years. When the emphasis was on cost-cutting in order to stay within reduced corporate budgets, companies demanded and obtained discounts on hourly fees, in turn placing economic pressures on outside law firms. With no change in their costs of production, these firms now faced declining revenues from long-time clients. As a result, they were forced to become more aggressive in marketing, seeking to hold or obtain clients by offering reduced fees.

It is a fair statement that the initial impact of the recession was primarily monetary, the need of companies to reduce legal expense to stay solvent, and the pressure on outside firms to hold position in the industry by becoming more competitive. It was a focused problem, but it did not deal with the underlying causes of inefficiency or the disincentives for efficiency of the hourly billing approach.

One corporate counsel reported that she is assigning cases to smaller firms, often in nonmetropolitan areas where fees tend to be lower. The attempt is made to match the type of cases being assigned to the talents of the firm, having concluded that most cases do not require the highest level of expertise or the resources of a megafirm. Alternative billing approaches are used wherever appropriate. (Counsel requested not to be identified.)

The expansion of in-house law departments and the employment in law departments of lawyers who had been in outside law firms that billed predominantly on a straight hourly basis meant that law department lawyers responsible for the management of outside litigation knew how hourly billing worked, knew the temptations, knew the abuses. Consequently, outside lawyers who previously had dealt with the president of the corporation (who may not have been a lawyer) now found themselves dealing with general counsel who knew exactly how the hourly billing game was played.

Examination of what has transpired in the past five or six years shows that because of the recession and the pressures on law departments to cut the cost of legal services, corporate counsel have played a dominant role in the changes that have taken place. Indeed, it has become more than cost containment, developing into a search for new relationships and better ways to meet the needs of clients.

The Corporate Legal Times *reported that Dorsey & Whitney (300 lawyers) with its principal office in Minneapolis has offered customized billing methods including flat fees with built-in percentage discounts after certain total fees have been paid. The discount is payable in cash back to the client, not applied against future services. For commercial litigation the firm has offered modified contingency approaches tied to the outcome.* (Corporate Legal Times, *January 1992.*)

It is not just the law departments of large corporations that have forced changes. Individual clients have become more sophisticated, consumerism has been influential, and nonlawyer competitors have added to the pressures on lawyers. Even lawyers who preferred not to change have been forced to do so, an unremitting pressure that promises to continue.

The good news is that progressive, far-thinking, innovative lawyers have received the message and deem it in their own interest to change the way law is practiced.

But let's review what corporate counsel have been doing to bring about change.

In 1988 Shelby R. Rogers, then senior vice president and general counsel of Texas Commerce Bancshares, Inc., in Houston, Texas, a bank holding company with 125 banks throughout Texas,[1] became concerned about lowering the legal expense of his company without sacrificing quality. Having been a commercial litigator in the private sector for ten years, he knew the problems of outside counsel and was acutely aware of the objectives of his company. He has been the most innovative corporate counsel in experimenting with and using alternative billing methods. In doing so, he reduced his company's legal expense considerably, yet he forged ongoing mutually satisfactory relationships with the outside firms that continued to provide legal services.

Shelby Rogers's premise is that clients who receive value will be satisfied clients, and satisfied clients make for a profitable and successful law practice. His major concerns about hourly billing were the total cost of legal services, the lack of predictability of fees, the cost efficiency of services, and the absence of risk-sharing between lawyer and client.

The full text of an agreement for fixed fee representation with a bonus clause for early resolution as used by Texas Commerce Bancshares appears at page 174 in *Win-Win Billing Strategies*.

Rogers has written:

> One method of billing for legal services which our bank holding company has found particularly successful over the past five years is the employment of a contractual retainer agreement with three law firms, with offices in several Texas cities.
>
> In summary, this retainer agreement allows any bank officer from any one of our 125 banks in Texas to call any attorney of these retainer law firms and receive up to two hours of legal services on a defined matter without being billed directly for that service. In turn, the law firm and I negotiate annually a flat monthly fee payable by the holding company's legal department to the law firm for this legal service arrangement.
>
> Although the exact terms of each retainer contract are slightly different, in general the following terms and conditions apply to this type of arrangement:

> Effective January 1, 19__, this Retainer Agreement shall cover all work performed by ABC Law Firm for XYZ Corporation, *except* the following items:
>
> 1. Work in connection with actual loans or extensions of credit which is customarily charged to the borrower, including the preparation of loan documents. (General legal advice on loan structuring and basic strategy for troubled loan workouts *is covered* by this retainer.)
> 2. Work for the bank's Trust Department which can be appropriately charged to the account involved; and, review of wills and trusts prepared by other legal counsel for bank customers.
> 3. Work in connection with actual litigation, examples of which are collection matters, garnishments, foreclosures, bankruptcy proceedings, arbitration, suits brought by the bank, labor matters and representation of the bank before governmental agencies, all of which work will be billed to the particular bank organization involved, provided, however, general legal advice in the areas described above *is covered* by this Retainer Agreement.
> 4. Any single matter (including, without limitation, any matter referred to in paragraphs 1 through 3 above) consuming *more than two hours*. If a matter exhausts the two-hour limit, the time devoted thereafter must be authorized by the bank organization involved, and if approved, the work thereafter will be charged under the established billing procedures and invoiced as directed by the organization engaging the work.
>
> The amount of the monthly retainer paid by XYZ Corporation shall be $_____ plus expenses, if any. This arrangement is terminable by either party on 60 days' notice to the other.
>
> Our six-year experience with this retainer agreement has shown that our "retainer" law firms have also substantially increased their proportionate share of regular bank-paid and customer-paid legal work for our bank officers. This fact gives validity to the premise that a contractual retainer agreement is an effective "loss leader" for a law firm. In return, our bank officers receive general and preventative legal advice on a wide range of subjects without feeling the pressure of being billed by the hour from our outside lawyers.

Shelby Rogers has successfully used several other types of billing arrangements, among them a defense contingency contract. He described this approach as follows:

> The factual scenario surrounding this arrangement involved one of our banks being part of a bankruptcy action relating to a borrower with an outstanding debt of $2.0 million to our bank. The borrower had $1 million in cash collateral at our bank which was offset against the borrower's debt within the 90-day bankruptcy preference time period.
>
> The bankruptcy trustee filed an action seeking recovery of the $1 million back into the bankruptcy estate. Without belaboring the pros and cons of the relative merits of the legal issues involved in the case, let me just say that our in-house bankruptcy lawyers and our outside

bankruptcy trial counsel agreed that $1 million was our maximum exposure in the matter and that $500,000 was an acceptable exposure level for the bank in the matter. And, in fact, a $500,000 settlement offer had been tendered by the bank and rejected by the trustee.

Based on that joint assessment, we agreed with our outside law firm that they could represent us in the bankruptcy preference action on the following basis:

■ Maximum exposure	$1,000,000	
■ Acceptable exposure agreed to by bank and its outside law firm	$500,000	
■ Actual damages assessed by court or agreed to in settlement	$750,000	Law firm fee 50% of regular hourly charges
■ Actual damages assessed by court or agreed to in settlement	$500,000	75% of regular hourly charges
■ Actual damages assessed by court or agreed to in settlement	$400,000	Regular hourly charges plus ____% of $100,000
■ Actual damages assessed by court or agreed to in settlement	$0	Regular hourly charges plus ____% of $500,000

The bottom line of this specific factual situation is that we settled the action with the trustee post-hearing but pre-decision for $350,000, which gave the law firm its regular hourly rates plus a percentage bonus of the $150,000 difference between the actual settlement and the $500,000 "acceptable exposure" figure. The total settlement and outside counsel's fee was *less than* our initial settlement offer to the trustee, and the law firm *received more* compensation than its regular hourly rate, which prompted both our outside law firm and our client to deem this a "win-win" situation.

David B. Garten, general counsel of NL Industries, a multinational chemical company, contends that long-term relationships with outside firms are critical, particularly where those firms have made a commitment to efficiency-enhancement technology. Alternative billing methods must do more than price-cutting. There must be significant savings as the result of increased efficiency. He also contends that alternative relationships must be good for both companies and efficient outside counsel. Thus, fee arrangements must be open to reassessment and adjustment in the event of unfairness.[2]

NL Industries has to deal with a large number of environmental matters. The company contracted with an outside firm to computerize and manage environmental work previously done by in-house lawyers, subject to the condition that the legal department must be tied to the firm's computer network to provide instant communication. The arrangement combined a flat fee with bonuses based on cost savings.

Of Counsel *in 1994 reported the Snell & Wilmer (Salt Lake City) fixed fee annual retainer arrangement with a large corporation. The innovative feature was that if actual costs of services calculated using normal hourly rates exceeded or were less than the fixed fee by 15 percent there would be an adjustment.* (Of Counsel, *September 5, 1994.*)

The *Chicago Lawyer* in April 1994 reported that Jerry Aufox, general counsel of A. M. Castle & Co., disclosed that about 80 percent of his company's legal work is done on a flat or fixed fee basis. In the same issue, it was reported that Sam Eberts, corporate counsel in the office of the general counsel of Baxter International, also uses fixed fee arrangements. Both indicated that the approach for litigation was to divide the matter into tasks or stages with a negotiated fixed fee or cap for each task or stage.[3]

Karl Ege, general counsel of the Frank Russell Company, and Shelby Rogers while at Texas Commerce Bancshares, Inc., have both used the "Rent a Lawyer" approach, whereby for a fixed period of time a lawyer with specific desired skills was "rented" from an outside firm to work on a designated project. The cost to the company was less than the normal hourly rate, yet the company obtained assistance in meeting a temporary overload or had access to the expertise needed at that time. The advantage to the outside firm was that the firm became more familiar with the business of the client and developed closer personal relationships.

The Wall Street Journal *in July 1994 reported that a group of California banks had banded together to require a uniform method of billing by outside counsel, listing activities by tasks. The article suggested that this requirement would permit comparisons from one firm to another and ultimately could be a basis for requiring fixed fees.* (Wall Street Journal, *July 1, 1994.*)

Peter D. Zeughauser, senior vice president and general counsel of the Irvine Company in Newport Beach, California, has for years been one of the foremost advocates of alternative billing methods. Both while president of the American Corporate Counsel Association and thereafter he has lectured and written extensively on the benefits of nonhourly innovative fee arrangements. He, too, realizes that billing methods are but a part of the wider subject of how legal services can be delivered to provide value to clients. He is mindful of the impact of technology in reducing lawyer time and is cognizant of the leverage enjoyed by corporate counsel in the current buyer's market. In making work assignments to outside law firms he stresses the importance of aligning the client's and outside lawyer's interests. In his writings, Mr. Zeughauser has articulated some significant philosophical concepts.[4] He wrote, "In-house counsel may also desire to use alternative fee arrangements to allocate two of the principal risks inherent in purchasing legal work; to wit, the risk of a bad result and the risk of a cost overrun." This points out the significance of selecting the right skills and quality level to minimize the risk of bad results (or to maximize the chance of good results!) while maintaining predictability of cost, the wedding of quality and value.

Mikel R. Bistrow at Luce, Forward, Hamilton & Scripps, in San Diego, has used monthly retainers allowing in-house counsel to call as many times per month as they wish; discounted hourly rates when annual billings reach a certain level; and capped rates based upon level of expertise (e.g.; one rate for first- through third-year associates and another rate for partners). (LRP Publications, *October 1993, p. 34.*)

A realist, Mr. Zeughauser is keenly aware that the choice of billing methods can be used to align the interest of the client and outside counsel. Because corporate clients have budget constraints, alternative fee arrangements can provide cost predictability. He refers to the American Bar Association Section of Litigation's Committee on Corporate Counsel surveys, which indicate that most clients are willing to pay a premium in exchange for a predictable fee. He has a firm conviction that each alternative fee arrangement should be tailor-made for each transaction or litigation, or for similar types of transactions and litigation. He also stresses the importance of explicitly including "reopeners," allowing both lawyer and client to reexamine and recast the agreement to ensure that their interests are aligned.

In recognizing the advantages of capped fee arrangements Mr. Zeughauser points to one possible disadvantage if the cap is too low—namely, if the cap restricts or discourages careful analysis and investigation at the early stages of representation, the cap may prove costly at a later stage. Flat fees differ from capped fees in that flat fees truly encourage efficiency and create the possibility of increased profits for outside counsel. With respect to contingent fees for both plaintiffs and defense lawyers, he again refers to the ABA Corporate Counsel Survey showing that the use of contingent fee arrangements in the defense of litigation was one of the fastest areas of growth in the use of alternative fee arrangements between 1984 and 1992.

To illustrate these principles, Mr. Zeughauser suggests a hybrid fee arrangement that could be used in litigation and transaction work:

> In a litigation, a client and outside lawyer might agree on a hybrid "discount/not to exceed/contingent" fee. As an example, a client may have a $5,000,000 claim. After developing a case analysis, strategy, and budget, the client and lawyer conclude that it will likely cost $300,000 to $500,000 to take the litigation through trial and that a likely result is a $3,000,000 verdict or settlement.
>
> To allocate the risk of a cost overrun and to encourage efficiency, the client may only want to expend $300,000. In addition, the client may want the lawyer to continue working on the matter after the $300,000 threshold is surpassed, even if the likelihood of a big payout seems remote at that time. In this situation, to allocate the risk of a bad result and incentivize a good result, the client and the outside lawyer might agree that the client will pay only the first $300,000 out of pocket. To further shift the risk of a cost overrun to the outside lawyer, the hourly rate on the $300,000 might be discounted to one-half or two-thirds the typical hourly rate, an amount that would cover the lawyer's overhead. In this scenario, the outside lawyer has little at risk, other than profit, up to the first $300,000 in fees.
>
> To allocate some of the risk of a cost overrun, the client and the outside lawyer might agree that the "profit" (the difference between the discounted hourly rate and the full hourly rate) plus any excess will be paid first to the outside lawyer, from the proceeds of any recovery over $3,000,000, before splitting the contingency.

> The amount of the contingency could increase or decrease with the size of the award, depending on the level of difficulty and amount of time and effort involved in getting the higher amount and the amount of the total fee paid, including the hourly fees and contingency. Thus, the contingency might increase from 10 to 20 percent of the amount over the sum of $4,000,000, or if the case goes to a verdict as opposed to settlement.
>
> In transactional work, to allocate the risk of cost overruns and bad results, a lawyer might be paid a flat fee for a first set of transaction documents. A discount can be built in if the client has a need (for instance, a start-up business). If the deal closes, an additional amount, or bonus, might be paid, either reflecting the full hourly cost or something more, depending on the level of difficulty, the imposition on the lawyer's time, the importance of the transaction, the degree of risk of not closing, and other similar factors.

The *National Law Journal* reported a survey of corporate law departments indicating that measures taken to control outside legal costs included staffing, fee arrangements, and methods of doing business. Blended hourly rates have gained in popularity. Task coding on bills and electronic reporting of billing details are increasing. The use of electronic mail and computer networking with outside firms also are increasing.[5]

The results of the *1994 Price Waterhouse Law Department Spending Survey* were reported in the *National Law Journal*. The article attributed the decline in spending for outside counsel to a variety of techniques, one of which was the use of alternative billing methods. The survey for the prior year revealed that more than 50 percent of the respondents had never experimented with alternative billing and that 85 percent used hourly rates for more than 50 percent of their total outside fees. In 1994 30 percent of the respondents indicated that more than 30 percent of their total outside fees were based on discounted rates. More than 60 percent used some type of fixed fees and more than 40 percent used retainer and contingency techniques. More than 25 percent expected to increase the use of alternative billing methods in the coming year.[6]

NOTES

1. Shelby R. Rogers is a senior vice president and general counsel of Texas Medical Center in Houston, Texas. He has consented to the inclusion of his materials.

2. *National Law Journal*, October 17, 1994, p. C24.

3. Jill Chanen, "Hourglass Is Running on the Billable Hour," *Chicago Lawyer* (April 1994).

4. *The Use of Alternative Fee Arrangements to Achieve Smart Results and Improve Outside Counsel Relationships*, Copyright 1994, Peter D. Zeughauser, who has graciously consented to the use of his materials and ideas.

5. *National Law Journal*, July 4, 1994, p. A5.

6. *National Law Journal*, October 17, 1994, p. C14.

The Present—News Clippings and Reports from Here and There

Having been actively involved in the alternative billing crusade for the past eight years, my ongoing curiosity caused me to clip news articles and obtain reports that demonstrated the acceptance of innovative methods. Here are some of the gleanings:

"Billable Hour, a Centerpiece of American Law, Is Fading," wrote Margot Slade in the *New York Times.*[1]

• • •

James H. Riley II wrote in the *National Law Journal* that contingent fee agreements are appearing more frequently in patent infringement litigation.[2]

• • •

An insurance defense firm entered into an agreement with an insurance company to handle all litigation within the state for a fee based on a percentage of the premiums on policies written by that carrier in that state.

• • •

With respect to the percentage of total billings using alternatives to hourly billing, five firms reported:[3]

— McGuire, Woods, Battle & Boothe (406 lawyers), Richmond, Virginia —50%.
— Thompson & Mitchell (178 lawyers), St. Louis—41%
— Cozen & O'Conner (195 lawyers), Philadelphia—40%
— Lewis, Rice & Fingersh (143 lawyers)—35%

• • •

A major insurance carrier worked out an arrangement for fixed fees for certain classifications of assigned risk litigation, using a three-tiered pricing depending on type of case for a given volume of cases. The unique feature was reported to be the "option out" clause, which gave the outside law firm the right not to be bound to the pre-agreed fixed fee arrangement for a specified limited number of files each year.

• • •

One firm by agreement with the client bills for 95 percent of its normal hourly rate and asks the client to pay only that amount while litigation is pending. Upon completion, the client alone determines what, if any, part of the 5 percent should be paid depending upon the satisfaction level of the client.

• • •

The *National Law Journal* in the December 19, 1994, issue, reporting the results of its 1994 survey, listed 88 law firms by name, size, principal office, and the types of alternative billing methods offered by each firm.[4]

Firms are listed in alphabetical order. The number appearing after each firm's name is its total number of attorneys.

Arent Fox Kintner Plotkin & Kahn (217), Washington, D.C.: Special fees are negotiated in certain instances.

Armstrong, Teasdale, Schlafly & Davis (156), St. Louis: Blended rates, flat fees, contingent basis.

Baker & Daniels (198), Indianapolis: Fees charged to clients are dependent on the nature of engagement and services provided. Many methods of billing are employed in consultation with individual clients.

Bell, Boyd & Lloyd (168), Chicago: Blended rates, volume discounts.

Benesch, Friedlander, Coplan & Aronoff (138), Cleveland: Fixed fee, blended rates, result-based.

Best, Best & Krieger (115), Riverside, Calif.: Fixed fee, contingent litigation.

Beveridge & Diamond P.C. (82), Washington, D.C.: Retainers, contingency, volume discount, fixed fees, contract rates, value billing arrangements.

Bond, Schoeneck & King (145), Syracuse, N.Y.: Various methodologies and combinations of methods depending upon client and matter.

Briggs and Morgan P.A. (135): Fixed fees, blended rates, discounts for growing companies.

Brobeck, Phleger & Harrison (387), San Francisco: The firm uses all billing methods.

Brown & Bain P.A. (113), Phoenix: Contingent, fixed fee, reduced hourly rates with performance bonus.

Bryan Cave (411), St. Louis: Fixed fee, contingent fee, incentive fee.

Buchanan Ingersoll P.C. (241), Pittsburgh: Various, based on client needs/requests.

Buckingham, Doolittle & Burroughs (107), Akron, Ohio: Fixed fees, retainers, unit billing by task.

Burr & Forman (91), Birmingham, Ala.: Contingency.

Butzel Long (157), Detroit: Various methods. The firm structures specific arrangements in appropriate situations with individual clients.

Carlsmith Ball Wichman Murray Case & Ichiki (134), Honolulu: Contingency.

Chapman and Cutler (246), Chicago: Fee-schedule billings, negotiated fixed-fee arrangements, not-to-exceed fees (in certain cases) for transactional work.

Cooley Godward Castro Huddleson & Tatum (210), San Francisco: Individually negotiated.

Covington & Burling (314), Washington, D.C.: Used occasionally in special circumstances.

Cozen and O'Conner (195), Philadelphia: Contingency fee and fixed-fee arrangements.

Crosby, Heafey, Roach & May P.C.: (198), Oakland, Calif.: Budget with a charge per task, flat fee, discounted hourly rates with incentive payments, blended hourly rates for all professionals, open to client-proposed arrangements.

Cummings & Lockwood (123), Stamford, Conn.: Fixed-fee and incentive-based billing, among other alternative billing arrangements.

Davis Wright Tremaine (232), Seattle: Fixed fee, contingency, blended rates, volume pricing, etc.

Davis, Graham & Stubbs L.L.C. (102), Denver: Wide variety of billing arrangements based on needs of clients.

Dickle, McCamey & Chilcote P.C. (122), Pittsburgh: Contingent-fee basis.

Dickstein, Shapiro & Morin (159), Washington, D.C.: Discounts, caps, fixed or blended rates, partial contingencies, retainers for certain types of work.

Duane, Morris & Heckscher (228), Philadelphia: Many varieties.

Fennemore Craig P.C. (111), Phoenix: Fixed-fee agreements, result billing, contingent fee agreements in which payment is based on a percentage of the award or settlement.

Foster Pepper & Shefelman (139), Seattle: Fixed fees, blended rates.

Gardner, Carton & Douglas (225), Chicago: The firm has used most of the methods that are prevalent on the market.

Goodwin, Procter & Hoar (295), Boston: Blended rates, flat fee, negotiated cap, etc.

Graham & James (302), San Francisco: Various methods.

Greenberg, Glusker, Fields, Claman & Machtinger (89), Los Angeles: Fixed fee, blended rate, volume discounts.

Greenberg, Traurig, Hoffman, Lipoff, Rosen & Quentel P.A. (222), Miami: Success fees, partial contingencies, blended rates.

Gunster, Yoakley & Stewart P.A. (84), West Palm Beach, Fla.: Fixed Fee, contingent fee.

Hahn Loeser & Parks (86), Cleveland: The firm strives to accommodate the client, taking into consideration the type of work and complexity of the matter. The firm uses fixed-fee and blended-rate approaches.

Harris Beach & Wilcox (141), Rochester, N.Y.: Fixed fees, contingent fees, value billing, reverse contingent.

Heller, Ehrman, White & McAuliffe (323), San Francisco: Fee volume discount, fixed fee, maximum fee, contingent fee, blended billing rates.

Holland & Hart (225), Denver: Fixed/flat fees, blended rates, contingent fees, discounted hourly rates for high volume.

Holme Roberts & Owen L.L.C. (197), Denver: Contingent, discounts, fixed fees, blended, result-based.

Howrey & Simon (321), Washington, D.C.: The firm uses a full range of alternative billing methods.

Hughes Hubbard & Reed (225), New York: Fixed fees.

Hunton & Williams (445), Richmond, Va.: Fixed fees, fee caps, blended rates, contingency fee approaches.

Husch & Eppenberger (127), St. Louis: A variety of alternative billing methods are used.

Johnson & Wortley P.C. (167), Dallas: Occasionally uses fixed fee or percentage of proceeds.

Jones, Day, Reavis & Pogue (1,078): The firm has used certain alternative billing arrangements as appropriate to specific situations.

Kilpatrick & Cody (199), Atlanta: Discounted billing rates, some fixed-fee work on a limited basis.

Lewis, Rice & Fingersh (143), St. Louis: Fixed fees, blended rates, results-based value billing.

Locke Reynolds Boyd & Welsell (76), Indianapolis: Flat fee.

Luce, Forward, Hamilton & Scripps (141), San Diego: Fixed fees, blended rates, volume discounts.

Manatt, Phelps & Phillips (145), Los Angeles: Fixed fees, blended rates, and occasionally result-based billing methods.

Marshall, Dennehey, Warner, Coleman & Goggin (180), Philadelphia: Flat fee, blended rate, contract pricing, value billing.

McCarter & English (202), Newark, N.J.: Fixed fees, blended rates.

McGuire, Woods, Battle & Boothe (406), Richmond, Va.: The majority of matters handled are billed by special arrangements tailored to the requirements of the client, the subject or the circumstances of the particular case.

Meyer, Hendricks, Victor, Osborn & Maledon (74), Phoenix: Contingency fee, flat fee, various other arrangements.

Miles & Stockbridge (204), Baltimore: Fixed rate, average rate, contingency, negotiated rate.

Miller, Canfield, Paddock and Stone P.L.C. (248), Detroit: Various methods.

Miller, Johnson, Snell & Cummiskey P.L.C. (67), Grand Rapids, Mich.: Negotiable on a case-by-case basis.

Montgomery, McCracken, Walker & Rhoads (142), Philadelphia: As requested by clients.

Nixon, Hargrave, Devans & Doyle (254), Rochester, N.Y.: Fixed fees, retainers, blended rates, result-based, negotiated.

O'Melveny & Myers (554), Los Angeles: Blended rates, result-based.

Peabody & Arnold (98), Boston: Fixed fees, blended rates.

Pepper, Hamilton & Scheetz (272), Philadelphia: Blended rates, fixed fee for transactional business.

Phelps Dunbar (193), New Orleans: Contingency and fixed fee arrangements.

Piper & Marbury (265), Baltimore: Blended rates, fixed fees, percentage of hourly rates plus incentive.

Pope, Cahill & Devine Ltd. (70). Chicago: Blended rates.

Reed Smith Shaw & McClay (361), Pittsburgh: Willing to consider alternative billing methods.

Ropers, Majeski, Kohn, Bentley, Wagner & Kane (166), Redwood City, Calif.: Flat fees, flat fee or reduced hourly rates plus percentage.

Ross & Hardies (203), Chicago: In particular cases the firm uses blended hourly rates, capped fees, task billing.

Saul, Ewing, Remick & Saul (142), Philadelphia: Blended rate, contingency, fixed fee.

Schiff Hardin & Waite (200), Chicago: Wide variety used in appropriate circumstances.

Schnader, Harrison, Segal & Lewis (192), Philadelphia: Variety of methods.

Sedgwick, Detert, Moran & Arnold (229), San Francisco: Fixed fees, blended rates, volume discounts.

Snell & Wilmer (225), Phoenix: Task-based billings.

Stoel Rives Boley Jones & Grey (256), Portland, Ore.: Standard rates, discount rates, retainers, fixed-fee arrangements, premiums, contingency.

Strasburger & Price L.L.P. (182), Dallas: Sometimes fixed fees.

Thompson & Knight P.C. (210), Dallas: Fixed fee, reduced rate.

Thompson & Mitchell (178), St. Louis: Various methods.

Thompson, Hine and Flory (321), Cleveland: Reduced hourly rate coupled with contingent fee incentive, fixed-fee arrangements, blended hourly rate, preferred rates for long-term clients, volume related discount hourly rate.

Verner, Liipfert, Bernhard, McPherson and Hand Chartered (149), Washington, D.C.: Various methods.

Vinson & Elkins L.L.P. (524), Houston: Flat rates, fixed fees, blended rates, results-based billing.

Warner & Stackpole (64), Boston: Fixed fee, value based, flat rates, blended rates, contingency, hourly plus fixed fee, hourly plus contingent.

White and Williams (140, Philadelphia: Fixed fee, blended rates, result-based.

Wiley, Rein & Fielding (195), Washington, D.C.: Variable methods have been used at clients' requests.

Winstead Sechrest & Minick P.C. (167), Dallas: Fixed fee, blended rates, contingency.

Winston & Strawn (465), Chicago: Yes (alternative methods case-by-case).

Wyatt, Tarrant & Combs (177), Louisville, Ky.: Blended rates, fixed fee, etc.

Another firm worked out an arrangement that when the annual fees paid by a client exceeded an agreed amount (e.g., $500,000), 2 percent of the agreed amount would be issued as a credit against future services by the firm.

• • •

A firm, emphasizing client satisfaction, guaranteed satisfaction and agreed that if the client is not satisfied with the services, the client may elect not to pay all or a portion of the fee that was charged.

• • •

Of Counsel in July 1995 reported that Coffield Ungaretti & Harris, an eighty-lawyer firm in Chicago, was offering a written service guarantee that guaranteed the services of the firm as a whole. This approach to marketing resulted from surveys indicating that a majority of nonlawyer clients would be more likely to select a law firm willing to give them a written guarantee. Coffield Ungaretti guarantees service, not results.[5]

• • •

Of Counsel in April 1994 ran an article reporting on the number of litigators or litigation practice groups that had broken away from large firms to form litigation boutique firms using nonhourly billing.[6]

• • •

The *Wall Street Journal* in July 1994 reported several new firms formed by former partners of large firms who departed in order to use alternative billing methods. Among them is Dombroff & Gilmore, which offers a percentage holdback from hourly fees payable if the client is satisfied with the services, or a percentage credit after fees reach a prescribed level applicable to future services.[7]

• • •

The *American Lawyer* in 1993 announced the fixed fee arrangement between LeBoeuf, Lamb, Leiby and MacRae and Alcoa for the law firm to handle all of Alcoa's litigation. The *Corporate Legal Times* reported the results of this experiment, which reflected a savings to Alcoa of approximately $6 million over a two-year period. The LeBoeuf firm reports heightened awareness of the Alcoa culture, increased efforts toward preventive law, recognition of repetitive processes, increased efficiency, closer working relationships between inside and outside counsel, decreased overhead from having an office in a less-expensive city, and an increased tendency to advise the client on steps to be taken to avoid legal problems. Alcoa knows the number of hours spent by the LeBoeuf firm and charges back allocated legal expense to the specific Alcoa unit or department requiring the services so that each unit or department is aware of the ultimate expense of litigation.[8]

• • •

Accounting for Law Firms carried an interesting article by Richard E. Rassel, CEO of Butzel Long in Michigan, stressing that alternative billing methods strengthen law firm/client relationships.[9]

• • •

The *National Law Journal* in July 1994 reported that a large conglomerate, FMC Corporation, had invited five firms to submit proposals to take over all of FMC's legal work for a fixed fee annually for three years, in which case the FMC in-house legal department would be dissolved.[10]

• • •

Wal-Mart designated Assistant General Counsel Ronald Williams to be in charge of a program for flat fees for Wal-Mart litigation involving simple liability cases.

• • •

Tom Alberg, executive vice president of McCaw Cellular Communications, Inc., stressed the importance of quality legal work, clearly stating the objectives of the client, fostering long-term relations between in-house and outside counsel, and effective communication as the keys to receiving value.[11]

Notes

1. *New York Times*, October 22, 1993.
2. *National Law Journal*, November 28, 1994, p. B5.
3. *Corporate Counsellor*, December 1994, based on a survey by *National Law Journal*, December 19, 1994.
4. *National Law Journal*, December 19, 1994, p. C3. Reprinted with the permission of *National Law Journal*. Copyright 1994, The New York Law Publishing Company.
5. *Of Counsel*, vol. 14, no. 13, July 3, 1995, p. 4.
6. *Of Counsel*, vol. 13, no. 7, April 4, 1994.
7. *Wall Street Journal*, July 15, 1994.
8. *American Lawyer*, September 1993; *Corporate Legal Times*, October 1995, p. 1.
9. *Accounting for Law Firms*, May 1994.
10. *National Law Journal*, July 11, 1994, p. A4.
11. *Washington CEO*, October 1993, p. 34.

CHAPTER 5

How Do We Measure and Evaluate the Change in Billing Methods?

HAVING READ THE previous chapters and the examples of innovative billing methods currently being used, you may ask, "To what extent are lawyers actually using some alternative billing method?" Several surveys by different organizations may provide some answers to this question.

By 1993 Altman Weil Pensa sensed the increased use of alternative billing methods. To substantiate this notion and to quantify the extent of change, a survey was conducted. Responses came from firms of all sizes and revealed some interesting information. Of the respondents, 43.4 percent stated they were developing billing and pricing alternatives in response to client requests or demands; 29.5 percent indicated that they were actively developing alternative billing and pricing policies; 22.5 percent said they were not pursuing alternative billing strategies.

The survey indicated that the most commonly used alternative to hourly billing was the fixed or flat fee for defined services. The practice area where alternative pricing strategies was most frequently used was litigation, notwithstanding the sentiments of litigators expressed in 1987 that hourly billing was the only way to bill. The survey also reflected that other predominant practice areas where alternative billing strategies had been employed included corporate, real estate, estate planning, banking, employment, and personal injury (in that order). The attitude about alternative billing showed that 51.2 percent felt it "somewhat necessary," 24.8 percent "not critical," 20.9 percent "critical to survival/success," and 0.8 percent "unacceptable."[1]

For the first time *The National Law Journal's Annual Billing Survey* for 1993 asked firms whether they used alternative billing methods, and if so, what kinds. More than one-third of the respondent firms used methods other than the straight hourly fee. The most popular types were the fixed fee, blended rates, the contingent fee, and an hourly rate combined with a contingency factor.[2]

In 1994 the Federation of Insurance and Corporate Counsel (FICC) asked Altman Weil Pensa to survey alternative billing methods in the insurance defense industry. The FICC is a national association of outside defense lawyers, in-house lawyers, and claims executives from the insurance industry. Among the findings, there was an identifiable trend toward more extensive use of alternative billing from fiscal 1991 to 1992. The plaintiff's contingent fee was the most widely used alternative to hourly fees, with the fixed fee and volume discounts close behind. In descending order, the prevalence of use was blended hourly rate; hourly rate in conjunction with contingent fee; working retainer (deposit against future services); fixed fee in conjunction with hourly rate; unit fee; exclusive retainer; percentage fee; lump sum retainer; defense contingent fee; and retrospective fee based on value. For the purposes of this survey, discounted hourly billing was not regarded as an alternative method.[3]

The results of *The Fifth Annual Corporate Legal Times/Arthur Andersen & Co. General Counsel Survey* were reported in July 1994 in the *Corporate Legal Times*. Comparing 1993 averages to 1992 averages, increases were noted for discounted individual billing rates, fees based on outcome of the matter, and fixed fees for a particular matter. Fifty-seven percent of the respondents found fixed fees effective in controlling costs and managing outside counsel.[4]

In a July 1994 survey directed to ways to cut companies' legal bills, the *National Law Journal* reported that the following approaches (in descending order) were "gaining in popularity": blended hourly rates; task coding on bills; e-mail with firms; computer networking with firms; and electronic reporting of bill details. This trend is interesting in that it indicates the movement to deal not only with the *cost* of legal services, but also with the *way* inside and outside counsel legal services interrelate.[5]

In October 1993 *California Lawyer* published the results of The Fax Poll of 150 respondents reporting as of July 1993. While 86 percent of the respondents billed by the hour, 73 percent agreed that hourly billing fails to reward efficiency and expertise, and actually provides a financial incentive to "pad" or "create" hours. Of the alternatives to hourly billing, 47 percent of the respondents used fixed fees, 26 percent used "value" billing rewarding positive results, and 27 percent used caps on total fees.[6]

In late 1994 a report by David Michaelson & Associates prepared for Mead Data Central entitled *Managing a Modern Law Office* was released. The scope of this survey was significant. In addition to determining the extent of use of alternative methods and the revenues resulting from those types of billing methods, the survey asked about the relative profitability of alternative methods compared to hourly billing and about changes in operational methods that accompanied changes in billing techniques. The five stated research objectives were

- Changes in billing practices.
- Impact of changed billing practices on firm profitability.

- Actions taken to increase firm profitability.
- Use of office automation and computerization.
- Effect of computerization on law office operations.[7]

The summary of findings discloses that hourly charges remain the dominant billing system at large U.S. law firms (77% of billings). Among all firms, 62 percent of total billings and 80 percent of all hourly billings are derived from standard hourly billing methods. While the proportion of total billings remains small, half of all large U.S. firms reported an increased use of standard project billing (51%), flat fees (51%), and task-based billing (48%). Forty-eight percent reported an increased use of blended or average rates during the past five years, and 45 percent reported an increased use of discounted hourly rates during the same period. Virtually all large firms reported using each of the various types of alternative billing systems.

The Mead Data Central survey indicated that the shift toward alternative billing methods appears to be accelerating. Forty-three percent of the firms anticipated a decreased use of *standard* hourly billing. When the responses are grouped by firm size, however, the anticipated decline in standard hourly billing increases in likelihood as firms increase in size and annual billings. Anticipated decreases in billings from standard hourly rates are 25 percent for firms with ten to fourteen lawyers; 39 percent for firms with fifteen to twenty-nine lawyers; and 67 percent for firms with thirty or more lawyers. Anticipated decreases in billings based on standard hourly rates are 22 percent for firms with annual billings of less than $2 million; 42 percent for firms with annual billings $2 million to less than $5 million; and 60 percent for firms with annual billings of $5 million or more.

Overall, 48 percent of America's largest law firms have made operational changes as a result of a shift in their billing methods. Large firms (those with thirty or more lawyers) are the firms most likely to have made these changes. A high percentage of these changes are in administrative functions within the firm.

Firms that made operational changes in response to changes in billing practices are just as likely to say that profits increased as a result of changes in billing practices (45%) as they are to say their profits remained the same (44%). Fewer than one in ten (9%) large firms reported that profits decreased due to changes in billing practices. Computerization is the action most commonly taken to maintain or increase firm profitability. Half (54%) of large firms reported increased profitability due to changes in operations and technology. Even though relatively few firms derive a majority of their income from alternative billing methods, those that rely most on those methods appear more likely than other firms to report increases in profitability.

The Mead Data Central study acknowledges that the business of law is changing. Law firms are beginning to respond to the demands of the market.

The *National Law Journal* reported a survey of corporate law departments indicating that measures taken to control outside legal costs had to do with staffing, fee arrangements, and methods of doing business. Blended hourly rates have gained in popularity. Task coding on bills and electronic reporting of billing details are increasing. The use of electronic mail and computer networking with outside firms also are increasing.[8]

The results of the *1994 Price Waterhouse Law Department Spending Survey* were reported in the *National Law Journal*. The article attributed the decline in spending for outside counsel to a variety of techniques, one of which was the use of alternative billing methods. The survey for the prior year revealed that more than 50 percent of the respondents had never experimented with alternative billing and that 85 percent used hourly rates for more than 50 percent of their total outside fees. In 1994 30 percent of the respondents indicated that more than 30 percent of their total outside fees were based on discounted rates. More than 60 percent used some type of fixed fees, and more than 40 percent used retainer and contingency techniques. More than 25 percent expected to increase the use of alternative billing methods in the coming year.[9]

The 1993 Altman Weil Pensa survey, mentioned above, was based on replies from 129 respondents from law firms of all sizes. Since the results of that survey were released, law firms have been under strong pressure from clients to provide quality service for a reasonable price that reflects the value of those services.

For comparative purposes, a similar survey questionnaire was sent in 1995 to a cross section of law firms, with two additional questions. The survey summary compares 1995 results from 210 respondents to those of the 1993 survey. The number of respondents (expressed as a percentage of the total of 210 respondents) by firm size was as follows:

3.3%—Solo practice
40.5%—2–12 lawyers
29.0%—13–49 lawyers
13.3%—50–100 lawyers
13.8%—Over 100 lawyers

Significant highlights include the following:

- More firms are developing alternative methods, either by law firm initiative or at the request of their clients.
- The fixed or flat fee remains the most commonly used alternative, increasing from 72.9 percent to 76.2 percent of the respondents.
- The use of all nine major alternative methods increased.
- Hourly billing remains the predominant revenue source despite increased use of alternative methods.
- Alternative pricing strategies were mutually initiated by lawyers and clients (52.9% in 1995).
- Litigation remains the practice area in which alternative methods are most frequently used.

- 64.3 percent of the respondents use alternative methods for both litigation and nonlitigation matters.
- 36.2 percent of the respondents believe that alternative billing is critical to survival/success, compared to 20.9 percent in 1993.
- In 1995, 79.5 percent of the respondents expect the use of alternative billing strategies will increase.[10]

It can be fairly concluded that although straight hourly billing remains the predominant billing method in terms of both frequency of use and revenues produced, the use of alternative billing methods has increased and is anticipated to continue to increase.

Of Counsel, in the June 5, 1995, issue,[11] comments on the results of its 1995 Of Counsel 700 Survey showing generally an increase in hourly billing rates over the prior year for most levels of partners and associates. With the economic pressures as they existed, this is a bit of surprise. The commentary suggests the following possible explanations: (1) rates are less significant as firms move to alternative billing; (2) law firm managers take direct charge of negotiating alternative billing methods; (3) clients place less emphasis on cost per hour than on cost-efficient staffing and job performance; (4) there has been a reduction in assignment of less experienced lawyers to client matters; (5) the talents of high-end associates are being used to a greater extent; (6) law firms have reengineered their practice in response to client demands; and (7) law work has been delegated upward to higher billers or downward to paralegals.

If the future bears out the validity of these explanations, it will confirm the ideas expressed in this book.

NOTES

1. Altman Weil Pensa Publications, Inc., Newtown Square, PA.

2. *National Law Journal*, December 20, 1993, p. S1.

3. *1994 Survey on Alternative Fees and Alternative Dispute Resolution*, (Newtown Square, Pennsylvania: Altman Weil Pensa Publications, Inc., May 1994), prepared for the Federation of Insurance and Corporate Counsel.

4. *Corporate Legal Times*, July 1994, vol. 4, no. 32.

5. *National Law Journal*, July 4, 1994.

6. *California Lawyer*, October 1993, p. 13.

7. *Managing a Modern Law Office*, prepared for Mead Data Central by David Michaelson & Associates, Nov. 1994.

8. *National Law Journal*, July 4, 1994, p. A5.

9. *National Law Journal*, October 17, 1994, p. C14.

10. *Alternative Billing Strategies: A Survey of Current Practices* (Newtown Square, Pennsylvania: Altman Weil Pensa Publications, Inc., May 1995).

11. "Of Counsel 700 Survey Shows Steady and Surprising Rise in Billing Rates," *Of Counsel* (Englewood Cliffs, New Jersey: Aspen Law & Business, June 5, 1995): p. 1.

CHAPTER 6

The Fixed Fee—The Favorite Alternative Billing Method

BOTH THE 1993 AND THE 1995 Altman Weil Pensa surveys of alternative billing strategies reported that the most frequently used alternative to hourly billing was the fixed fee. From the client's point of view, the fixed fee enables the client to know in advance the charge that will be made. From the lawyer's point of view, fixed fees provide an opportunity to charge for value, not for hours spent. For both lawyers and clients, the switch to fixed fee billing provides a way to end the thought process that equates time spent with value.[1]

If you are buying an automobile, do you really care how much time it took to install the hood of the car?

Before you jump to fixed fee billing, however, there is an analytical process you should go through to make certain that you—and ultimately the client—know what is involved. Setting a fee properly requires knowing two things:

1 ▪ The scope of the services that will be included in the fixed fee.

It is essential to itemize or describe specifically the services that will be included. Often it will be useful to state expressly what will not be included. It is important that both the lawyer and the client have a clear understanding of what will be required and to agree that the described services are what the client wants. If there are foreseeable variables, you should do one of the following:

- Add a contingency or plus factor that would account for the variable, if one occurs.
- Quote two fixed fees, one if the variable does not occur, one if the foreseeable variable does occur.
- Provide for renegotiation if the variable occurs (like a change order in a construction contract).

2 ■ Your cost of providing those services.

You should do some cost accounting to determine approximately what it will cost in terms of time, services, and dollars to perform whatever is defined in the scope of the engagement. It is prudent to limit fixed fees to situations where you have done the same or similar transaction before so you know what is involved.

Unique or extremely complex services do not lend themselves to a fixed fee as easily as "commodity" services or those that occur more frequently, can be systemized, use paralegals, or employ technology.

Do your estimating based on each stage or phase of the proposed fixed fee agreement for each of the specific services included within the scope of the total engagement. A case plan or transaction plan setting forth all the steps that must be taken to complete the assignment will be helpful. As you do this, you can realistically estimate the cost of each step. You can add a timeline to ensure timely completion of the assignment.

When you are considering doing fixed fee work we strongly suggest that you review old or closed files involving similar or identical services. See what the patterns were, the variables, the constants, and the range of charges that were made.

Your cost of producing the services does not per se set the price. It tells you the minimum price you need to charge to break even. The marketplace determines the *price* you should charge. The ultimate issue is the *value* of the services, the benefits conferred on the client resulting from your services.

To sell a fixed fee the primary benefits to the client are certainty, predictability, and the sharing of risk. All clients, personal and business alike, want to know in advance what their cost will be. Business clients are normally subject to internal budgeting. In addition, the fixed fee provides a basis on which the client can weigh the cost of proceeding against the cost of settlement or abandoning the transaction. The risk-sharing characteristic is that the lawyer assumes the risk that the fixed fee is too low or that the cost of producing the services will prove to be greater than anticipated. My contention is that most clients, if given an estimate of what the fee will be when the fee is to be charged on an hourly rate basis, will choose the fixed fee even if the quoted fixed fee is greater than the best estimate. Whenever the client requires a maximum fee to be quoted (assuming hourly billing), it is better to quote a fixed fee with the hope that the engagement can be completed with lower than anticipated costs. The lawyer may lose if the fixed fee is too low, but there is at least the possibility of a higher level of profit if the matter can be completed more economically.

If the trend towards fixed fee billing continues (as I believe it will), cost accounting will be even more important. As suggested, the law firm of the future may have a "fee estimator" on its staff, following the example of the construction industry, where estimators have long been used to work up bids for construction projects. Another practice that can be borrowed from the construction industry is the "change order," which permits additional fees to be negotiated if unforeseen events occur or the client expands the scope of the engagement beyond what was originally agreed on.

These are the characteristics that should be emphasized in selling a fixed fee. Sometimes arguments for the use of the fixed fee include the statement that you can "still make a profit." I submit that the emphasis should be that fixed fees enable you to increase your profits. The negative connotation may be accurate for lawyers who have little idea of what their costs are. Most law firms have not engaged in any effective cost analysis. Further, many lawyers are guilty of not thinking through exactly what will be required to complete an assignment.

Hourly billing makes lawyers sloppy and provides little motivation for efficiency, effective delegation, the development and utilization of systems (either manual or based on the use of technology), or early resolution. Fixed fees provide just the opposite incentives.

If you agree to do a high volume of work for a fixed fee, it is probable that on some of those cases you will have some overruns, but on others you may have an above-average margin, so that the two even out if you have been at all accurate in setting the fixed fee in the first place. In my own experience as a practitioner handling a high volume of nonjudicial deed of trust foreclosures, that proved to be the case. Nonetheless, there was the incentive to use legal assistants, systems, standardized forms, and procedures and to be as efficient as possible.

But don't think that fixed fee billing is only for simple matters. Even in complex and highly sophisticated transactions, if you are familiar and experienced with the total process, know your costs, anticipate the variables, and work efficiently, a fixed fee in substantial amount can be used with all the benefits to both the client and the lawyer flowing from that approach. In using all billing methods except those involving partial or complete hourly billing, these incentives for efficiency exist.

It is especially important for firms with a heavy investment in technology and the processes related to technology to move away from hourly billing towards charging on the basis of value conferred. After all, systematization and technology are directed towards reducing the human time required.

To expand on how fixed fee billing can benefit the law firm, you should consider how you can be innovative to take advantage of the inherent characteristics of the fixed fee. For example, the quoted fixed fee can be a useful device for penetrating a new market. Pricing will determine the level of profitability, but even if there is a small profit margin in the early use of the fixed fee, other work may flow from clients attracted by the fixed fee. As your efficiency increases, it may be possible for you to reduce the fixed fee to become even more competitive in an increasingly competitive marketplace.

If you engage in total quality management to constantly improve the quality of your services, pricing for included services can be revised upward to reflect improved quality or downward where you are confronted by strong competition.

Keep in mind that the fixed fee need not be used solely for the total services in the engagement. The fixed fee can be used for segments of the total services whenever it is reasonably clear what is required for that segment. Think in terms of billing on an hourly basis where there is uncertainty about what will be required, then go to the fixed fee when the transaction has been defined and the course of action has been charted.

As you continue to invest in technology to reduce the human time required, it becomes even more important to think in terms of fixed fee billing. The quality of the product, the timeliness of delivery, and the value to the client become the criteria for measuring the value of the services.

Albert L. Moses, a lawyer practicing in Columbia, South Carolina, and a longtime computer enthusiast and expert, wrote a compelling article entitled, "Warning! Fixed Fees Ahead (Engage All Systems)," which was published in the March 1995 issue of *Law Practice Management*.[2] He believes that this is what is now happening:

1. Our clients—especially corporate clients—to cut costs are forcing us lawyers to leave hourly billing behind, as much as possible, and move to fixed fees and variations thereof, as much as possible.
2. A fixed fee environment absolutely requires lawyers to be as efficient and productive as possible.
3. The computer industry is producing new computer programs in a new way that makes them significantly easier to learn and use.
4. Lawyers who learn to use computers effectively will have a large competitive edge in a fixed fee environment.

Mr. Moses recognizes the pressures on lawyers brought by clients to use systems and efficient procedures. By consulting management reports on such procedures as task-based billing it will be possible to compare an individual firm's performance of a given task with group averages. This information will force compliance with standardized fees. As law firms employed by these corporate clients learn how to operate profitably in a fixed fee environment, they will be able to apply these lessons to other practices and practice areas, increasing their ability to compete effectively with other law firms.

He outlines the evolution of computer technology and observes that through the increased hardware power of computers and the increased ease of use of software, lawyers can become more productive and able to respond to the demands of clients. Two categories of software or computer programs can have a fairly immediate impact on a law practice: (1) document assembly that automates the production of documents, and (2) information retrieval that allows the recycling of old products. For example, for a corporate client that requires a great many specialized agreements, one firm known to Mr. Moses uses document assembly and information retrieval techniques to quickly produce a rough draft *for a fixed fee*. At the point when the contract is presented to the client, the firm switches to an hourly rate for consultation with the client necessary to fine-tune the agreement. Firms that develop an information base can, by use of computers, assemble all relevant information necessary for performance of the task. Mr. Moses states:

> As we develop systems to allow us to operate under fixed fees, we may find that in fact, we are selling what the client perceives he or she is buying—a product. In producing that product, the systems contribute materially to the value of what is being sold and should be considered an investment by the firm. In fact, systems that produce a product for the client have been referred to—properly, I think—as the firm's intellectual capital. The lawyers who contributed that system have made a contribution to the firm's intellectual capital, and when that intellectual capital produces a return for the firm, the contributors should be rewarded.

Mr. Moses contends that properly used, computers can handle the routine portions of law practice, thereby freeing lawyers to think creatively for their clients, a proper and challenging role.

Another combination of billing methods is to use the fixed fee as the basic fee, with a bonus to be paid contingent upon attainment of a specified result. Here is a real-life example of what a lawyer specializing in land use planning did for his clients. The lawyer in question realized that his land developer clients in undertaking the purchase of raw land with intent to plat the land into residential lots always thought in terms of the cost per developed lot. The cost of the raw land, the cost of surveying and engineering, and the cost of utilities and roads all were computed on a per-lot basis. The only major cost item not computed on a per-lot basis was the expense of legal services for rezoning. The lawyer decided to set a fixed fee for rezoning legal services at a fixed amount per lot as finally rezoned. The client sought maximum density in zoning. The more lots approved in the rezone, the more lots to sell and the higher the profits from the venture. With this fixed fee arrangement both the lawyer and the land developer client benefited from pushing for maximum density.

Just as the billable hour invaded the billing process, it has become embedded in the internal compensation systems of law firms. Fixed fee billing may become the method whereby efficient, systems-oriented lawyers who are working smarter, not longer, can influence changes in compensation system philosophies that emphasize hours worked. Fees received, not hours worked, will increasingly be recognized in the management of law firms.

Final shot. Do *not* stop recording your time. You need to keep or extend time recording in order to determine your *cost* of providing your services. The problem is that the majority of law firms are unable to respond to client requests for fixed fee alternatives because they do not have historical case cost or budgeting information on which to base accurate business decisions.

If you don't know your cost, how can you intelligently set the price?

When you know your costs, are aware of the competitive market, and use efficient methods including technology, fixed fees provide an opportunity for increased profitability. When you have freed yourself of the limitations of selling your time, you can concentrate on selling results and value, which, after all, are what your clients have always desired—and are increasingly demanding.

NOTES

1. Portions of this chapter first appeared in *Report to Legal Management* 20, no. 6 (Newtown Square, Pennsylvania: Altman Weil Pensa Publications, Inc., March 1994).

2. Albert L. Moses, "Warning! Fixed Fees Ahead (Engage All Systems)," *Law Practice Management* (March 1995): 60. Mr. Moses has generously consented to the embodiment of his ideas into this chapter.

CHAPTER 7

Especially for Litigators, the Original Skeptics

WHEN OUR FIRST TWO BOOKS on billing methods were published in 1989 and 1992, litigators expressed the strongest objections to any billing method other than the straight hourly method. They pointed out that there are many unknowns in litigation, and no way to anticipate a multitude of factors beyond their control. Outside counsel and corporate counsel alike were vocal against any change in billing methods. Their stance was that hourly billing works, so why change it?

By 1993 and again in 1995, however, the Altman Weil Pensa survey showed that litigation was the practice area using alternative methods most frequently.

Why, then, this change from skepticism to the most widespread use of alternative billing methods?

The apparent answer results from a complex of factors. Litigation (both the payment of claims and the cost of legal services) is the major legal expense for corporate clients. The delays and uncertainties of litigation make it the most difficult to manage. With the highest expenditures, the opportunities for savings are also the greatest. Client pressures caused litigators to become an early and major target for cost reduction.

This chapter will attempt to deal with issues specifically relating to litigation in the larger setting of the buyer's market.

The trend towards the use of alternative billing methods accelerated in the early 1990s because of the business recession that first struck law firm clients and ultimately the law firms themselves. Litigators were the major target. With increased economic pressures, clients became more cost-conscious. The waste and inefficiencies that had been tolerated in the 1980s were no longer acceptable. Practices that did not increase value were suspect. Loyalties disappeared as clients sought improved quality and lower costs of legal services. Life for lawyers, particularly litigators, became real with the switch from a seller's to a buyer's marketplace. Accompanying the decline was increased competition among lawyers for available work with more aggressive marketing and reduced prices.

What many thought originally was theory concerning alternative billing methods became reality. Nonbelievers at first contended that the recession was but a passing phase and soon conditions would change so that the firm could go on with its practice in the same old way. Some of these nonbelievers were shocked when longtime major clients began to demand proposals for alternative billing methods and sought in various ways to control legal costs. Increasingly, clients demanded higher-quality services at lower prices. Discount billing is not a billing method; it is pressure to lower the pricing level.

With particular reference to litigation, the trend towards greater use of alternative billing methods is evidenced in numerous ways. The extreme example of fixed fee billing occurred when a major corporation, Aluminum Company of America, agreed with outside counsel, LeBoeuf, Lamb, Leiby & MacRae, to pay a fixed annual fee to have all litigation (more than five hundred cases) handled by that one firm.[1] Another was the agreement of Blackwell Sanders Matheny Weary and Sanders with UtiliCorp United described in chapter 3 where the firm took over the whole function of UtiliCorp's fourteen-lawyer legal department for a fixed annual fee with a sharing of savings clause.

Some corporate counsel are analyzing the cases handled by outside law firms to determine categories of basically similar cases. By examining closed files, a range of fees for cases within a category can be determined, with the next step being negotiating fixed fee agreements for cases that are substantially similar.

Litigators are the major targets of task-based billing and of the demands of sophisticated clients that time entries be grouped in a way that enables reviewing counsel to determine how much a given task should cost. Even if the basis for billing now is hourly, this approach will provide some guidelines and a basis for comparison of the charges made by outside counsel. The next logical step is for the corporate client to set maximum charges per task or to determine that some tasks are irrelevant to the legal process and should not be performed. The present state of task-based billing is to force the presentation of information in a way that can be more accurately analyzed, but undoubtedly it is only the first of a series of steps that will be taken to bring legal expense under control. The Uniform Task-Based Management System Litigation Code Set issued April 7, 1995, is set forth in the Appendix. It is an attempt to standardize the format, which, if successful, will provide an even wider basis for comparison of legal costs.

With the type of review and analysis now being done by progressive corporate counsel, many corporations are reducing the number of firms they will use around the country. Some of the reduction may be based solely on price, but it appears that quality of service and the cost of service are increasingly the basis for selection or retention of outside counsel. In many instances, existing outside firms will be asked to submit a proposed alternative billing method as part of the selection-retention procedure.

Another trend is the heightened awareness that litigation varies from routine cases to extraordinarily complex cases with much at stake. With this realization case assignments are being made based on the degree of expertise required and the relative cost of handling.

A good example of innovation is described in *Win-Win Billing Strategies* (a copy of the fixed fee agreement is included in that book). The type of cases essentially involved collection cases for a bank holding company within a specified range for the amount claimed. For the handling of each case a fixed fee was paid, *plus a bonus for early resolution by settlement or trial*.

Some litigators have agreed to bill based on an agreed percentage of their normal hourly rate (typically in the range of 60 to 80 percent), with a bonus to be paid based on the results. How the bonus is to be computed is set forth in the representation agreement. This type of agreement provides cash flow during pendency of the litigation, involves some risk-sharing between lawyer and client, and provides an opportunity for receiving a fee higher than normal hourly rates, if the efforts are successful. It has been used in the normal contingency context based on amounts recovered, but also as a defense contingency, if defending counsel holds down the recovery to a specified amount, either by trial or by settlement.

Real success in the art of billing lies in crafting an arrangement that fits the needs of the clients and the willingness of the lawyers—and it can be done and is being done in litigation! The representation agreements included in chapter 3 illustrate how some of the largest firms in the country are customizing and negotiating fees for litigation.

Corporate counsel often try to impose a cap or maximum amount that will be charged for the matter being handled using hourly billing. The author's personal philosophy is that it is generally unwise to agree to a cap. It can only work to the disadvantage of the lawyer, if there is an overrun. When confronted with a demand for a cap on a matter that you really would like to handle, it is better to attempt to negotiate a fixed fee rather than a cap. That way, if you can increase efficiency, settle or try the case sooner, work more effectively, or are just lucky, you at least have an opportunity to be better compensated. It does not mean you do not still have the prospect of receiving less than the desired return for your services, if the fixed fee has been set too low. You can win or lose with a fixed fee, but with a cap you cannot win, but may lose. Nonetheless, caps or maximum fees that set the outside limits for the services are being used, thereby providing for corporate budgeting purposes some predictability of the charges that may result.

Here are a couple of twists in billing techniques that have been reported. One firm, by agreement with the client, bills for 95 percent of its normal hourly rate and asks the client to pay only that amount while the litigation is pending. Upon completion, the client alone determines what, if any, part of the 5 percent should be paid depending upon the satisfaction level of the client. This reflects a desired blending between quality of service (as perceived by the client) and billing method. Undoubtedly, this approach is intended to keep existing clients happy and to attract new clients as a marketing device.

The linkage between quality of service and alternative methods of billing has some interesting ramifications. In a 1990 survey, corporate counsel reported that poor-quality work would be more influential in their decision to drop an outside law firm than the amount of the fees or the method of billing. In the five years since *Beyond the Billable Hour* was published urging consideration of alternative billing methods, many law firms have become involved with total quality management (by whatever name it was called). TQM rests on delivering legal services that solve the problems clients want and need to have solved. Both TQM and billing for value are client focused. The end product of TQM and alternative approaches to billing is the building of trust and confidence between lawyer and client. We have noted that firms that have invested in the quality movement have typically developed a closer, more trusting relationship with their clients and because of this relationship are more easily able to move in the direction of alternative billing methods. The quality movement has special applicability to litigation where the focus has been on wasteful, inefficient practices.

Another twist involves an emphasis on client satisfaction. The firm in question guarantees satisfaction, agreeing that a client who is not satisfied with the services may elect not to pay all or a portion of the fee that was charged. This is an extreme approach that many may be reluctant to take. It puts you to the test as to whether you really believe that you do quality work and that the fee you charge is fair to the client.

About now some readers are asking, "How can I, as a litigator handling a long and complicated matter, foresee all of the problems and issues that may arise?" The answer is that you cannot know in advance what will occur in the handling of that type of case. New parties may come in, new issues may surface, opposing clients and their lawyers may make life complicated, or the court may make the trial vexatious. The best answer is that complex litigation can be broken down into phases, making it possible to foresee with reasonable accuracy what will take place in the next few months or until a certain stage of proceedings has occurred. Once you begin thinking in phases of litigation, billing ingenuity and innovation are possible. For example, you can agree to a fixed fee during the initial evaluation stage of the case. You can specify for the discovery phase that your fixed fee covers a prescribed number of depositions or interrogatories. You can negotiate for a fixed fee for motions, possibly with a bonus if the motion is successful. If the trial phase occurs, you might want to switch to hourly billing, since this where a lot of variables can occur. This type of budgeting is now being required by many corporate counsel. To do it, the lawyer must thoroughly analyze the case, determine the issues that can be foreseen, consider the variables, and work effectively towards goals as set mutually by lawyer and client. Budgeting gives some predictability of costs for purposes of corporate budgeting. Budgeting stresses efficiency and provides incentives for appropriate staffing and work methods. The innovative litigator will consider combining elements of hourly billing, results obtained, fixed fees for defined services, and evaluation of value added.

The moral for litigators is that once you get away from hourly billing you have greater control over how a matter is staffed, what steps you take for the client, and how much time you are permitted to spend on behalf of the client. You will be judged by the quality of your services or benefits conferred, not the tick of the clock. You will be more the judge of what needs to be done for the client and not be second-guessed or managed by a claims person or in-house counsel.

No matter what billing method you use, it is critical to remember that the ethical rules in every jurisdiction require a lawyer's fee to be reasonable. It is good practice, and may be a requirement, that the lawyer spell out in the representation agreement how the fee will be determined. For example, if you intend to bill using the unit system, be certain that your client clearly understands that the charge you make per unit is not dependent on time spent. If your fee agreement has a contingency factor, it is critical to set forth in your fee agreement the way the bonus will be calculated. If the case does not have a known monetary aspect—for example, if you are seeking injunctive relief, not damages, or if the payment following settlement or judgment is in a form other than money—agree on a dollar figure in advance that would be the bonus if certain prescribed relief is obtained.

Litigators are frequently asked to respond to a request for proposal. The RFP can require submitting a preliminary analysis of the case, a description of the proposed staffing, an indication of familiarity with the subject matter, references, and a proposal for the fee arrangement. Some RFPs seem to be primarily price-shopping, but others are oriented towards building a long-term relationship. Often the client who issued the RFP uses arrangements proposed in several responses to negotiate a representation agreement with one of the responding law firms. Whatever the use by the requesting party, the request requires immediate response. The firm that knows its cost of operation through cost accounting is better able to respond. Litigators who have had a longtime relationship with a client and a steady flow of case assignments can panic when a request for proposal arrives. All of a sudden, it becomes apparent that competitors are being considered for the representation. This, too, is part of the world of competition for litigators as well as for transactional lawyers.

Progressive law firms and lawyers have invested substantial sums in hardware, software, the creation of technology-based systems, and the training of personnel, including the lawyers. The litigation practice area is well adapted to use technology in a variety of ways. Litigators can help clients avoid litigation by use of electronic checklists to ensure compliance with contract terms or governmental regulations. Document assembly systems can provide guidance to clients on basic contract terms in the early negotiating stage. The use of decision trees as part of risk analysis helps both lawyers and clients in early evaluation of claims that actually or potentially are going to be litigated. Electronic communication or direct computer access is useful for good communication between litigators and their clients. Technology in the courtroom to enhance the effectiveness of litigators is another application. Effectively used, technology should produce a better-quality product and increase timeliness in the delivery of services. Keep in mind, however, that one of the key advantages of technology is to reduce the human time required to produce the services.

The use of technology in law practice may be merely an extension of manual systems, but increasingly technology is being used to reengineer legal processes to create better ways to accomplish a desired result.

The use of technology is an especially appealing and applicable tool for litigators, but the reduction of human time also reduces the number of billable hours. There should be every incentive for those using technology to get away from hourly billing to some other method that measures value. The more you invest in technology and the more you reduce the human time required, the less you earn if you continue to bill by the hour.

Here are the steps that litigators can take to move away from straight hourly billing towards some other billing method:

1. Know the characteristics of your law practice.
   a. The nature and needs of your clients and potential clients.
   b. The nature and abilities of your firm; its expertise; its practice areas.
2. Analyze the types of litigation that you have handled for the past three years, using closed files as well as open files, to determine whether there are categories of cases, either by subject matter or by client, that show patterns that might permit an alternative billing method.
3. Learn your cost of producing legal services so that you can make intelligent decisions as to pricing and billing methods.
4. Analyze the identity, nature, strength, and location of your competitors for each practice area or type of case that you have.
5. Examine who your clients are, the type of work you do for each, and the possibility that the clients would accept some other billing method. Of those clients that you feel might accept some different billing method, determine which are most likely to be willing to innovate. Do this before you decide which new billing method you wish to propose. For example, can you agree on a fixed fee for certain representations, if you are assured of an increased volume of business from the client? Consider proposing to your most innovative client a test of billing methods as was done in the fixed fee plus a bonus for early resolution example mentioned earlier. In that situation, corporate counsel and one of the firms handling collection work agreed that ten cases of the agreed-on type of case would be assigned to the outside firm on the regular hourly billing basis; ten cases would be assigned on a fixed fee basis. When all cases had been completed, the respective counsel would confer to see what the results had been and to make any adjustments that were mutually agreeable. The punch line is that once this was done, that outside firm began to receive more cases than before because of the im-

proved relationship, trust, and confidence that had resulted from the experiment.

6. Get in the habit of developing a case plan for every case that you handle. A case plan is the written plan for handling a specific representation. Done at the outset and continually revised, the plan identifies issues, sets forth the goals of the client with respect to the case, maps strategies, prescribes anticipated staffing, and reflects agreement between lawyer and client on how the case will be managed.
7. Experiment with a few cases. Do not expect to change all of your practice or all of your firm members to new billing methods immediately. Experience will guide you after you have tried alternative methods. If you are using fixed fees, be sure to define in the representation agreement precisely what is included. If you are using a contingency factor, evaluate carefully the risk you are taking and the magnitude of possible benefit if you prevail.
8. Stop thinking in terms of billable hours for both billing and compensation purposes. Think value to the client and dollars received for the lawyer.

Another approach is to go back and read the fee agreements in chapter 3 for inspiration to be innovative.

In summary, litigators are particularly subject to demands for alternative fee arrangements. The high cost of litigation, delays in resolution, and the excesses in the discovery process have prompted serious consideration of alternative means of dispute resolution. Traditional litigation as a practice area may disappear unless changes are made to meet the insistent demands of clients.

NOTE

1. *American Lawyer*, December 1993, p. 5.

PART 2

How to implement innovative billing

The relationship and importance of client trust and satisfaction

Motivating lawyers to change how law is practiced

Overcoming lawyer resistance to alternative billing methods

The imperative for change

Designing for the future

CHAPTER 8

Transitioning from the Present into the Future

LET'S PAUSE FOR A MOMENT as we move to Part Two by thinking about where the profession is headed and reflecting on what has occurred, why it has taken place, and what the ultimate quest is.

What have the firms whose innovative fee agreements you have now read done to implement their new approach to law practice? The agreements themselves may be innovative, but more important, they reflect an understanding that the focus for success must be to understand client objectives, to consider value from the standpoint of the client, to provide services that meet the client's perception of quality, and to devise an approach to billing and pricing that meets the client's criteria of value. It becomes apparent that you cannot separate billing and pricing from the totality of the law firm's operation.

When lawyers truly understand the objectives and needs of clients and commit to solve the problems that the client needs to have solved, a miraculous transformation occurs—the client has a feeling of trust and confidence in the lawyer. Hourly billing had an inherent basis for distrust because of the conflicting interests of lawyer and client. Where there is client trust and competent performance by the lawyer, there will be the strong likelihood of ultimate client satisfaction. Client trust and client satisfaction can lead to long-term, mutually beneficial relationships.

Major client concerns about hourly billing include the following:

- The total cost of legal services.
- The lack of predictability of what the cost will be.
- The absence of risk-sharing between lawyer and client when hourly billing is used.
- The relationship between the fees charged and the value to the client of the services provided.

The overriding concern of clients is to receive value in the sense of receiving services that provide a benefit to the client. Value in this context means that the fee charged equals the benefits received by the client.

The only value that counts is the value perceived by the *client*. The only services that bring a benefit to the client are those the client needs and wants to receive.

As we have seen in prior chapters, alternatives to straight hourly billing are being used increasingly, even though hourly billing continues to be the predominant method both in frequency of use and in revenues produced.

But look at what has happened when clients accept and lawyers continue billing by the hour. Early on, corporate counsel began to require budgeting, sometimes for the whole matter, other times by individual phase. Penalties were imposed if budgets were exceeded. For the most part, clients that required budgeting retained the right to approve the budget. The mere act of approving the proposed budget for a case was based on the decision of the client that for the contemplated services the amount budgeted represented value to the client. "I will pay you, Mr. Lawyer, $\$x$ for the first phase of the case."

Another approach taken was task-based billing, which, in reality, is not another billing method but rather a means whereby the client could determine what fee was being charged for a specific task. It arose because clients could not decipher the complicated itemized bills sent by their lawyers. Grouping services by tasks in the billing statement enabled the client to determine whether the charge was equal to the value to the client of the task that had been performed. Task-based billing held out the possibility that the client could compare one firm's services against another's, could determine whether the services were beneficial on a cost/benefits basis, and, in some instances, whether the hourly charges were pumped up by inefficiency. Once again, the issue was whether for a given task the client had received value. Another fallout was that the client could ask whether certain steps taken were even necessary to be done at all.

Another development was the increased use of legal auditors to review minutely the bills of firms that billed by the hour. Can there be any stronger evidence of clients' lack of trust in their lawyers? These audits looked for duplication of effort, padding, changes in staffing, excessive time spent, and occasionally fraudulent practices. Legal audits of hourly billing were an attempt to control the symptoms of inefficiency, not the causes. The weak spots in the use of legal audits are that a grandstand quarterback not charged with responsibility for handling the matter can opine that a given task should have taken less time to perform than was billed and that many legal auditors were compensated based on the "savings" they found in a bill, a direct conflict of interest. Despite these weaknesses, the real reason for employing a legal auditor was to determine whether the client had received "value."

It is sometimes contended that discounted billing is an alternative billing method. Discounted billing relates to pricing, not to billing method. Discounts based on volume are another matter, however, and are often tied to other approaches to innovative billing.

Choice of hourly billing with a maximum or cap is another sign that clients are willing to pay up to a certain level, but no more, because to go beyond that level would mean that the services have exceeded the value to the client. It may on first impression seem to be a matter of cost control, but in reality the insistence on a cap is one way that the client discloses the limit of value. In addition to being the client's expression of value the maximum fee or cap does provide the certainty or predictability of what the fee will be, or at least the upper limit of what will be charged.

Electronic access to the law firm's billing system certainly has obvious advantages, such as providing a quick way for the client to know what is going on, the cost to current date, the opportunity to intervene if matters are being badly handled, and the elimination of the cost of preparation of bills by the law firm. It is a bit like being seated in a taxi at a spot where you can see the meter, or like being able to call up your hotel bill on your hotel room TV screen. In either situation, you can keep abreast with what the charges are. If the taxi fare is too high, you can get out and walk or take a bus. If the hotel charges are too high, you can question those charges or move to cheaper quarters.

Another technique is the use of a request for proposal. These are used for different purposes. One legitimate use of RFPs is to locate a lawyer or law firm whose talents fit the needs of the client. Another legitimate use is to invite alternative billing proposals that may open the door to new and beneficial relationships. Sometimes RFPs are used purely for price-shopping, which may or may not lead to long-term mutually beneficial relationships.

All of these efforts to control the excesses of hourly billing appear to have the common objective of keeping the price charged to a level that equals the value of the services to the client.

When lawyers and clients get into the use of alternative billing arrangements it forces thinking about value. When a fixed fee is quoted, the client must determine whether that proposed fee equals the value of the included services. If there is a contingency or bonus factor, does the bonus or the amount that would be received under the contingency reflect value? The client must evaluate what he or she is getting in the way of a service and what it is worth.

One of the major benefits of considering appropriate alternative billing methods is that it forces both lawyer and client to think through and communicate the objectives of the client and the services that will be required to meet those objectives. Inherent in this process is the importance of determining the fairest way to measure the value of the services.

Even where the primary method of fee charging is tied to hourly billing, but with some limitation on the total charges that will be made, there is a clear movement towards fees that in some way reflect the clients' perception of value. When there is a dollar limitation on the fee that will be charged, or if the fee is to some extent based on results or benefits (not straight hourly billing), there is an incentive for efficiency.

Lawyers who use hourly billing try to include some element of profit in their hourly rate. The hourly rate may or may not equate with the value conveyed by the services. Lawyers are beginning to recognize that alternative billing methods may enhance, not decrease, profitability. The incentive to improve quality, foster efficiency, and reduce the cost of production creates an opportunity to reduce the cost of legal services for clients while improving the profitability of the lawyer.

In the transition to innovative billing another concept has evolved called the life cycle of a product. When a new, highly sophisticated legal product first appears, it falls within the unique category because of its newness and the fact that only a few law firms can produce that product. As volume increases and more and more law firms develop the capability of providing that specific bundle of services, the product ceases to be unique and becomes a commodity. As will be seen in chapter 11 relating to the value curve and pricing, commodity services are price sensitive. The problem is that many lawyers fail to realize the rapidity with which unique services become commodity services. To state it differently, in today's legal marketplace the life cycle of many legal products becomes shorter.

Technology permits tasks that previously could be performed only by large firms to be handled by solo practitioners or small firms. Thus, the effective use of technology is becoming an equalizer. In this transition the level of competition increases, in turn making pricing more sensitive.

CHAPTER 9

What Do Clients Want from Their Lawyers?

A CLOSE LOOK AT the comments about alternative billing methods reveals that clients are not concerned only about what they are charged for legal services. Concerns about value and whether they are receiving value uncover deeper and more-subtle desires of sophisticated clients.

The ultimate objective of any client is to have legal assistance in solving a problem. Lawyers often do not realize that the business of lawyering is to find ways to solve the problems that clients want and need to have solved.

Clients express a desire for *quality* of services. Just as "value" is the value as perceived by the client, "quality" is also as perceived by the client. Neither value nor quality as perceived by the lawyers is the relevant standard, although most lawyers believe that they can define both value and quality.

From the standpoint of the client, legal services should

- Solve the client's problems.
- Be delivered in timely fashion.
- Be provided for a fee that reflects true value to the client.
- Recognize that the justification for the existence of lawyers is to serve clients and to solve their problems.
- Have a high level of lawyer-client communication.

The total cost of legal services often appears to be a primary objection of clients. Some clients appear to be concerned only about reducing or controlling legal expense. These clients may be willing to accept a lower level of quality in order to save money, although normally they want quality of services, but at a lower price. What they really may be saying is that they need a simpler, less costly solution to their problem.

If the client does not make it clear what the problem to be solved is, or if lawyers do not take the time and make an effort to understand

and define the problem and the objectives of the client, there is no meeting of the minds. This points to the need for good communication from the start of the representation to the conclusion.

I have pondered over the years the wall that exists when a client/potential purchaser has not defined or is not able to define clearly what is desired. Part of the problem is that the seller/lawyer may not understand what the customer/client needs or would be happy to purchase, while the customer/client does not understand what product or services exist or could be made available. Is this a chicken-or-the-egg dilemma? To give a simple example, for years we had a TV set that we used and enjoyed. Then someone had the foresight to develop the VCR, recognizing that viewers would buy a device that recorded TV shows for later viewing and that enabled prerecorded videotapes to be enjoyed in the home. Someone anticipated and developed the VCR at a time when I, the viewer, had no idea I would like to have such a thing.

For another example, I never lamented that I had to keep my foot on the gas pedal of my car throughout long trips, even though a leg cramp or two may have been caused by the constant pressure on the accelerator. At one point I bought a car that happened to come equipped with cruise control. Someone anticipated that a device that would make it unnecessary to keep your foot on the pedal would be attractive to drivers. Once I had cruise control, I realized the comfort and the benefits, and it became a necessity.

The point is that there may be problems out there that clients do not even know are problems, or there may be possible solutions that clients do not realize are or could be available.

These two simple examples apply to the relationship between inside and outside counsel. Both owe a duty to the corporate client to find ways to solve a corporate legal problem. Each has knowledge and resources that can be brought to bear with good communication and dedication to the common goal of solving the problem at hand. This approach, termed "partnering," is an attempt to cooperate in the use of expertise and skills for the benefit of the client.

To continue this theme, one of the comments frequently made with respect to alternative billing methods is that a level of trust and confidence between inside and outside counsel is important for success. Some observers have stated this in terms of the need for better case management by corporate counsel, greater involvement, better communication, and so on.

These conditions are not easy to bring about where corporate counsel, operating under a mandate to reduce legal expense, are overly aggressive in their drive to beat down the fees charged by outside counsel and are thinking only in terms of reducing the bill rather than developing close, long-term, mutually beneficial relationships. What is needed is a change from an adversarial to a cooperative relationship between inside and outside counsel. Where such a cooperative relationship exists, there will be a win-win situation.

With hourly billing there is an inherent conflict. Outside counsel have a dollar incentive to maximize the number of hours spent, since each additional hour increases the size of the fee; inside counsel, knowing that fewer hours means lower fees, have every incentive to question the hours billed and to question whether those hours were spent doing things that were necessary, were performed by the correct person, and were used effectively and efficiently.

While many of the complaints about legal services are about the cost, clients want a level of expertise and services that fits their needs. Clients do not want a thirty-page legal brief delivered at a high cost if a one-page memo or a phone call will tell them what they need or want to know.

Another thing that clients want is timely performance. Delays hold up business and personal decisions, add to the cost, prolong frustrations, and keep the client occupied so that other activities cannot be pursued. This is referred to as the "client's cost of carry," the ongoing need to keep people involved pending resolution of the problem. When there is a legal problem to be solved, either in litigation or in a transaction, there are in reality two costs that vitally affect the client. The first, and most often discussed, is the amount paid to lawyers for their services. The second is the internal cost to the client in searching for documents, attending depositions, waiting in court, traveling back and forth, and spending time resolving the pending problem or transaction rather than carrying out more productive services for their business or personal affairs. In addition, there is the "worry" factor—sleepless nights, concern about the outcome, nervousness that affects daily business and family life resulting in personal stress, frustration, and often impaired health. Unreasonable delay has a cumulative negative effect on the participants.

One of the irritants clients most often complain of is the failure of lawyers to be available, to return phone calls or respond promptly to requests. Sitting at home awaiting a phone call that does not come at the time promised or waiting in a reception room beyond the scheduled appointment time has a negative impact on the life of the client. Lawyers will be smart to recall how they react when kept waiting to see a doctor who is apparently indifferent to patients' schedules or when they take time away from the office to wait at home for an appliance repair person who fails to show up at the promised time.

Clients are willing to pay for expertise, timely performance, good communication, and a fee that fairly reflects value. To deliver what knowledgeable clients want will require new approaches to the delivery of legal services, new methods, new quality standards, and new approaches to meeting client needs. That is what the rest of this book will be about. The billing process is not a separate, compartmentalized part of the lawyer-client relationship. Objections to fees are symptoms of underlying problems needing resolution, frequently the result of poor lawyer-client communication.

The innovative billing methods described in chapter 3 illustrate how important it is to have good communication between lawyer and client. In crafting a specific representation agreement the ability of the client to describe the problem to be solved and to express the client's objectives is important, but even more critical is the ability of the lawyer to understand and be well aware of the meaning of what the client has said.

During the course of the representation the communication skills of the lawyer are vital in several respects—lawyer to lawyer in negotiations, lawyer to court in trials, lawyer to witness in discovery and trial, lawyer to government official in obtaining permits and licenses, and, last but not least, lawyer to client and the reciprocal client to lawyer, all of which involve communication skills.

The start of the communication process is when the client first comes in contact with the law firm, whatever the nature of that first contact—in writing, by telephone, or in person. Each person in the law firm can influence the representation by the way communication occurs. Whether it is the telephone operator, the receptionist, or the legal assistant, impressions are formed that may be positive or negative. Communication in this sense should be interpreted to include both verbal and nonverbal exchanges, for impressions can become indelible by the image that is conveyed.

Just a few days ago a new friend asked, "What kind of clothes did you wear to the office when you were in law practice, Dick?" Since we were sitting on the beach in Maui when this question was posed, I was somewhat surprised. My answer was that it depended on what was scheduled for that particular day. We talked further about the appropriateness of clothing and demeanor and how influential unspoken communication through images that are created can be.

High-level communication skills can differentiate lawyers. The ability to converse, exchange ideas, display empathy, listen, truly understand, probe for true meaning, inspire confidence, evidence your care and concern for the other person's problems, recognize moods, honor different points of view, use appropriate language, manage inflections, be conscious of body language, pitch at the appropriate level—all of these are aspects of effective communication.

Why are we talking about communication skills when this book is about billing methods and pricing?

From the selfish monetary point of view of the lawyer, excellent communication skills can put dollars into your firm bank account.

Starting with the initial interview with the client, the client-lawyer-client communication process commences. Communication can impute value. Excellent communication is in itself value. If throughout the representation the client feels informed about what is planned and what has been accomplished and feels benefited by what the lawyer is doing, the billing is not just conveyance or expression of value, but confirmation of the value that the client has recognized throughout everything that occurred before the sending of the statement.

Milton W. Zwicker, an Orillia, Ontario, solicitor, has written many useful and insightful articles and books on the art of communication. For example, chapter 7 in *Win-Win Billing Strategies,* entitled "Billing as Part of the Communication Process," contains many useful hints on the communication process between lawyer and client.[1] Another version of the materials was published in *Law Practice Management.*[2] Quality in law practice includes more than documents, pleadings, and advice. In my definition, "quality" includes the totality of the relationship of the client and lawyer. Likewise, "value" results from the totality of that relationship. Intangibles like steadfastness, availability, reliability, loyalty, faithfulness, courtesy, concern, friendliness, and other intangibles all contribute to and are a part of both quality and value.

Communication is enhanced when you understand the background, the activities, the personality, and the environment of the other person. To the extent possible an attempt should be made to know as much as possible about the client. If the client has a business, knowing the problems of the industry generally, visiting the plant or office, and understanding problems or opportunities unique to that business add to the ability to communicate and to understand. Similarly, the lawyer-client relationship is enhanced if you know about the family, hobbies, and other interests of the client. Whether it is genuine interest or a marketing ploy, a profile of each client on your personal computer permits instant recall.

Clients do not often take the initiative in disclosing how they feel about the services that have been rendered or about the relationship. Surveys of clients often reveal true feelings. Increasingly, law firms are doing client exit surveys when a matter is concluded. Periodic visits to major clients, often by a partner who has not been directly involved in doing the work for that client, flatter the client because it shows that the firm cares about and values the relationship. Likewise, such interviews may bring out any grievances not previously expressed, or may confirm the solidarity of the relationship.

Increasingly, law firms are having client surveys done by outside organizations so that anonymity can be preserved. Some years ago our firm, the Reed McClure law firm, participated in such a survey. The respondents included a wide cross section of the community, both clients and nonclients. The results confirmed some things that we liked and revealed some things that surprised us. Respondents who were identified as our firm clients generally were pleased with our services. Nonclients who had heard of the firm generally reported that the firm had a reputation for doing good work. The surprise to us was the large number of respondents who had never heard of the Reed McClure law firm even though the firm had been in existence for more than seventy years! Speedily our marketing plan turned to steps to increase name familiarity.

Another aspect of communication involves determining what problems clients or prospective clients have or are likely to have in the future. Market research is an aid to strategic planning, marketing, branching, or the creation or enhancement of practice areas. For example, if you have done market research you may be able to direct your continuing legal education dollars towards topics that will benefit your practice, or you can be on the lookout for specific backgrounds of your applicants for employment when you are interviewing. Where the lawyer has knowledge of facts generated by market research, the level of communication is raised because the lawyer and client are now able to converse on subjects of mutual interest.

The development of your own database of facts relevant to firm clients or industries with which clients are involved can also provide a basis for effective communication, especially the ability to recall information quickly when the need arises. This is in addition to information available on computer networks that can be researched. The advent of the personal computer and the accessibility of information on a vast number of subjects enables the small-firm practitioner to compete with the larger firms. Enhanced communication is the result.

Henry W. Ewalt, experienced in both private law practice and as corporate counsel, authored an excellent book, *Through the Client's Eyes*.[3] Chapter 12, entitled "Billing: A Valuable Communication Tool," sets forth the requirements for a statement for legal services that will show what was done, when it was done, who did it, and how it was done. Mr. Ewalt's contention is that the bill itself provides an opportunity to express and confirm value. As part of the total lawyer-client relationship, lawyers should ascertain the preferences of their clients on how statements will be submitted. Where the client has been kept informed or, better yet, participated in the handling of a matter, including participating in critical strategic decisions, the statement will serve as confirmation of the services provided and the approach that was taken. This is even better than the use of the statement to *inform* the client of what has taken place. Client development involves showing clients and prospective clients how bills for legal services will assist the clients in managing their legal fees. Through the billing processes envisioned by Mr. Ewalt, statements become a positive, proactive technique for cementing relationships, rather than the conveyance of the bad news of what the charges are.

The scope of this book precludes a treatise on communication techniques, but that in no way diminishes the importance of the message that is sent, namely, that improved communication between lawyer and client will produce benefits in marketing, cement client relationships, preserve a competitive position in the marketplace, make more pleasant the contacts between lawyer and clients, permit more effective strategic planning, and most of all make billing a part of the total process.

If you examine complaints against lawyers or lawyer disciplinary proceedings, you will note that a high percentage result from poor communications. The failure to inform in a timely manner, the failure to return calls or respond to letters, the lack of clarity in discussing matters with clients all result in negatives to be avoided. Try to turn these into affirmatives.

NOTES

1. Milton W. Zwicker, "Billing as Part of the Communication Process," Chapter 7 in Richard C. Reed, ed., *Win-Win Billing Strategies: Alternatives That Satisfy Your Clients and You* (Chicago: Section of Law Practice Management, American Bar Association, 1992).

2. Milton W. Zwicker, "The Power of Communication on the Billing Process," *Law Practice Management* (July/ Aug. 1992): 23.

3. Henry W. Ewalt, *Through the Client's Eyes* (Chicago: Section of Law Practice Management, American Bar Association, 1994).

CHAPTER 10

Economics—The Relentless Pressure

THE SUBJECTS COVERED THUS FAR, the numerous fee agreements set forth or described, and the results of the numerous surveys demonstrate that there have been tremendous changes in the legal profession since our first book, *Beyond the Billable Hour*, was published in 1989. It is clear that what some people thought was billing theory has become reality and that the trend away from straight hourly billing will continue. The recession and the swing from seller's market to buyer's market have unleashed economic forces with compounding effects.

At the time of writing, recent surveys show some resurgence in law firm profits. Closer observation of those survey results, however, shows that there were many ups and downs among the larger firms. In an article, "Turmoil beneath the Surface," in the July/August 1995 issue of the *American Lawyer*,[1] Steven Brill opined that the legal marketplace is fundamentally different in that buyers are no longer buying lawyer hours, they are demanding and buying solutions to problems and this is changing the structure of law firms, a theme that this author and others have expressed during the recent past.

If the legal profession had continued to have a seller's market, the probability of any significant change in the way law practice was conducted would be slight, with the possible exception of the influence of technology. The continuing flow of law graduates increased the supply of lawyers available to compete for available legal work. The economy of the country does go up and down, so the recession should not have come as a surprise. The impact of the recession on businesses and individuals was greater than many anticipated, especially some law firms that acted as though prosperity for lawyers was guaranteed forever. Many thought the recession in the legal profession was a passing phase and soon the good old days would return. Those lawyers waited and did not change.

The movement toward nonhourly billing methods that some regarded as both logical and desirable existed before the recession. It was, however, the economic downturn and resultant pressures that accelerated change in the profession, a pressure that will have long-term and lasting effects.

Economic pressures are the force for change; technology will be the means. Actually, to back off a bit, technology in itself will not bring about the major change in law practice; rather, the willingness and ability of lawyers to devise and use new approaches to providing legal services will be the key to the future, and one of the principal tools will be computers. To change individuals and to alter law firm cultures will not be easy, but those that do will be the survivors.

The economic squeeze on law firms comes from above and below, the constant problem of increased costs of operation on the expense side, declining revenues on the income side. Corporate counsel are not the only clients seeking to reduce legal expense. Individual clients are deeply concerned about what seems to be the high cost of having a lawyer. Other providers (nonlawyers and nontraditional competitors) are entering the scene, causing additional pressures on revenues. Some services traditionally provided by lawyers are being performed by others or by the clients themselves.

In Tucson a client can use a computerized, fill-in-the-blanks program for marital dissolution complaints. Recently, an expert lawyer in the Tampa area spotted a computer software program on will and trust drafting offered for sale at $9.95. Since he specialized in estate planning and elder law, he was curious about just what would be included in this software. He bought the program and had a legal assistant in his office try it out. She filled in the blanks and shortly had produced what this lawyer reported was a reasonably acceptable instrument. His conclusion was that lawyers can no longer make a living by selling paper.

Firms have designed or acquired expert systems for use in their offices believing that the skill and expertise of the senior lawyers in setting up the system would permit delegation to less experienced junior lawyers or paralegals. This being the case, it will be but a short hop to having systems available that will not require any lawyer, or at least not any lawyers who charge premium prices.

We previously observed that the life cycle of new legal services is shortening and the transition from unique to commodity services occurs more rapidly. The consequence is that prices will come down to the commodity level, where competition is the most intense and prices are the most sensitive.

When we speak of the actions taken by corporate counsel to reduce outside legal expense, we are not speaking only of the megacorporations dealing with the megafirms for massive litigation or huge transactions. There is evidence that the smaller corporations are among those most aggressive in seeking to lower outside legal expense. Many small firms do insurance defense work, collections, and product liability cases. These firms are also subject to pressures from the clients that engage them.

We read of task-based billing requiring legal services to be grouped so that comparisons can be made from lawyer to lawyer or firm to firm. The immediate objective is to enable the client to know exactly how much a given task costs, who did the work, and whether unnecessary steps were taken. This analysis will lead to further changes in how law is practiced. Task-based billing is but the first step in a long evolutionary process that will change law practice.

General Motors was one of the first major corporations to announce and require task-based billing. Others followed suit to the point that law firms were forced to deal with numerous independently developed formats. Many, if not most, time and billing systems could capture billing information, but to comply with the various task-based formats required by corporate clients it was necessary to manually rearrange the billing data, a slow and costly process.

Several separate efforts were made to standardize the task-based billing format, but these varied in the amount of detail required and in the coding requirements inherent in this approach. The most definitive approach to standardization was developed by the American Bar Association Section of Litigation, the American Corporate Counsel Association, and a sponsoring group of major corporate law departments and law firms.

On April 7, 1995, the final draft was released. To fully explain the requirements and, hopefully, to jar lawyers into recognizing that a major change is here, not just coming, that draft, the Litigation Code Set, is reproduced in the Appendix.

This draft has no official sanction and is not compulsory. It remains to be seen how corporate law departments adhere to the standardized format. The good news is that the discipline imposed by the Litigation Code Set may force law firms to analyze their methods, learn their costs, recognize the importance of planning case strategy, eliminate unnecessary and unproductive steps, and perfect the art of budgeting. Honing these skills will enable skilled lawyers to meet the demanding requirements of their sophisticated clients. The bad news for lawyers is that this is in all probability only the first step in what will be a traumatic change as further pressures are applied.

Economic pressures on law firms have caused a lengthening of the partnership track, additional requirements for billable hours, reduction in new hiring, elimination of "nonproductive" partners, downsizing, and other belt-tightening measures. The pressure for billable hours has reduced the time available for training of junior lawyers, especially when clients are unwilling to pay hourly rates for untrained lawyers. These efforts to maintain leverage are early symptoms of things to come.

There is no reason to believe that the economic pressures on the legal profession will be reduced in the foreseeable future. A massive readjustment in the ways legal services are provided will be an imperative. To survive, lawyers must recognize the economic realities, devise new and better ways to practice law, and be prepared for a global change in the legal environment. It will be more than a gradual evolution; the forces of revolution are stirring and will not go away.

NOTE

1. Steven Brill, "Turmoil beneath the Surface," *American Lawyer* (July/August 1995): headnotes.

CHAPTER 11

Pricing of Legal Services

THERE IS MORE in the legal literature about billing methods than about pricing, yet pricing is one of the more difficult aspects of law practice. With hourly billing, pricing was simpler, limited to the key decision on the level of hourly rates for each fee charger.

Billing methods and the pricing of legal services are separate and distinct. No matter what billing method you employ, your pricing can be at the high end or the low end. Suppose your billing method is the fixed or flat fee method for defined services. If you price or charge $100 for those services, you may be at the low end in pricing. If you charge $1,000 for those same services, you may be at the high end. Each billing method has advantages and disadvantages for the client and the lawyer, so you should strive to find the right method for a given representation. No matter which *method* you use, you must determine the pricing level, a factor that will be influenced by the type of service, the kind of client, and the competitive market in which you practice.

THE VALUE CURVE

The value curve was set forth and discussed in chapter 3 of *Beyond the Billable Hour* in a chapter written by William C. Cobb and was also included in chapter 5 of *Win-Win Billing Strategies* with considerable amplification of its significance and application.

The value curve continues to be useful to demonstrate how different services have different value. The curve shows relative differences in value—and, hence, price—but does not give you precise information on how you should price your services.

So that we have a common basis for understanding, the value curve is shown once again on the following page.

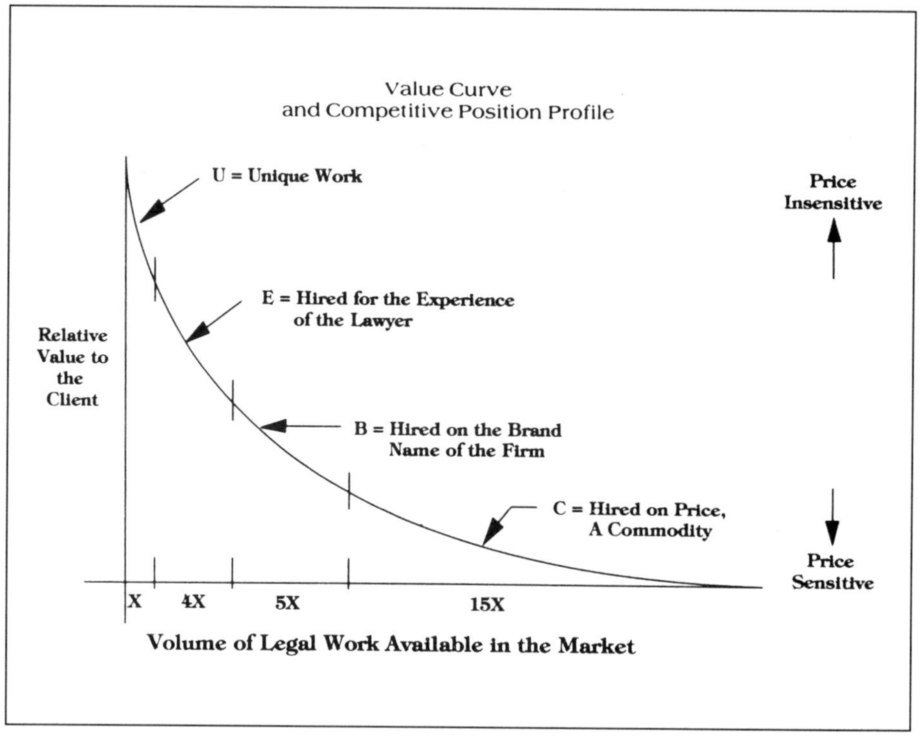

Adapted from William C. Cobb's Value Curve. Used with permission.

At the high end of the curve, unique work is limited in volume of work in the market to a quantity of 1x. By its nature, unique work is price insensitive. With matters of extreme importance, complexity, or potential for disaster, clients do not shop for price. Moving to the right, or downward on the curve, experiential work has a volume of 4*x*, is of less value than unique work, and is less price insensitive. This category is of increased significance today because of the growing tendency of sophisticated clients to hire not a firm but a lawyer who has the specific experience or expertise they want.

The brand name of the firm has a volume of work available in the market of 5*x*. Note that this 5*x* quantity equals the volume of unique and experiential combined, but is one-third of the volume of the next category, commodity work. With a volume of 15*x* commodity work has the lowest value, which is extremely price sensitive. Commodity work is more routine, can be systematized in most instances, and can be performed satisfactorily by any of a large number of lawyers.

There is nothing wrong with doing commodity work; indeed, it is the work that lawyers do most commonly. The processing of commodity work must be done efficiently, usually on a noncustomized basis by less expensive units of labor. It is important for law firms to recognize that some of their services may fall into any one of the four categories and to staff and price appropriately. This applies to every lawyer who may work with different categories of services in the course of his or her law practice. From the value curve, you learn the following:

- The volume of available work in the market varies by category.
- The value of services varies by category.

- Price sensitivity varies by category.
- Competition for work varies by category.

The value curve has significance both in the choice of billing method and in the pricing of legal services. Knowledge of the value curve and its significance aids in the development and use of innovative billing approaches.

Various methods of billing have been discussed in earlier chapters, and the value curve and its significance in showing the *relative* value of legal services have been explained. However, neither billing methods nor the value curve instruct you on how to price legal services.

CLASSICAL PRICING THEORIES

In classical economics much has been written about pricing theories, most of which were applied primarily to manufacturing industries or service industries other than the professions. Traditionally, law firms have charged "fees" and sent "statements" to their clients. *Webster's New World Dictionary, 1990 Edition,* for example, defines *price* as "the amount of money, etc., asked or paid for something" as the primary definition, and *fee* as "a charge for professional services." The secondary meaning of *price* is "value or worth."

Among the classical pricing definitions are

- Cost pricing (fixed + variable + profit)
- Value pricing (what the market will bear)
- Penetration pricing (to win market share)
- Competitive pricing (average market price)
- Skimming pricing (improved quality and image)
- Dumping price (below cost)
- Loss-leader pricing (attract other profitable business)
- Contract pricing (determined by negotiation)

HOURLY BILLING PRICING

Most lawyers are not very scientific in pricing their services. With hourly billing, only two, or possibly three, factors are involved. The first is the hourly rate of fee chargers, typically including an amount to cover overhead plus a desired level of profit. The second is the number of hours expended as recorded with varying degrees of accuracy. Multiply the hourly rate by the number of hours and you get the price or fee. A possible third factor is to make a judgment for upward or lower adjustment, primarily subjectively. Unfortunately, this method of pricing often has very little relationship to the value of the services. Straight hourly billing worked when the seller's market prevailed.

Whatever your billing method and whatever your pricing theory, it is imperative that you know your *cost of production of your services*, a topic that will be explored later in this chapter. Unless you know your cost, you will be flying blind.

Peter F. Drucker suggests that the primary question may not be price but rather, "What is value to the customer?"[1] Value, according to Drucker, is the sum of all of the aspects of a service that are deemed important by the client.

An interesting article, "Pricing Opportunities—And How to Exploit Them," by Hermann Simon appeared in 1992 in the *Sloan Management Review*.[2] Although not directed to service industries or the professions, the article includes some thought-provoking comments that may apply to pricing in the legal profession—for example: "Price and value are cornerstones of every transaction." In discussion of one company's practice Simon observes, "Light users were much less price sensitive than heavy users, so [the firm] offered pronounced quantity rebates and a bonus system," suggesting that quantity discounts should be given only to heavy users of legal services, not to the occasional client. The author stresses that price and the effect on market share should always be considered together. A price increase can decrease market share possibly to the point of diminishing profits, while a price decrease where competition does not require it can also reduce total profits. The search then is for optimal price levels. A change in pricing should involve intense study based on expert analysis, client interviews, and observation of market behavior. One way to test market behavior is to experiment with changed pricing on a limited basis to see the reaction of the customer or client before expanding the new pricing generally.

A skimming price often is higher than the market at the time since the services being offered are not generally available. As competitors begin to offer similar services, a price reduction will be necessary (a downward movement in the value curve, which makes the services more sensitive to price). The downward movement may be delayed if there is differentiation in the service, even though basically the same service is offered by others. Loyalty to the lawyer or firm, client inertia, or the internal cost to the client of moving to another firm may explain the delay that occurs. An opposite approach is penetration pricing, where the price is consciously set below market levels to increase market share with the hope that a reasonable profit level can be maintained. Professor Simon suggests that when an incumbent producer is confronted with a newcomer producer of a similar product or service, the incumbent has three options:

- To reduce price before competitors enter (proactive price cuts).
- To reduce price after entry, usually after some market share losses (reactive price cut).
- To maintain high price and accept a market share erosion (harvesting strategy).

The question to be considered is whether these notions apply to the legal profession. It is submitted that they do. What is probably the case is that most law firms do not spend much time thinking about the philosophy or realities of pricing. Thoughtful law firm managers may wish to study articles such as this one by Simon to become more aware of pricing methods. Considering the increasing pressure on law firms to reduce the total cost of legal services and the strong competitive forces that law firms face today, this type of analysis may become a prerequisite for success in the future.

PRICING BASED ON PROFITABILITY

A series of bells rang for me when I read "Financial Analysis for Profit-Driven Pricing" by Gerald E. Smith and Thomas T. Nagle in the *Sloan Management Review* in early 1994.[3] One of the reasons the bells rang out was that I had pondered for some time the tendency of lawyers using alternative billing methods to judge the success or failure of such efforts by whether they had earned more or less than their hourly rates. My contention is that the setting of hourly rates, a cost-plus profit method, was often done without much accurate information on the cost of providing a given service. Typically, firm statistics show hours billed, fees billed, and fees realized and collected. Assuming two lawyers within the same firm with identical year-end statistics, how often do firms then go on to measure the relative profitability of those two fee producers? One lawyer's practice may have required a high level of staff support, high-level advance of costs, and delayed collection of fees. The other lawyer, with the same total statistics, may have had substantially lower cost of production and hence greater profitability. For the most part, law firms using hourly billing tended to charge an established hourly rate (or possibly more than one rate) pretty much across the board without regard to differences in cost of production of certain services, including benefits conferred or the exposure to malpractice risks.

Another phenomenon that I noted on numerous occasions while in private practice is that when several partners gathered to set or review billings, there was a tendency to feel that fees to the clients of other partners should be raised, but not those to one's own clients. The analogy relates to the observation by Smith and Nagle that there are antagonistic forces in pricing decisions. They contend that financial people allocate costs to determine how *high* prices must be to cover costs and to achieve profit objectives. Marketing and sales people determine how *low* prices must be to achieve their sales objectives. Is this akin to the relative roles of the law firm partners in a billing meeting?

Consideration of pricing in the context of value as perceived by the client pushes pricing to the point of view of the client (market-driven forces). Unless the lawyer knows the cost of production, how far can consumer pressure for price reduction go without causing the law firm to become unprofitable? One quick answer is that whatever the firm can do to reduce the cost of production will enable the firm to withstand outside pressure for price reduction.

Smith and Nagle observe, as did Professor Simon, that pricing decisions must be undertaken with an awareness of the impact on market share or volume, since it is the combination of the two that ultimately determines profits. They call their approach "profit-driven pricing" and suggest that competing forces within the organization should together address the more general question "What changes in price, and in the marketing program, could make this product more profitable?"

As I continued to read the Smith and Nagle article, the ringing of the bells became a clanging when I came to a graph entitled, "Constant Profit Curve Plotting the Tradeoff between Price and Sales Volume Required for Constant Profitability." It looked for all the world like the value curve. The left or vertical axis related to price expressed in dollars in five-dollar increments. The horizontal axis related to unit sales volume expressed in thousands of units. As a baseline the authors used a price of $60 for 400,000 units. The illustration was that if there were a 10 percent price reduction, from $60 to $54, to maintain constant profitability it would be necessary to have an increase in sales volume to 500,000 units. By using the constant profit curve, a similar computation could be made showing the effect of an increase or decrease in price on the volume of sales required to maintain constant profitability.

PRICING BASED ON AVAILABILITY OF WORK

For this concept to be useful in law practice, it is important to determine to the extent possible how much legal work is available in the marketplace. This will not be easy to do because there are no readily available sources for making an accurate prediction of how much work might be attracted with a pricing change. But these principles and concepts can be used in making some broad, undetailed analysis. For example, assume that your law firm is pretty much limited to practice in one county; that you have developed a system using technology for mass producing deed of trust or mortgage foreclosures at a very low cost; that you have done this type of work for a fixed fee; and that you have existing in-house capability of handling more of this kind of work. The issue then is: If you reduced your price but still maintained a reasonable level of profitability, how much additional foreclosure work is available in your market? Even though you cannot be precise in your analysis, you can certainly consider the number of public recordings of foreclosure actions and whether the trend was upwards or downwards; the number of banks, savings and loan, or insurance companies in your marketplace who might need this type of service; the economic conditions prevailing that might indicate whether individuals would be likely to default because of bad times or be able to make loan payments because times were good; the relative price now charged by your firm and your major competitors for a foreclosure; and how much price reduction would be needed to induce clients to change to your firm.

Among the many thought-provoking ideas suggested by Smith and Nagle is that pricing decisions should be made with an awareness of both short-term and long-term consequences, suggesting that a dip in profitability might be justified if there would be recovered or increased profits in the long term, or if the change in pricing could lead to new and different opportunities—such as becoming the major legal counsel to the bank for whom you had only done routine foreclosures. A pricing decision made in this way is, in a sense, a kind of penetration pricing.

PRICING RELATED TO COST OF PRODUCTION

Another writer, David H. Maister, has recognized that in setting the price for fixed fee billing it is essential to know the cost of providing the services in the specific matter being handled. His article "Measuring Profitability Matter by Matter" appeared in the *American Lawyer* in mid-1994.[4] He suggests that this measuring process can be accomplished by using information normally contained in time and billing systems that track cash receipts by subject matter and record both hours logged and standard billing rates for each timekeeper. By changing the billing rate column to the cost per hour of that timekeeper, you have both revenue and costs for that matter. Maister's article gives a detailed description of the methodology and the significant issues that such an analysis opens for discussion. His major contention is that measuring profitability by his suggested method, compared to traditional methods, will disclose instances where the profitability level will be different than previously thought. The constructive use of this information is that it may lead to changed approaches that will be beneficial to the firm in the longer term. This article is recommended reading. It relates to matters that will be discussed in the next chapter with regard to determining your costs and to the chapter on fixed fee billing.

The most focused article on the pricing of legal services is "Alternative Pricing Options for Law Firms" by Silvia L. Coulter and Andrew Shulman, which appeared in the *Legal Administrator* in mid-1993.[5] These authors suggest that the first step in the pricing process is to analyze all base and variable costs. Base costs are those expenses of the law firm that cannot be changed in the short term. Variable costs are those that increase or decrease as the workload changes. The next step is to analyze profitability of practice groups, types of service, branches, etc. The next step is to determine whether the profitability of any of the subgroups could be increased by changed work methods.

Before determining price, client expectations and competitive reaction should be studied. For new work, cost-plus pricing is advantageous. Once price and cost of production have been established, the firm can move to fixed fees and, thereafter, to some incentive-based pricing. The final step, according to Coulter and Shulman, is to examine pricing impacts on volume, profits, market share, and overall image.

Internally, determining cost of production can be accomplished with effort. Typical problems that may be encountered include allocation of overhead costs and the inertia of some partners who do not really want the level of profitability of their own work to be determined. Suffice it to say that intelligent pricing cannot be accomplished without a good knowledge of costs. Internal analysis, however, is only half the process.

The more difficult part of pricing is to assess client reactions and the reaction of competitors to pricing changes. In some legal communities there are surveys that can provide some information on prevailing pricing levels. Another approach is a client survey, often with outside expert assistance, that includes questions to elicit clients' feelings about pricing. Valuable information about existing firm clients can be obtained in this manner, but that leaves unresolved information about market share and the potential availability of suitable legal work in the marketplace. This area of inquiry is the most obscure. Earlier we have talked about the need to customize billing approaches. One pricing theory was negotiated pricing. One of the more effective ways to determine the acceptability of your proposed pricing is by direct communication and negotiation. When you are dealing one-on-one with a prospective client, you will be able to tell whether you have set prices too high if you fail to land the client because of price. Responding to a request for proposal is another way you can learn whether you are competitive in your marketplace, if you are consistently underbid.

Using the terminology of the value curve, technology and the accelerating pace of law practice shorten the transition from unique legal work to experiential, to brand name, to commodity services. Consequently, you should reassess your pricing policy periodically, considering the relatively shorter life cycle of pricing. Even with new services that may be innovative or the product of improved technology, you should always think in terms of client benefit and value in setting the price. It is critical to fine-tune your pricing to meet perceived value and the relationship of your services to those provided by your competition.

Later in this chapter we will discuss what may be a new career in law firm operations, the position of estimator, a specialist who will have expertise in cost accounting and in determining the price to be charged.

Because billing and pricing are one of the six component functions of a legal organization, it is critical that billing and pricing strategies fit and be internally consistent with the overall operation of your organization.

You should analyze by practice areas the position on the value curve where those matters fall, and price your services appropriately. If your analysis of your practice reflects that many of your services are commodity services where systems and technology can be used and where the scope of the engagement is reasonably fixed, you should move towards fixed fee billing.

If you have a contingent fee practice, you should refine the pre-engagement procedures to ensure careful screening of the cases you take in, and you should monitor your cost of production even though your fee will be contingent on results. Contingent fee billing, because it is not keyed to billable hours, provides an incentive for efficiency, making it important to use whatever systems or technology promote efficiency. Think of the benefits of litigation support systems and case management programs in streamlining the process of preparing for and trying lawsuits. Although the ultimate fee is dependent upon results obtained, every reduction in the cost of processing the work either adds to the profitability to the firm or makes possible a reduced cost to the client.

In your litigation practice, you should concentrate on early strategic planning of the matter at hand, budget by phases in complex litigation, and consider whether some hybrid arrangement involving a contingency based on results would be acceptable to you and to your clients. Where you have a volume of litigation with substantially similar cases involving similar issues and exposure, fixed fee billing may be appropriate. With this choice you accept the risk that some cases may be closed with less involvement than others, so you should be prepared to accept variations with the hope that on balance your fixed fee will bring the desired level of profitability.

You should remember that not all legal services are of equal value and avoid charging uniformly from practice area to practice area or from matter to matter.

To find a mutually acceptable and beneficial billing arrangement, you should select the clients you feel are the most flexible and innovative and work with them. As lawyers experiment and innovate in billing methods, it is helpful to work with clients who are open to change. It has become apparent that the most successful innovation occurs where there is a long-standing relationship between lawyer and client that has resulted in a feeling of mutual trust and confidence. There is an interesting parallel where outside firms and corporate law departments have both gone through the total quality management discipline. Although it has not been demonstrated quantitatively, there is evidence that the chances of successful innovation in billing is greater where TQM or its equivalent has been a mutual experience.

Proposing alternative billing approaches is also useful in obtaining new clients, many of whom will be grateful to hear something new from law firms seeking new business. Alternative approaches can be proposed in the courtship of a prospective client or in response to a request for proposal. Flexibility in billing methods may be a means for differentiating your services from those of a competitor, even those whose services may be at the same quality level as yours.

The point to remember is to fit your billing methods and pricing techniques to match your approach to the type of practice now being conducted and also to be prepared to adopt billing methods and pricing techniques that will fit your strategic plan as to the types of clients that you hope to have and the different practice areas that you wish to develop in order to meet the goals of your strategic plan.

In general, systematization and the use of technology will be more applicable for routine, repetitive matters that you are handling, namely, commodity work. That is not to say that systematization and use of technology are not important for other types of work. Wherever you can improve efficiency and whatever your practice area or billing method, there will be benefits to both the lawyer and the client—lower charges for the client, higher level of profitability for the firm. Those who adhere to straight hourly billing should have the incentive to increase efficiency even though the number of human hours expended is reduced. The benefits are that lawyers and staff will be able to handle increased volume and to meet competitive pressures from other providers to reduce charges to clients. Those lawyers who can do quality work at a price that reflects value as perceived by the clients, that is, the marketplace, will prosper.

It is important to recognize that the strategic plan sets the objectives of the firm (or an individual lawyer) and the quality of services (the work product in its total context) will provide the niche for the firm and will determine the position of the firm generally. Therefore, it is imperative that billing methods and pricing techniques be fine-tuned to be consistent with these other component functions.

Another caveat and reminder is that you can, and perhaps should, employ several different approaches for your legal work. Most practices will have clients with varying needs and different types of matters, which makes it possible to vary your approach to fit those idiosyncratic differences. That is true not only for the firm but for individual practitioners in a group practice.

From the standpoint of corporate or governmental law departments assigning work to outside legal counsel, these considerations are also valid. Analysis of the work being assigned should suggest to assigning counsel the methods of billing that would be appropriate. In proposing or considering suggested alternatives, the same type of fit between the goals of the assignor and the type of practice of the assignee should be seriously considered. An interest of corporate clients is to know in advance what the cost will be. Fixed fees aid in predictability and facilitate internal budgeting.

The lessons of the value curve are that (1) different types of services produce different positions on the curve, and (2) firms that in the past have done hourly billing across the board traditionally have undercharged for unique work and overcharged for commodity services, not recognizing the degree of price sensitivity of the two extremes.

Another approach to controlling legal cost relates to differences in lawyering skills and their effect on total legal expense even for lawyers using the straight hourly method. As I recall the news item in the legal press, U.S. Fidelity and Guaranty Co. was concerned about the total legal expense including both amounts paid to outside counsel and amounts paid in settlements or from court judgments.[6] They found that of the total dollars paid out, about 10 percent was for defense cost and 90 percent for payment of claims. They decided to concentrate on the ninety percent portion. After carefully evaluating the performance of their numerous outside lawyers, they culled the list and sought individual lawyers with the best and most compatible skills even though some of those individuals charged at a higher hourly rate than those customarily used as outside counsel. They shopped for skills, not just price. The startling results showed that the amount actually paid for claims dropped $35 million below budget and that the total outside legal expense also dropped $15 million below budget, meaning that there was a marked overall reduction in legal expense. The stated conclusion was that the more experienced and effective lawyers worked more efficiently and achieved better results in holding down the amount being paid in settlement or in payment of judgments. Assuming that this was not an aberration, this is another thought-provoking notion that relates to quality of services (expertise and skills) and approaches to pricing.

It poses the interesting theory that perhaps a curve like the value curve (which is based on value to the client) exists that would reflect the expertise and skills of lawyers. In all probability there are a few lawyers with unique expertise and skills and many more at the lower end of the curve whose competence is more keyed to the commodity level.

Earlier we commented that the more recent trend in billing and pricing is characterized by innovation. Ingenious lawyers are using their imagination and flexibility to customize their billing and pricing methods. The fee agreements set forth in chapter 3 illustrate the importance of crafting an agreement that meets the situation at hand. It is clear that hybridization, customizing, and tailoring in billing have occurred and undoubtedly will continue to occur.

In summary, billing and pricing involve mixing and matching. It is critical to mix by using a variety of approaches and to match the type of work with the needs and preferences of your clients and, most of all, to ensure the compatibility and consistency of your approach with the other component functions of your practice.

Exhibit 11-1 is a checklist designed for individual self-assessment that may help you to ask the right questions in selecting an appropriate billing method. It is your task to provide the answers that are right for you. Each member of your organization can do this self-assessment, or you can do it collectively.

EXHIBIT 11-1: Self-Assessment Checklist for Selecting a Billing Method

Before you jump in to change your methods for the billing and pricing of legal services, you should consider each of the following:

1. *Objectives and goals must be clearly defined.*

   (a) The solo practitioner, firms of all sizes, and in-house counsel need to set objectives and goals. Do you have firm objectives and goals?

   (b) What are your strengths and weaknesses?

   (c) What services do you now provide?

(continued on next page)

EXHIBIT 11-1 (continued)

(d) What services should you provide in order to meet your goals and objectives?

(e) How do you as owner(s) of the firm or organization perceive your organization, its competitive advantages and disadvantages?

(f) Is your perception realistic and supported by the facts?

(g) How does your perception fit with your clients' perception? How will you find out?

(h) Who are your lawyers and what are their talents?

(i) What is your lawyer experience mix and how does it fit the needs of your clients?

(j) Who are your clients and what are their legal needs now or in the foreseeable future?

(k) How do your firm's talents meet the needs of your clients?

(l) Do your clients perceive that you or your firm has the skills to meet their needs as perceived by your clients?

(m) Where does your practice fit on the value curve?

(continued on next page)

EXHIBIT 11-1 (continued)

2. *What is your present and future market?*

   (a) What are the market trends?

   (b) What is the demography of:

      (1) your firm

      (2) your clients

      (3) your legal community?

   (c) Who are your competitors and where are they located?

   (d) In what practice areas do they compete?

   (e) What are the prevailing rates for the types of services you provide in your market, especially if you are providing services that are price sensitive?

   (f) Who are your clients?

   (g) What are the needs of your present or potential clients?

3. *What are your present billing methods?*

   (a) Do your present billing methods enable you to achieve a desired level of profitability?

   (b) Do your billing methods meet client needs and preferences?

   (c) Do your billing methods enable you to compete effectively?

(continued on next page)

EXHIBIT 11-1 (continued)

(d) Do they enable you to further your firm goals?

(e) Do they fairly measure value to the client?

(f) Are they consistent with trends?

(g) Do they promote effective marketing?

(h) Are they based on written fee agreements?

(i) Have they been innovative? flexible?

(j) Are the billing methods different for different types of services?

(k) Are they competitive in your market area as to price?

4. *Things to examine in your practice.*

(a) Examine how many manual or computerized maxisystems or minisystems already exist in your practice. In a "minisystem," you or someone in your organization follows a preestablished system of performing certain actions or producing certain documents for a phase of a transaction. In a "maxisystem," the preestablished system exists for substantially the whole transaction.

Example of a maxisystem: The preparation of simple articles of incorporation, bylaws, the oath of directors, and minutes of the organizational meeting for a small corporation.

Example of a minisystem: Getting out and serving notices of a deposition, including subpoenas, arranging for a court reporter, and reserving a conference room.

(b) Analyze your practice to see if there are recurring representations where the value to the client will be materially increased if a certain result is obtained.

Examples: A merger or acquisition occurs; there is early resolution of the matter being handled; a rezone is obtained or a plat is approved with certain approved densities.

Where you are willing to share risks with the client, a contingency factor in a price to be charged may be appropriate.

(c) Do you have some high-volume, reasonably similar matters that can be handled on a routine basis by legal assistants or junior associates?

Example: Nonjudicial deed of trust foreclosures.

(continued on next page)

EXHIBIT 11-1 (continued)

5. *Are you willing to try innovative billing?*

   (a) Have you analyzed your practice to determine those practice areas or types of services where alternative or innovative billing methods might be beneficial?

   (b) Are you or some members of your firm willing to innovate?

   (c) Do you have clients who might be willing to accept alternative billing methods?

   (d) Are you willing to take the time and make the effort to bring about a change in how you bill for legal services?

   (e) Will your organization support the effort?

6. *List five or more situations in your practice where you can use alternative billing methods.*

7. *What immediate steps do you propose to take to change your methods of billing or pricing?*

When you have completed the self-assessment checklist, you can use the second checklist in Exhibit 11-2 for your further analysis.

EXHIBIT 11-2: Further Guidelines for Selecting a Billing Method

1. Gather some of your most forward-looking colleagues together and urge them to join you in thinking globally about how law practice is and will be changing. Think conceptually.

2. Abandon any notions that law practice in the future will be as it has been in the past or is at present.

3. Read everything that you can about alternative billing methods, total quality management, and current practices of corporate legal departments in moving towards "partnering" with outside law firms.

4. Think about the information you have or can gather about the cost of providing legal services for specific representations. Act to improve the cost-accounting aspects of your practice. Concentrate on determining the cost to produce legal services where the scope of the engagement can be reasonably defined.

5. Analyze the systems you now employ, whether manual or technology based, to determine the commodity services you routinely perform. Commodity services are services that are repeated regularly and often can be done by legal assistants or associates following prescribed practices or procedures.

6. List the twenty clients that produce the most fees for your firm. Then think of what services are involved and how well you meet what you perceive are those clients' legal needs.

7. Then do a client survey or client audit of those key clients and ask them how well they feel you are meeting their legal needs. Your perception of their legal needs may differ from their perception. Indicate a willingness to discuss ways that you could improve in order to meet those needs.

8. When you begin to feel that certain matters could be billed on other than an hourly basis, collect closed files that involved comparable services and analyze what was involved, the charges you made, the common elements, and the variables. Determine whether there is enough similarity in the scope of the previous work to predict the cost of providing those services currently.

9. Depending on the size of your firm, determine whether there are specific lawyers, practice areas, or practice groups that might be particularly amenable to innovations in billing methods. Concentrate on those rather than trying to make the whole firm change initially.

10. Think about value and how it can best be measured. Are there clients who are extremely results oriented? Ask yourself if you would be willing to share some of the risks, if there is a good possibility of getting a bonus based on favorable results.

(continued on next page)

EXHIBIT 11-2 (continued)

11. Attend all the seminars offered on alternative billing methods. Talk to those in attendance, both speakers and registrants, to learn how to use new methods and to hear of their personal experience. Many small-firm practitioners have already successfully developed innovative billing and pricing methods. Learn from those who know it works.

12. Think about how your marketing efforts could be enhanced by using innovative billing and pricing methods. Clients like to know in advance how much services will cost so they can judge whether the effort will be worth the cost and can plan ahead for their legal expense.

13. If your client insists on having a cap or maximum fee quotation and you are inclined to agree, rather than agree to hourly billing with a maximum, switch to a fixed fee.

14. Constantly ask yourself how your efficiency could be increased, including not only eliminating unnecessary work but also decreasing the time for resolution of the client's problem.

When you have completed the checklists, including determining whether your environment is such that innovation in billing has a chance to succeed, you are ready for the next step—determining the cost of producing legal services. Whatever your billing method and whatever your pricing level, it is critical that you have some idea of *your cost* of producing those services. The difference between the price you charge and your cost of production determines *profitability*.

THE NEED TO KNOW YOUR COSTS—AN IMPERATIVE

Choice of billing method and setting of prices are both dependent on knowing the cost of producing services. You should not intentionally set a price that does not produce some profit, unless you are adopting a penetration pricing or loss leader pricing policy. Whether your billing method is hourly, fixed fee, contingent, or some variation thereof, it is imperative that you know your costs.

Time recording will remain important and indispensable. In fact, efforts should be made to increase the accuracy and completeness of entries. Ensure standardization to the extent possible and extend the requirement of keeping time to others in the organization who have not been regarded as producing billable time. Apart from any use of time recording for purposes of hourly billing, the function is *to determine cost of production*.

There are two significant statistics that are easy to determine under existing typical law firm bookkeeping systems. By comparing total revenues with expense of operation, including compensation to lawyers who are not owners of the firm, you know your overhead percentage. On an across-the-board basis, this percentage of every dollar of revenue is what it costs to keep open for business before any compensation to partners/shareholders. The remainder equals total firm profits. Dividing total firm profits by the number of partners/shareholders gives profit per partner/shareholder. For comparative purposes, profits per partner will indicate increases or decreases from year to year and the impact of additions or subtractions in the number of partners. These simply derived statistics deal only with total firm operation; they are not specific enough to disclose costs and profitability of certain services or the expense or profitability of individual lawyers or, more important, individual partners/shareholders.

Determining the cost of production by type of transaction, department or practice area, or individual lawyer becomes more complicated, because it will be necessary to make some arbitrary allocations of total expense. Because you must make these proratings or allocations on a somewhat arbitrary basis, you should remember—and make it clear to everyone—that the resultant figures are approximate, even though useful. For example, if you are attempting to determine the cost of a partner based on some share of the total rental cost for space, and you do it on a per capita basis, some will be quick to point out that office size differs from lawyer to lawyer. On the other hand, if you prorate or allocate based on exact size of office, some may complain that they would not have chosen a large office but were forced to accept one. Another difficult allocation is the cost of the library. The size of the library, and hence the rent expense, is easy to determine. As to the books in the library, some may say they never use the library, or that the specialized texts it contains should be charged to the practice area or department that uses that particular set of books. That is why you should not try to be precisely exact (for example, don't count the number of legal tablets each partner used), and do not expect any result that is not approximate. The big items of rent, technology, and people costs can be defined fairly accurately, as is the cost of carry for such things as advance of funds for out-of-pocket disbursements. In his discussion of pricing in "Measuring Profitability Matter by Matter," David Maister suggests a way to determine profitability without precise cost allocation. In "Alternative Pricing Options for Law Firms," Coulter and Shulman emphasize the distinction between fixed overhead costs (expenses that cannot be changed quickly) and variable costs (which vary with the caseload).

Chapter 6 of *Win-Win Billing Strategies*, entitled "What You Need to Know in Selecting a Billing Method," describes in greater detail the mechanics and methods of determining costs.[7] Another source is a book by Robert J. Arndt, *Managing for Profit: Improving or Maintaining Your Bottom Line*.[8] An excellent treatise on law firm financial management was written by John G. Iezzi, *Results-Oriented Financial Management*.[9] How to set billing rates based on analysis rather than hunch and how to do cost accounting are explained in detail.

The growing use of fixed fee billing demonstrates the importance of determining the cost of producing defined services that are included in the fixed fee service agreement. Two steps must be taken with as much precision as possible. The first is to define exactly what services are included within the scope of the representation. The second is to calculate how much it will cost to produce those defined services. Then set the price depending on the pricing policy you are following.

Cost accounting as a basis for pricing and cost analysis for determining relative profitability have some similarities. Once you have allocated cost figures for each component needed for legal services (much of which will be the allocated cost for each person, use of technology, or function that is required) you can begin to calculate how much should be charged on a given matter to recover your costs. In that process it is necessary to analyze exactly what will be required by way of services, if you are billing on a fixed fee basis or taking in a contingent fee case. Because you will have detailed cost figures, you can calculate either prospectively or retrospectively the amount of profit that can be anticipated or actually received based on knowledge of the total revenue produced in that representation.

We previously spoke of the difficulty and disruptive effect of going into too much detail in allocating costs. The computation of total firm overhead (gross revenues collected minus all expenses including all employees and nonpartner/shareholder compensation equal profits to the owners of the firm) is relatively easier. To determine cost of producing a given matter there is a way to avoid precise cost allocation that will provide a good guide. The expense of people involved with handling a given matter is typically the major expense. The first step is to determine the cost to the firm of various categories of people who work on a case, particularly those who are timekeepers. This includes paralegals, researchers, associate lawyers, partners/shareholders, and any others whose time can be identified. Two approaches exist. The first is to determine *by individual* the cost to the firm per year in the form of direct compensation plus any fringe benefits. That individual's cost to the firm can then be divided by either the number of billable hours established for each category of employee or, if you wish to be even more precise, by the *average* of the total number of billable hours for the preceding two or three years.

You now know the direct compensation cost per billable hour for each individual. Originally, we included the cost of all employees of the firm other than partners/shareholders as part of overhead. Now you should deduct the total employee expense of all timekeepers from the total overhead. You now have firm overhead exclusive of the cost of the designated employees. You should note that the employee costs for nontimekeepers are included in general overhead. To test this approach, take a closed file where all work has been performed and all fees have been received, so you are working with precise figures. For all timekeepers you multiply the cost of that timekeeper per hour by the hours spent on the matter and total these individual computations. Deduct that total from gross revenue received on the matter being analyzed. Then deduct the general overhead using the adjusted overhead percentage. At this point you have the cost of producing those services for all but the partners/shareholders. Total the cost per hour for each partner/shareholder who worked on the matter and deduct the total from the revenue received on that matter. If that subtraction results in a negative figure, the firm failed to recover its cost of production. If the subtraction results in a positive figure, that transaction had a level of profitability higher than the level used in computing partner/shareholder compensation.

You can use this process to estimate the cost of producing the services required in a prospective matter. The cost per person and the general overhead percentage remain the same. You must estimate the number of hours that will be required and project what the total will be.

In my own experience in more than forty years of law practice during which our firm grew from six to sixty lawyers, as our degree of sophistication grew in financial management, we were able to budget both fees to be received and expenses for the coming year quite accurately, thanks to the expertise of our financial manager. Granted that in the Reed McClure law firm our cash flow was pretty even from month to month, that our realization rate was high, that we billed monthly on most matters, even those that extended over several years, and that we did not have many windfall fees based on contingent fees. In that time period many law firms expressed doubt that revenue could be budgeted, even if expenses could be fairly well predicted. In our firm, the reason budgeted revenue figures proved to be quite accurate was the ability of our financial manager to fine-tune the figures. For example, she knew the past billing histories of the various partners. If the billable hour goal was 1,750 hours, she knew from past years' records that certain partners consistently billed fewer hours than 1,750, so she would reduce the expected billable hours for that partner downward to reflect more realistically what in all probability would be the contribution for the coming year. She also knew that certain partners consistently would record more than 1,750 hours, so she made an upward adjustment. She also knew that the realization rate varied from partner to partner, but with a fairly consistent pattern. She then did some tweaking and tuning for that partner. An additional refinement was that certain partners worked in practice areas where the profitability was higher than that of other areas. Once again she did some fine-tuning. As the result, her budget figures more often than not predicted the future with a high degree of precision. Her master's degree in statistics, attention to detail, and computer skills gave our firm a high degree of sophistication in an era when not many firms did this kind of budgeting.

The moral of this is that in determining costs with today's sophisticated tools, with the right kind of financial management you can produce figures that are sufficiently accurate to provide a sound basis for knowing your cost of production.

Increasingly, corporate counsel are requiring budgets either for the total matter or in phases. Even if your client does not require a budget, it is good fiscal practice to have such a budget as soon as the scope of the undertaking can be defined or foreseen. Breaking a matter down into pieces makes visualization easier. One of the greatest benefits of budgeting or planning the representation is that it forces the lawyer to think through the whole process and not plunge blindly into steps that may or may not be essential. It should also require communication between lawyer and client to determine not only all relevant facts but also the objectives and targets of the client. Thinking through the representation should help in risk-assessment, whether it is the risk of the client, the risk of the lawyer in charging with an element of contingency, or the combined risk, if there is to be risk-sharing.

This analytical approach leads to other good things. Examining the steps that need to be taken provides an atmosphere conducive to asking, "What steps are absolutely essential and what steps could be eliminated without impairing the possible level of success?" Now you are into the areas of quality management, improvement in efficiency, and possibly into reengineering of your practice. You cannot do any of these if you do not have cost data to work with.

The types of analysis suggested here can be done manually or expedited through the use of computer technology. Setting up customized computer programs requires a step-by-step analysis of the events that must occur and the actions that must be taken to accomplish a given task. This systematization of the thought process forces planning.

Stephen J. Dutton is an Indiana lawyer who has developed a high level of competence in the use of computers. With his permission a project plan for a securities private placement transaction is reproduced as Exhibit 11-3.

Under the heading/task column at the left is listed each of the steps that must be taken. The critical path lines show the sequence and duration of each task. Included in the diagram are milestone symbols. The fourth column from the right shows the estimated duration of the task. Under the plan the scheduled start and scheduled finish of each task are shown by month, day, and year. These can be used as target dates for the lawyer, but also serve as a clear indication to the client when certain steps will occur. The rightmost column shows the scheduled total cost of each step that is chargeable and includes steps that must occur (usually involving action by others or required waiting time). The bottom in this column is the total cost expressed in dollars. If this representation is undertaken on an hourly basis, this total can be considered as an estimate of the total fee. If the representation is a fixed fee representation, the cost calculation can be a guide for setting the fixed fee. In the unlikely event that this representation would be on a pure contingency, the total would serve as a guide to how the contingency fee representation should be structured if the law firm is to realize its normal return.

If there were possible, although not inevitable, conditions or possible complications that might affect the project, this could be programmed as a contingency or modification that would then specify the changes in time for performance and the total cost. Think in terms of an "extra" or "change order" in the parlance of the construction industry.

EXHIBIT 11-3: Short Task Outline w/Cost

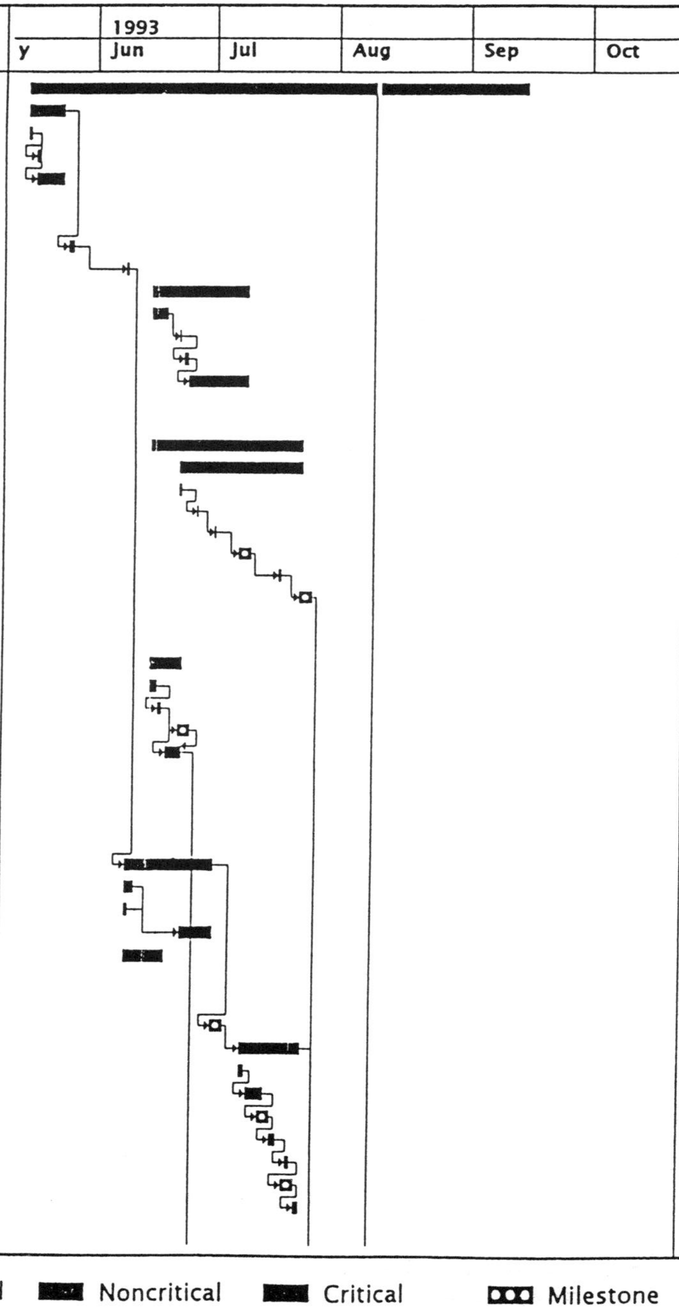

Heading/Task 3 Days Per Column	Est Dur	Scheduled Start	Scheduled Finish	Scheduled Total Cost
PRIVATE.PJ		05- 14- 93>	09- 15- 93	
Initial Information		05- 14- 93	05- 23- 93	
Request Information	2hr	05- 14- 93	05- 14- 93	380. 00
Assist Assemble	1dy	05- 16- 93	05- 17- 93	800. 00
Assemble Information	5dy	05- 16- 93	05- 23- 93<	0. 00
Subtotal Initial Info				1180. 00
Initial Due Diligence	10hr	05- 24- 93	05- 25- 93	1900. 00
Initial Meeting	3hr	06- 07- 93-	06- 08- 93	570. 00
Short Term Financing		06- 14- 93	07- 08- 93	
Outline ST Financing	6hr	06- 14- 93-	06- 15- 93	1140. 00
Approve ST Financing	2hr	06- 21- 93	06- 21- 93	0. 00
Documents for ST Fin.	8hr	06- 22- 93	06- 23- 93	1520. 00
Secure ST Finance	10dy	06- 23- 93	07- 08- 93	0. 00
Subtotal Short Term F				2660. 00
Clean Up		06- 14- 93	07- 21- 93	
Option and Stock Plan		06- 21- 93	07- 21- 93	
Draft Plan	6hr	06- 21- 93-	06- 21- 93	1140. 00
Comments on Plan	2hr	06- 25- 93	06- 25- 93	0. 00
Revised Plan	4hr	06- 30- 93	06- 30- 93	760. 00
Board Adopts Plan	0dy	07- 06- 93	07- 06- 93	0. 00
Indiana Plan Filing	6hr	07- 16- 93	07- 16- 93	1140. 00
Plans Effective	0dy	07- 21- 93	07- 21- 93	0. 00
Subtotal Option and S				3040. 00
Stock Check		06- 14- 93	06- 22- 93	
Review Transactions	16hr	06- 14- 93-	06- 16- 93	1600. 00
Draft Certificates	8hr	06- 16- 93	06- 17- 93	800. 00
Certificates Executed	0dy	06- 22- 93	06- 22- 93	0. 00
Stock Check Memo	12hr	06- 18- 93	06- 22- 93	1200. 00
Subtotal Stock Check				3600. 00
Subtotal Clean Up				6640. 00
Draft Filing		06- 08- 93	06- 30- 93	
Due Diligence	15hr	06- 08- 93	06- 10- 93	2850. 00
Assist Due Diligence	1dy	06- 08- 93	06- 09- 93	800. 00
First Draft	5dy	06- 22- 93-	06- 30- 93	7600. 00
Financial Statements	10dy	06- 08- 93	06- 18- 93	0. 00
Subtotal Draft Filing				11250. 00
Distribute 1st Draft	0dy	06- 30- 93	06- 30- 93	0. 00
Revisions		07- 07- 93	07- 22- 93	
1st Mark Up Mtg	1dy	07- 07- 93	07- 08- 93	2320. 00
Second Draft	2dy	07- 09- 93	07- 13- 93	3040. 00
Distribute 2d Draft	0dy	07- 13- 93	07- 13- 93	0. 00
2d Mark Up Mtg	1dy	07- 15- 93	07- 16- 93	2320. 00
Final Draft	1dy	07- 19- 93	07- 20- 93	1520. 00
Distribute Final	0dy	07- 20- 93	07- 20- 93	0. 00
Final Mark Up Mtg	1dy	07- 21- 93	07- 22- 93	2320. 00

EXHIBIT 11-3 (continued)

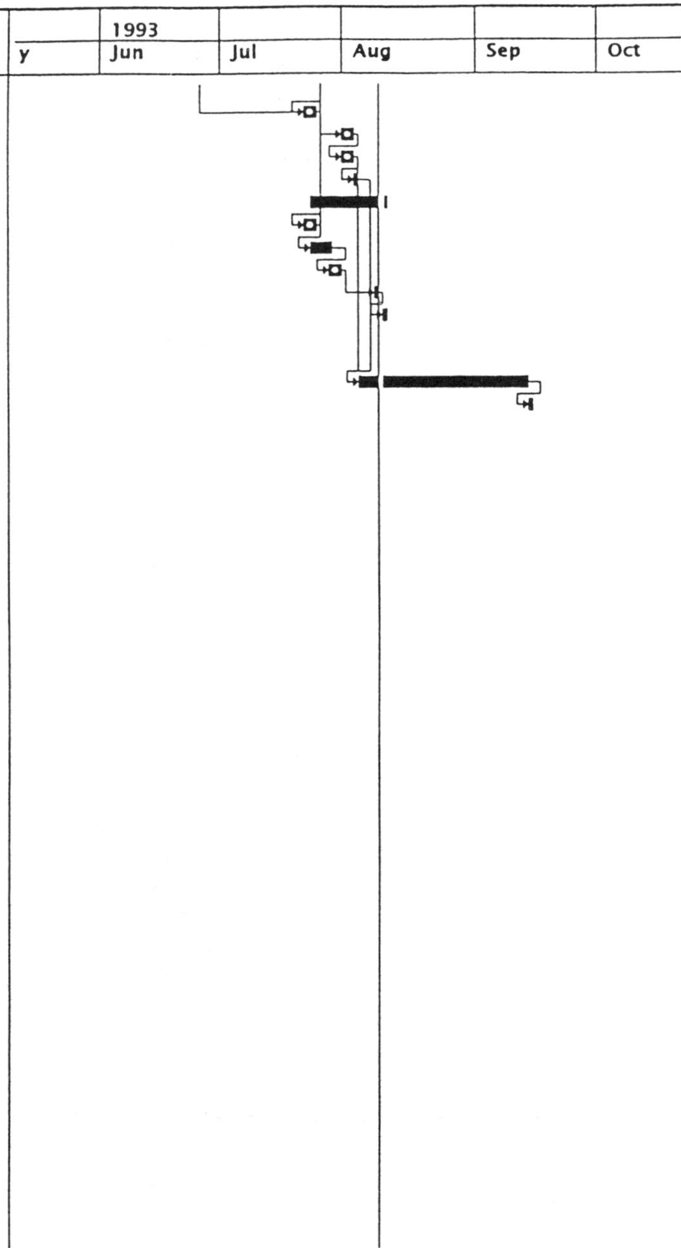

Heading/Task 3 Days Per Column	Est Dur	Scheduled Start	Scheduled Finish	Scheduled Total Cost
Subtotal Revisions				11520. 00
File Prelim. w/ Ind	0dy	07- 22- 93	07- 22- 93	0. 00
Indiana Comments	0dy	08- 01- 93	08- 01- 93	0. 00
Effective in Indiana	0dy	08- 01- 93	08- 01- 93	0. 00
Initial Closing	1dy	08- 02- 93	08- 03- 93	2320. 00
State Filings		07- 22- 93	08- 10- 93	
Determine States	0dy	07- 22- 93	07- 22- 93	0. 00
Prepare State Filings	20hr	07- 22- 93	07- 28- 93	3800. 00
Submit State Filings	0dy	07- 28- 93	07- 28- 93	0. 00
State Comments	1dy	08- 07- 93	08- 07- 93	0. 00
Final State Filings	10hr	08- 09- 93	08- 10- 93	1900. 00
Subtotal State Filing				5700. 00
Remaining Sold	30dy	08- 03- 93	09- 14- 93	0. 00
Closing	1dy	09- 14- 93	09- 15- 93	1960. 00
TOTAL				$ 45700. 00

THE POSITION OF ESTIMATOR

I am joined by two distinguished lawyers in predicting that one of the key positions in the law firm of the future will be that of estimator. Peter Zeughauser, general counsel of The Irvine Co., has thought a great deal about the importance of getting outside estimates of the cost of litigation or transaction as a precondition to hiring counsel. His approach is to force outside counsel to analyze the matter proposed to be handled and to come up with an accurate estimate of the fee. John Larson, chairman of Brobeck, Phleger & Harrison in San Francisco, has been quoted in the legal press as envisioning specific employees, partners, or financial officers whose sole job will be to estimate fees to be charged.[10]

The estimator will have to have multiple talents. The essential skills are not necessarily possessed by any, or at least many, individuals. It may be that to obtain the necessary skills, the estimating function will have to be done by more than one person. The requisite skills are:

1 ▪ **Financial.** The ability to compile and analyze cost data in the financial records of the firm, refining financial records to meet the needs for estimating.

2 ▪ **Computer.** The ability to utilize computer technology, to play "what if?" using reliable financial data in variable form, to build a database that can be understood and used, and to keep abreast of future developments in technology.

3 ▪ **Systems.** The ability to recognize where systems can be used, to force the use of systems, and to recognize critical steps that need to be maximized and noncritical steps that can be modified or eliminated.

4 ▪ **Market awareness.** The ability to sense changes in the legal marketplace, to appraise the strength of competition, and to judge which billing method or hybrid arrangement will meet the needs of clients.

5 ▪ **Substantive understanding.** The ability to know how law is practiced, the way lawyers think and act, and the perils and uncertainties of litigation and transactional work.

6 ▪ **Risk assessment.** The ability to judge the risks to the law firm of using different types of billing methods, using reliable data upon which to make risk judgments, and to bid accurately and realistically.

7 ▪ **Objectivity.** The ability to act in a cool, impartial manner that inspires the confidence of the lawyers of the firm, to avoid internal political pressures, and to justify the faith and reliance that the firm has placed on the skills of the estimator or estimating team.

The transition to nonhourly billing methods requires different skills. Economic forces increase the importance of price setting and costing. It will be difficult, but exceedingly important, for law firms to change to this approach.

Some law firms have attempted to analyze profitability on a profit center basis. Examples of profit centers include practice areas, departments, offices, type of clients, individual partners, or some other unit or combination of units selected by the firm. Typically, this involves the use of spreadsheet computer software that can segregate and report items of expense and revenue by profit centers. Those firms that have made an effort to do profit center analysis will have a head start in determining costs for purposes of setting price, as the same cost data is a prerequisite for profitability analysis. The profit center approach permits an analysis of how profits by each center would be affected by increased revenues, which, of course, are a function of price and volume. For additional information, see *Focusing on What Resources Yield Best Results* by Ronald L. Seigneur.[11]

You have a wealth of information in your closed files. With a closed file you know exactly what work was done, what happened, what events transpired that were not expected at the outset, who worked on the file, what technology or manual systems were used, what results were obtained, what fee was charged, and what the level of profitability was. Using the cost allocation system that you have developed, you can apply that system to the file that is closed. Closed files also provide information useful to improving efficiency. Repetition of material in files involving similar issues may suggest methods of standardization and development of systems. You come to the realization that there are similarities in the way matters are handled.

NOTES

1. Peter F. Drucker, *Management Tasks, Responsibilities, Practices* (Harper & Row, 1973): 83.
2. Hermann Simon, "Pricing Opportunities—And How to Exploit Them," *Sloan Management Review* (Winter 1992): 55.
3. Gerald E. Smith and Thomas T. Nagle, "Financial Analysis for Profit-Driven Pricing," *Sloan Management Review* (Spring 1994): 71.
4. David H. Maister, "Measuring Profitability Matter by Matter," *American Lawyer* (July/August 1994): 38.
5. Silvia L. Coulter and Andrew Shulman, "Alternative Pricing Options for Law Firms," *Legal Administrator* (July/August 1993): 20.
6. "Have Big Legal Bills? Maybe You Should Pay More for Attorneys," *Wall Street Journal*, January 7, 1994.
7. Richard C. Reed, ed., *Win-Win Billing Strategies: Alternatives That Satisfy Your Clients and You* (Chicago: Section of Law Practice Management, American Bar Association, 1992): chapter 6.
8. Robert J. Arndt, *Managing for Profit: Improving or Maintaining Your Bottom Line* (Chicago: Section of Law Practice Management, American Bar Association, 1991).
9. John G. Iezzi, *Results-Oriented Financial Management* (Chicago: Section of Law Practice Management, American Bar Association, 1993).
10. *Of Counsel*, April 4, 1994, p. 4.
11. Ronald L. Seigneur, "Focusing on What Resources Yield Best Results," *Accounting for Law Firms* (New York: Leader Publications, September 1993).

CHAPTER 12

The Merger of Quality and Value—A Significant Evolving Process

THE CONVERGENCE OR MERGER OF the concepts of quality and value is being confirmed in the legal marketplace.

Value has been defined as the *perception* of the *client* that a benefit has been conferred by the legal services. Quality has been defined as the *perception* of the *client* that a need of the client has been fulfilled. In this sense, the need of the client is a problem of the client that needs to be solved. *Price* or *the fee*, as indicia of value, ideally would equate exactly with value, though this may not always be the case.

Quality may exist in the context that a client's problem has been solved, yet value, hence price, may not fairly measure the benefit that has been conferred. For example, the client's problem has been solved, but the price or fee charged may be too high to satisfy the client and provide an incentive to the client to return to that lawyer the next time a similar problem arises.

To elaborate on the merger of concepts of value and quality, one of the complaints about the hourly billing method specifically or legal billing generally is that the cost or expense was too great. Yet sophisticated purchasers of legal services repeatedly state that quality service is what they want and will insist on. Corporate counsel when surveyed reported that in considering whether to retain or terminate outside counsel, the first consideration affecting their decision is the quality of the work, even more important to them than total price or specific billing method. Undoubtedly there are some clients who will feel that any legal expense is too high. What those clients are saying is that they want to be relieved of the problem that makes it necessary to hire a lawyer in the first place.

More astute clients realize the importance of quality legal service and generally are willing to pay a fair fee for quality service. What they do not want to do is to pay too much, to pay for inefficiencies, duplication of effort, or services that were not necessary. If you examine the reports of legal auditors or news clippings reporting those results, you will note that too much time for a given task, multiple staffing, working on irrelevant issues, use of inexperienced personnel, constant shifting of the file from one person to another, overbriefing on insignificant issues, and other examples of inefficiency are the targets, a literal crying out for lawyers to become more efficient. Clients want their lawyers to do the right things and to do things right. This goes to the heart of complaints against straight hourly billing, a method that does not provide any incentive to do only the right things or to do whatever they do right. The complaints are the converse of the earlier stated theme:

Any billing method that does not depend exclusively on time spent *as a measure of value* provides an incentive for efficiency and early resolution of the matter being handled.

Quality, like value, is a relative term that depends on the intended use and the perceptions of the client/customer. Mercedes and Cadillac automobiles are top-of-the-line, high-priced cars. Do they represent quality? Yes, but a customer who wants to haul lumber would be better advised to buy a much lower-priced pickup truck without amenities.

Following the publication of the two books on billing methods for the Law Practice Management Section, I became involved in my consulting practice with total quality management (TQM). Ultimately, I was editor and chapter author of a book entitled *Applying Total Quality Management to the Law Office*.[1] It was during this process that correlation of the concepts of value and quality became apparent, for many of the philosophical precepts seemed close, if not identical.

The concepts of total quality management evolved with the major players not always in agreement. The evolution is well described in a book *Quality or Else: The Revolution in World Business*, by Lloyd Dobyns and Clare Crawford-Mason.[2]

The key ingredients of the philosophy of the person most closely associated with the development of TQM, W. Edwards Deming, were continual improvement, knowledge, and constancy of purpose. Joseph Juran's definition of quality was "fitness for use," and he said that the first thing you need to know is what that means to your customer. What does the customer need from you to make your product usable to him or her?[3] Armand V. Feigenbaum defined quality as "what the buyer says it is." With this, Deming might disagree, because the customer doesn't know what you can do; that is, are you offering everything you have, or can you develop something better or even something new?[4]

If we accept the notion that the business of lawyering is to solve the problems clients need and want to have solved, the horizons expand to go beyond present problems of clients and to anticipate and be able to solve problems that may not yet have arisen, and to do so by means and techniques that may not yet have been invented or developed. Certainly this includes the use of technology in law practice. Theoretically, the use of technology saves or reduces the human time required.

Traditionally in law practice, the transcripts of depositions were indexed and summarized by lawyers or paralegals to enable quick and accurate access to pertinent portions. Manual systems were devised to organize and index exhibits that might be needed in litigation or had been admitted into evidence. Today, computerized scanning and search capability enables lawyers to locate the place in a deposition transcript where the needed information can be found. Exhibits in complex litigation can also be listed, categorized, indexed, and retrieved using technology. In both cases, technology has replaced human hours.

The purpose of writing *Applying Total Quality Management to the Law Office* was to demonstrate that the principles of total quality management that were developed for the manufacturing industries were applicable to the operation of a law office with appropriate adaptations. Some have contended that applying TQM to the legal profession is a passing fad, coined by consultants for their own gain and not of great significance. As applied to law firm operation and also to industry, other organized programs intended to improve quality have been developed. One of these, labeled reengineering, was promoted for use in law firms and continues to the present. The major difference between reengineering and total quality management is that the latter aims to improve the way you are doing things, while reengineering suggests that the slate should be cleaned and that you start from scratch to devise the best, most efficient ways of conducting your business. In this way it is somewhat akin to the concept of zero-based budgeting.

Whatever the label such a program carries, it is my strong conviction that improved quality of legal services will be a continuing quest. Law firms that improve efficiency will survive; clients will go to the firms that are in fact efficient and produce the best results for the dollar.

Let me give you a personal example. In a winter storm, several large fir boughs had fallen in our yard that I needed to cut and remove. I took my electric chain saw to a company that sells and repairs power equipment. My problem was that the oil filler cap that screws into place had become stuck so that I could not fill the saw with oil. I was afraid to force the filler cap for fear of wrecking the plastic oil storage cup. If the filler cap could not be removed or if the oil storage reservoir were damaged, it would be necessary for me to buy a new chain saw for several hundred dollars. The saw also needed sharpening and the tension adjusted, neither of which I wanted to pay for unless the filler cap problem could be solved.

The repairman had the same reluctance that I had to force the cap, but agreed to do so after I said I would release him from liability if it wrecked the oil storage reservoir. A couple of minutes later, he came back smiling. The cap would unscrew and the reservoir had not been damaged. I then asked him to sharpen the blades and adjust the tension, expecting him to tell me that it would be done in a week. "I'll do it now," he said. Shortly, my renewed and usable chain saw was in the trunk of my car and I was headed homeward. Before departing, I paid my bill, a modest charge of $10, plus 77 cents for the state of Washington.

What did I get? My problem was solved, the saw was usable. I had avoided buying a costly new saw. The saw was sharpened for use on that very day. I did not have to drive to pick up the sharpened saw on a later day. And all it cost was ten bucks! What did I do? I took one of their business cards and as soon as I got home, I entered the name, address, and phone number of the saw repair company into my computer list of addresses for future reference the next time I have a similar problem. And I probably will never return to the company I had used before. They had refused to help me with my problem, saying that they sharpened saws but didn't want to touch the repair job.

Now don't tell me that you are in the business of lawyering, not repairing power chain saws. It has everything to do with the principle of solving client problems in timely fashion for a reasonable price.

Before leaving TQM and Deming's constancy of purpose notion, another TQM guru, Homer Sarasohn, said that you have to have some reason to be in business other than to make money.[5] You also have to know what business you are in and how to stay ahead of the customer's needs in that business. This may not appear to deal with the discussion of the merger of quality and value, but it does relate to some of the vices of hourly billing. The emphasis on billable hours has affected the feeling of clients about the legal profession, the way lawyers have been compensated, and indirectly the quality of the lives of lawyers who are pressed to produce an ever-increasing number of billable hours. Those are symptomatic of a profession that has making money as its goal rather than serving clients by solving their problems. It gets into the great debate over whether law practice is a business or a profession. In passing, my retort to this debate is that law practice is both a business and a profession, although I say it in a slightly different way. My answer is, "Law practice is a profession that should be run in a businesslike manner."

As earlier suggested, the component functions of any law firm are so interrelated that it is impossible to act with respect to any one function without affecting the other component functions. The work product—that is, the services provided to the client—is among the most important, if not *the* most important, of those functions.

The intertwining of the concepts of quality and value makes it impossible to discuss billing and pricing as measures of value without considering what constitutes quality in the minds of clients, since the perceived quality translates into perceptions of value by clients. Clients are demanding quality services at a reasonable price.

"Quality of services" includes the total work product of the legal organization. The definition includes not only what is furnished but also how those services are delivered. Quality in this sense focuses on providing those services that clients want and need to solve their problems, conferring a benefit that creates value in the perception of those clients.

The specific skills of a lawyer and the way in which the services are delivered to the client must be aligned to coincide with what the client wants and needs to have. Thus, instructing on how to provide quality of services must involve principles, methods, and attitudes rather than a one-size-fits-all prescription. Not only is the role of lawyers changing; the demands of clients are also in a state of flux.

The changing demands of clients in a buyer's market bring increasing economic pressures on lawyers at a time when the techniques available to lawyers are also changing rapidly, primarily because of the availability of technology to alter the way work is done. This double impact—economic demands and technological advances—promises to bring dramatic changes to the legal profession.

What better way to improve client trust than to always provide quality services that meet the needs of your clients? If services are well performed, clients will be less inclined to complain about the cost of those services. Where quality of services is high, client satisfaction, as well as trust, should be the end result. On the other hand, slipshod services at an unreasonable price can only generate unhappy clients.

The billable hour can properly be called the villain of the scenario, with insidious effects on how law has been practiced in the decades just past, how lawyers are compensated, the quality of personal and professional life, firm structures, the need for efficiency, training of lawyers and staff, and the public's perceptions of the legal profession. Billing for time spent, not for value provided, ignores the need of clients to have effective legal solutions at a predictable and reasonable price.

When the pendulum swung and the seller's market switched to a buyer's market, sophisticated clients balked at practices they had previously tolerated. This is not to say that clients are not willing to pay for quality legal services properly delivered; indeed, there is strong evidence that quality of service is of greater importance to clients than the size of legal fees.

When pressure on law firms began to mount and profits per partner began to decline, many firms started some cost-cutting and took steps to cut out some of the fat. Downsizing (an interesting euphemism), salary reductions, and discharge of nonproductive partners were early reactions to the new pressures. More effective collection policies and more active monitoring of receivables helped to some extent, but there is a finite limit to realization percentages. Commendable as those actions may be, only limited relief can occur. The changes must be more fundamental than the combined effect of these early reactions. There is some evidence that firms that downsized for short-term economic reasons are beginning to pay the price in terms of their current ability to provide quality services. They thought they were cutting fat, but ended up in some instances by cutting brainpower and depth of support.

Achieving quality of services may be positive or negative, positive in the sense of developing requisite skills and delivery techniques adequate to meet client demands, negative in the sense of attempting to eliminate practices that clients deemed objectionable. Major objections to hourly billing include lack of incentive for early resolution of the matter being handled; using more people than really necessary; shifting of individuals during the course of handling a specific matter, thereby necessitating increased familiarization time; charging for inexperienced personnel; failing to listen to clients to determine their objectives; having faulty time records; having time quotas that encouraged padding of time records; doing work that was not necessary or relevant; failing to keep the client informed; lack of any risk-sharing by the lawyers; lack of predictability as to what the client would be charged; incomplete planning and determination of strategy; delaying effective analysis of the probable outcome; inadequacy of communication between lawyer and client; excessive discovery; activity that does not add value to the client; poor mismatch between available expertise and level of expertise required for the matter; failure to delegate to the least expensive competent unit of labor; poor case management by both inside and outside counsel; and reluctance to determine levels of client satisfaction or dissatisfaction.

Taken together, these complaints are a strong indictment of the legal process. Simply stated, critics contend that many, if not most, lawyers do not do things right, do not do the right things, do not provide timely services, and charge too much for doing it!

In defense of practitioners it should be pointed out that some lawyers display a high level of expertise and provide services that satisfy the needs of their clients. It is apparent from seeing the representation agreements described in chapters 3 and 4 that some lawyers have made changes in how services are provided as well as in how those services are priced and billed. It should be noted also that lawyers are not solely responsible for the complexities of life today, with the myriad statutes, rules, and regulations that must be dealt with, nor are they solely responsible for the delays and inefficiencies of litigation or other governmental processes.

In thinking about what lawyers can do to reduce the complaints and how legal services can be improved by adopting new techniques, it is useful to review some of the changes that have taken place in law practice in the past five decades.

For example, years ago in litigation plaintiffs were required to state with particularity all requisite aspects of their claims. If they failed to do so, defendants would file a demurrer, a pleading by a party to a legal action that assumes the truth of the matter alleged by the opposite party and sets up that it is insufficient in law to sustain the claim or that there is some other defect on the face of the pleadings constituting a legal reason why the opposing party should not be allowed to proceed further. This required a claimant to prepare the claim carefully to determine whether a proper claim could be stated. When a demurrer was sustained, the court might allow an amended claim to be stated that would cure the defect. At some point when successive demurrers had been sustained, the court, in its discretion, could deny the right to further plead, in which case the claim would be denied with prejudice. Objections to this type of pleading were that it imposed technical requirements that could defeat an otherwise meritorious claim.

Since discovery was not widely used, a second objection was that this approach amounted to "trial by ambush."

The theories evolved, primarily in the federal courts, that the "search for truth" would be promoted if litigants were required to "turn up all cards on the table," that is, to make full disclosure that would enable the trier of facts to make a proper judgment. Instead of pleading in detail, a plaintiff could essentially say that an injury or transaction occurred causing damage and that the defendant or defendants were responsible. When the New Federal Rules went into effect there was also an expansion of the rules relating to discovery. Previously, depositions were taken, but now additional discovery was permitted including interrogatories, requests for admission, and the like. Thus the march towards voluminous, expensive, and time-consuming discovery began. Just as the medical profession reacted to more frequent claims of medical malpractice by increasing the number of tests they gave to patients, lawyers who were concerned about malpractice claims felt that if they failed to do complete and extensive discovery, they would be found liable.

As the years passed, the principles of the New Federal Rules were adopted in state jurisdictions, so that by the late 1940s trial practice had changed in most states. In the decade of the 1950s, billing for time emerged as a way to charge for legal services. With increased opportunities for discovery, the time spent by lawyers increased, thereby producing more dollars of revenue, irrespective of whether enlarged discovery produced anything of relevance. Keep in mind that the scope of discovery is usually defined as an inquiry that would reasonably lead to the discovery of admissible evidence. The scope was beyond what was directly admissible as evidence. More discovery, more time required to do it, more money in the lawyer's bank account.

Another event took place that also had an impact, the development of the copy machine. Before copy machines came into widespread use, carbon paper was used for making copies of letters, pleadings, and other records. Only a limited number of legible copies could be made using carbon paper. For multiple copies, printing or mimeographing was used, but this was not characteristic for routine production of paper documents. With the evolution of copy machines, copies proliferated. In business and in law practice, files became larger. Everyone even remotely involved in a transaction could easily be furnished with a copy. More documents, more discovery, more time required to do it, more money in the lawyer's bank account.

A sociological change also occurred with the passing of time. Claimants became more inclined to file lawsuits. Legislatures passed more laws, governments at all levels passed more rules and regulations, and life became more complicated and complex. More lawsuits, more documents, more discovery, more time required to do it, more money in the lawyer's bank account.

Concurrently, there was the information explosion. Throughout the world more and more information was produced and stored. With accelerating pace, more and more regulations were imposed, making it difficult for the average person—or the average lawyer—to keep informed and to know what needed to be done to comply with the myriad requirements of society. Moreover, as the amount of information proliferated, the means of accessing this stored data improved using technology and the means of disseminating the accumulated information expanded through new methods of communicating.

In this complex, expanding, often conflicting environment, lawyers, law firms, and law departments cannot afford to drift and be controlled unknowingly by forces that sometimes seem beyond control. In considering what services the lawyers should perform and how those services can be produced, it is critical to return to some basic questions.

Ask "Why do lawyers exist?" "Why are we a law firm?" "What is a law department supposed to do to justify its existence?"

If the answer to these questions is "To solve the problems of our clients," as I submit it is, then the issues become *Who are the clients? What problems do those clients need to have solved? How do we solve them?* Once these questions have been answered, the determination of what will constitute quality of services can be made. There are three ways to deal with these questions. First, there should be an in-depth analysis of old and pending files to study who the clients are (in this context the "client" of a governmental or corporate law department is the person, entity, or division that utilizes the services of the law department), classifying the files by subject matter, frequency of use, resources utilized, and revenues produced. While examining those closed or pending files, think about how those matters were processed and the extent to which there were recurring issues or documents that could be standardized.

The second step, determining what problems clients need and want to have solved, is to do what some, but not many, lawyers do routinely, that is, go to the major clients and ask them! Conducting client surveys and one-on-one interviews with clients, gaining familiarity with industry problems, attending law firm seminars where clients are the speakers, and developing an intimate knowledge of the business or activities of clients are useful techniques. Market research by outside consultants is helpful. As part of the client contact process, levels of client satisfaction with existing services should be ascertained, and, if there are reported complaints or deficiencies, ascertain what needs to be done to eliminate those complaints. One useful inquiry where legal work is split between law firms is to inquire of the client what the competitor does better than you do and what would it take for you to get a bigger share of that market. Inquiries such as these are part of the process of improving the communication skills of lawyers with their clients, a broad topic that includes not only written and oral skills of each person in the organization, but also an attitude of openness, helpfulness, empathy, concern, and understanding. Communication is a two-way street, and steps should be taken to ensure that clients feel you want them to communicate with you so that there is a full measure of understanding and communication in your relationship. This, of course, requires a willingness and ability of lawyers to *listen* to clients and to appreciate their concerns.

The third step for an individual lawyer, firm, or department is to THINK. Lawyers typically are so busy practicing law that they do not take the time or make the effort to reflect on what they are doing, whom they are serving, how they are practicing, and what they would like to achieve in the future. Thinking involves becoming knowledgeable not only about client needs but also about practice methods, going from the big picture as set forth in the strategic plan to the specifics on how the organization is to be structured, staffed, and operated.

Going back to step two, understanding clients' needs and establishing effective lines of communication, leads to the concept of "partnering," a concept developed initially in the relationships of inside law departments with outside counsel, but applicable in principle to all lawyer-client relationships. Outside counsel are employed because they possess skills or have capabilities not available within the legal department. However, in-house counsel have a greater knowledge of the problems of the business of the corporate client and often have been exposed in the past to legal problems similar to those currently existing. Partnering involves close cooperation between inside and outside counsel to use the knowledge and skills of each in concert to solve the problem at hand. In the successful use of the partnering approach, the relationship between inside and outside counsel ceases to be adversarial and becomes cooperative, mutually supportive, and team oriented.

It is my belief that the most productive and valuable lawyer-client relationships are those involving a high level of trust and confidence with mutual respect for the talents and skills of all involved. In the final analysis, the relationship of lawyer to client is a human relationship that, to be enduring, must be mutually beneficial.

We have defined quality of services very broadly to include the totality of the work product provided to the client by the legal organization. It is important for the lawyers to recognize each day of the year that it is not only *what* services are provided but also *how* clients are treated. Warmth, cordiality, concern, helpfulness, promptness, availability, loyalty, patience, and responsiveness are all qualities that can differentiate a firm from competitors who are furnishing essentially the same type of legal services.

As client demands became more focused and client complaints more vocal, some law firms sought ways to raise their quality level. In this regard, there has been an evolutionary process under the general banner of "quality."

As noted earlier, total quality management was developed initially for manufacturing concerns. Later it was picked up by corporate law departments and, more recently, by law firms.[6] Some were enthusiastic about the concepts but got bogged down by the process. Where bureaucratic process became more important than results, TQM faded. Others customized the approaches to quality, using some of the principles under programs given different names. Later, efforts at improving quality were called process reengineering. Essentially, process reengineering postulates that in law businesses the quality of people is not the problem, but that inefficiencies in the processes used create a level of costs that increases the charges to the clients to a level that clients will not accept. Instead of adding people or using technology to make a process go faster, firms must examine each process to determine whether there is a better way to accomplish the desired end. Advocates of process engineering state that to do so involves starting over. It means looking at a firm's legal and business processes with absolutely no preconceived notions about how to deliver the service.[7] The emergence of this approach has been well described by Ira D. Moskatel and Susan Resnick-West, who point out that there will be occasions when nothing less than redesigning a whole practice area will suffice to meet the efficiency gains demanded by the present business environment.[8]

By whatever label and with whatever variations, there is no question that present-day clients demand both quality of services and a cost that reflects value. Thus, in dealing with this component function of a legal organization, there must be constant focus on what clients want and need.

The most appealing definition of high-quality legal services that I am aware of was developed by Peter Giuliani, a consultant in Westport, Connecticut:

- The ability to perceive client needs or commercial objectives quickly and correctly.
- The expertise and diligence needed to facilitate the satisfaction of client needs or commercial objectives.
- The professionalism, training, and skill to ensure that client needs are satisfied in a manner that conforms to and is in compliance with applicable law and ethical standards.
- The delivery of cost-effective, timely, and responsive service that adds value or achieves a result whose value exceeds the fee charged.

The phrase "paving the cow paths" has been used to describe the early use of technology in law practice. Instead of inventing new ways to practice law, technology was developed that presumably improved the old way. But technology should not be used just to make old processes move "faster." In considering the services the firm wishes to provide and how to process those services, keeping an open mind, being innovative and futuristic, and "starting with a blank sheet of paper," there is an appeal in the concept of process reengineering as it relates to *processes*, although it may not be broad enough to cover all aspects of practice.

Meaningful concepts in trying to cope with the many changes that have occurred in recent years can be found in a book by Joel Arthur Barker, *Future Edge: Discovering the New Paradigms of Success*.[9] He defines a paradigm shift as a change to a new game, a new set of rules. The first person to accept the new paradigm has an advantage that lasts until others who later accepted the new paradigm have managed to catch up.

Even when not necessary for survival, taking new and innovative approaches to what and how services are to be furnished has an appeal. Take the evolution of document production. Traditionally, lawyers dictated and secretaries typed. The demarcation was so rigid that new lawyers, especially female lawyers, who by preference personally typed for their own use while in law school, refrained from using a typewriter in the law office because it just was not what lawyers were supposed to do. With the advent of automatic word processors, document production in many firms went to centralized word processing centers. Now, with personal computers on the desks of many lawyers, the lawyer who does not put fingers to the keyboard is at a disadvantage. Recent surveys indicate that the ratio of secretarial staff members to lawyers has declined as more and more lawyers are hands-on users of computers.

Whether it is starting with a blank sheet of paper or just keeping an open mind, the ultimate questions are what kind of law practice the lawyer/law firm/legal department wishes to have and what the best ways (processes) to achieve this are.

In terms of lurking shifts in paradigms, two have been suggested that could have significant effects. Delegation was thought to be sound practice in law firms. This often meant that many different staff people were working on the same matter. Clients found objectionable the constant shifting of people and the familiarization time required. Recently, there have emerged some spin-off small firms oriented to serve a specific industry or, in some instance, a specific client. Their claimed advantage is that a closer relationship will be established, knowledge of the client's business will be greater, and with constancy the client's interests will be better served. Another shift relates to firm structure. In a pyramidal firm structure, access to information generally was greater for those higher in the pyramid. With current technology, access to information can be available to many, making it logical that the steepness of firm pyramids may flatten or become diamond shaped. This will be discussed more fully in chapter 19.

Another change that is a response to the delays and high cost of litigation is the use of alternative dispute resolution. If new methods of resolving differences are used by clients or compelled by the courts, new skills will be required and adjustments will inevitably follow. Whatever methods can be devised for early resolution of contested matters will be consistent with providing, not prolonging, solutions.

Lawyers considering quality of services may well ask whether these changing paradigms are being forced by clients who are dissatisfied with existing practices, or by technology, or both. Specific planning cannot be done without an awareness of the total legal environment.

In shaping a practice now and in the future, the best attitude to take involves (1) an awareness of the changes that are taking place, (2) a willingness to create change in how you do business, (3) a recognition of the possibilities for successful change through the use of new technology and systems, and (4) an awareness of the ongoing importance of learning what services your clients want and need and finding ways to respond to those desires. Thus, this component of practice, quality of services, becomes a general attitude and approach with sufficient flexibility to quickly adapt to new circumstances.

It will be prudent in making changes to constantly ask, "Does it provide quality and value to the clients?"

With respect to unfolding and constantly changing technology, the questions to be asked are, "Am I being made a slave by this new technology (whatever it may be at the time), or will use of this technology be a useful tool that will enable me to be a better lawyer?"

There is little question that technological advances have made it possible for lawyers to change—and hopefully improve—the way legal work is processed. In reducing the amount of human time required to perform various tasks, technology has increased speed, scope, and timeliness. The whole array of communication techniques, mobile phones, voice mail, electronic mail, fax, teleconferencing, beepers, courier services, television, and the like, links the world for almost instantaneous communication. As clients require or are offered electronic access to law firm computers to monitor charges for services, case management, steps being taken, or documents stored in those computers, communication between lawyer and client can take place at will without the intervention of a request and a response.

The future promises even more mind-boggling technology. Pending is a proposal for 240 satellites that will make every person in the world reachable by phone. If speed of communication is rapid now, the proposal to use cable TV networks for electronic linkage will vastly increase the speed of transmission over even the fastest of today's modems.

Information is a resource used by lawyers. The scope of available information has grown dramatically. As Internet expands in usage or as other direct electronic access becomes available, information will increase exponentially. The firm must decide how much data is useful in the type of law being practiced and avoid being deluged by more data than is really necessary.

One major advantage held by lawyers is the confidential relationship between lawyer and client. As the firm plans its services, care should be taken to preserve confidentiality, notwithstanding the electronic linkage available. In meeting competition from nonlawyers, the statutory and ethical confidentiality requirements of the legal profession should be asserted as an advantage, and hence a means to differentiate the services lawyers alone can provide.

Two other significant developments have changed the world of law practice. The first is the use of technology to reduce human time in producing, controlling, and using information. Computerized research, document retrieval, litigation support, case management, budgeting, cost accounting, expert systems, and document assembly systems are illustrative. When used effectively, these can replace manual systems, thereby freeing lawyers and staff members to perform tasks not performable by machines. Any lawyer who prepared for and tried cases involving a large number of documents can attest to the benefits of litigation support systems. Look for technological tools that liberate. Select technology that best fits the type of practice being conducted.

The second significant development influencing law practice is mobility. Electronic linkage makes where you work of less importance than how you work. External and internal networks permit access to the intellectual capital of the firm with less regard to the geographical center of the firm. The firm should analyze how this mobility affects the products being produced. The firm should also be conscious of the impact of mobility on the personal lives of firm members and weigh the good and the bad. The ultimate test is whether mobility assists or hinders the provision of the services needed by clients. Many clients are not, and probably will not be, oriented to technology. Since the ultimate lawyer-client relationship is a human relationship, what may be an advantage for some clients is a source of major frustration for others.

Let me give you a personal example. While in law practice, I dealt with individual and small-business clients primarily on a very personal basis. I resisted voice mail because I did not want my clients to be forced into an automated phone answering system where all they could do was to "press 1" or "press 2." My belief was that my clients wanted a human voice, preferably mine, when they called. When I started my second career five years ago with a national consulting firm, however, my attitude about voice mail changed. Now my consulting colleagues were moving around the country almost daily, making direct phone or personal contact very difficult. With voice mail, accessible twenty-four hours a day, I could transact business with my colleagues more effectively. The conclusion I reached is that if the parties are both mobile or accustomed to one manner of communicating, voice mail works well. The moral I draw is that in deciding how you practice, it is critical not to have mismatches with your clients. If your clients prefer hard-copy letters, give them hard copies. If your clients want to punch a computer key to access your computer, give them the access code. Albert L. Moses, in his estate planning practice, dealt with many elderly clients whose eyesight had declined. He noted that some had difficulty reading the estate planning documents he had drafted. He now uses large type and wider spacing in the documents prepared for his sight-limited clients.

One thing to remember is that as ways of producing legal services change, the number and type of personnel in your organization will change. Different skills will be needed. Bureaucracies should be trimmed if the functions performed are no longer necessary. Lawyering skills may also be different. Depending on what type of services you provide, your recruiting and training practices may need to be changed. Just as you should choose technology to fit your practice needs, you need to match people skills to the needs of your clients.

In this chapter dealing with quality of services, we have spoken of the importance of knowing who your clients are, their present and foreseeable legal needs, your strengths and weaknesses, and your ability to serve your clients. We have dealt with the rapidly changing legal environment and the need to meet the challenges of change. In recognizing the technology that is available, we have stressed that the choice and use of technology should be made on a cost/benefit basis and that the total operation should be fine-tuned to match the preferences and needs of your clients. Speed, scope, and timeliness are words repeatedly used to reflect the pace of law practice and life in general. The common denominator of much of this has been that technology is intended to liberate by reducing the human time required for repetitive tasks, research, and the organizing and retrieval of information. If you do these things to reduce human time *and continue to bill by the hour*, you will experience firsthand the productivity paradox.

Let's talk about the nagging irritant of not-quite quality and its effect on billing for value. Little things can cause clients to feel that the services are not really quality.

Did you ever get a bill from your doctor or dentist billing you for services you couldn't quite understand even though you were pleased generally with the services you had received? Did you have trouble understanding some code or description that meant something to the doctor, the clinic statistician, or accounting department, but meant nothing to you?

Have you ever received a bill for legal services where you, even if you are a lawyer, still could not fathom what had been done to further your cause even though you were generally satisfied with the way the representation had been handled? Or the billing came so late after the services were performed that you could not remember what had occurred?

Even though you were pleased generally with the way the professional services were performed, the method of billing provided an irritant that detracted from your good feelings towards your doctor, dentist, or lawyer. Clear, expressive billings that demonstrate value and confirm that the billing method agreed upon has been followed accurately can become a positive.

Recently we hired three different contractors for some work at our home. All three contractors were reputable, responsible, and courteous. Two of the three were people who had done prior satisfactory work for us over the years. All three did what we asked them to do, and we were for the most part satisfied with the quality of workmanship—except for three minor, but nagging, shortfalls that detracted from the overall quality (that's where my term "not-quite quality" arose). Let me illustrate.

We needed to replace an old water line from the meter to our house. The corrosion that had built up over the years in the galvanized line had reduced water pressure, so we wanted a new copper line installed. After the copper line was in place, the water pressure did increase, but now the cold water tap in the laundry area slightly vibrates at one setting and makes a terrible noise, scaring the daylights out of you whenever it happens. It is a nagging irritant that makes us overlook the general level of quality.

Then we hired a carpet company to install some new carpeting in our family room and in one of the hallways. In putting down strips to anchor the carpeting, the workmen accidentally nailed a sliding pocket door at the entrance to the bathroom so that the door would not slide shut. The contractor responded immediately, and the carpet installer found and removed the nail that was causing the problem—almost but not quite. Now the door sticks slightly when the door is opened or closed. This irritant is enough to make me think of that carpet installer each time this happens.

We also hired a paving contractor to put an asphalt overlay on our driveway and inside the carport. As they laid down the overlay in two adjoining strips, the job required two truckloads of asphalt mix. After the roller had smoothed the overlay and the job was completed in a generally satisfactory manner, it was apparent that the two sections of the driveway were different in composition. The two truckloads of asphalt had slightly different mixes (one had more sand in the mix than the other, which made for a smoother surface). The contractor responded courteously and sought to remedy the problem. It was agreed that we hold back part of the payment until summer came, when the contractor had a top coat spread over the whole driveway to mask the differences and provide a uniform appearance. That was done, but to this day, it is apparent to me, if not to any visitors, that the job, even as rectified, was not as good as I had hoped for. Another nagging irritant of not-quite quality.

How does all of this apply to billing methods used by lawyers, you might ask. Here's how:

Value and quality of service are almost synonymous, or are virtually merged, in the perception of the client or the customer. Any deviation from quality detracts from value. My work in the past few years on the subjects of billing methods, billing for value, and total quality service have convinced me that you cannot realistically talk about value unless you talk about quality.

In billing for value, the lawyer and the client are involved in three critical stages. The first is the very outset of the representation where it is important for the lawyer and the client to define exactly what the client wishes to accomplish. This requires clear communication. At the same time, it is critical for a clear understanding to be reached on the method of billing.

The second stage is primarily the responsibility of the lawyer in performing the necessary services. The client should be informed on what is being done, problems encountered, the predicted time schedule for completion, and any changes in the probable outcome. Again, ongoing communication is essential.

The third and final stage is the billing process itself, where it is important to review the extent to which the objectives of the client have been reached as defined in the opening stage, continuing through the second stage where the lawyer should fairly evaluate how the legal services have brought benefit to the client. The culmination is the preparation of a statement that reflects the value of the services for which the billing is being sent. If the stage-two services included some "not-quite" quality performance, it is better to acknowledge the shortfall and to make amends in the billing process. Confront the issue; do not try to hide, if you wish to retain the client. Not everything runs smoothly in all representations. It is better to make a voluntary adjustment in your bill to minimize the nagging effects of less than quality performance.

If you and your client in stage one have not agreed on the objectives of the representation, how can you measure value when you get to stage three, the billing phase? How can you determine quality, if you were not clear on what the client wanted you to accomplish?

The truly interesting development in recent years has been the innovative ways in which some lawyers have adapted the generic billing methods to fit the specific needs and desires of their clients. Part of this process of innovation has led to creative marketing. It is now apparent that in competitive situations the ingenuity of law firms in crafting billing methods has made the difference in obtaining or maintaining clients. Innovation and the willingness to tailor the fee agreement to fit the specific situation are keys to holding old and attracting new clients. Don't take your existing clients for granted. Your competitors may be approaching them with innovative fee agreements as part of their aggressive marketing. By all means possible, do not allow "nagging irritants" to mar your relationships with your clients!

Remember that to the extent that your services do not meet quality standards, the value of those services will be less in the minds (and pocketbooks) of the clients.

In thinking about the impact of nagging irritants on value and client satisfaction, it is often the small, mechanical services that detract from a job that in its major aspects was well performed. For example, you have just completed a major estate plan for your client that was well done by the firm and well received by the client. You promise to send copies of key documents to your client, but forget to do so. The client, after waiting for a while, calls to inquire when the documents will be sent. These phone calls are not answered. Several weeks later, the client comes to the office and personally requests the copies, which you promise will be sent that day. The documents are sent to the wrong address. My guess is that the client in this circumstance will remember the frustration of not receiving the copies promptly and will forget the good work product you produced. As irritants remain, satisfaction declines.

Try to avoid quality shortfalls, so that no nagging irritant will remain with your clients.

NOTES

1. Richard C. Reed, ed., *Applying Total Quality Management to the Law Office* (Newtown Square, Pennsylvania: Altman Weil Pensa Publications, Inc., 1993).

2. Lloyd Dobyns and Clare Crawford-Mason, *Quality or Else—The Revolution in World Business* (Boston: Houghton Mifflin Company, 1991): 52.

3. *Ibid.*, p. 71.

4. *Ibid.*, p. 73.

5. *Ibid.*, p. 58.

6. See endnote 1.

7. For an excellent description of how and why process engineering should be undertaken, see Cynthia Munger, "Process Reengineering: Revolutionizing Legal Services," *Law Practice Management* (May/June 1995): 22.

8. Ira D. Moskatel and Susan Resnick-West, "Starting with a Blank Sheet of Paper: Reengineering Law Practice," *Law Practice Management* (May/ June 1994): 31.

9. Joel Arthur Barker, *Future Edge: Discovering the New Paradigms of Success* (New York: William Morrow and Company, Inc., 1992).

CHAPTER 13

Where Do We Go from Here?—Some Serious Considerations

WHY IS IT that so many lawyers and law firms that are still operating at a profit do not appear to recognize the dramatic changes occurring in the practice of law? How much does it take to move bar associations, individual lawyers, law departments, and law firms away from complacency? When will they get off the billable hour treadmill and realize that the legal world of tomorrow will be vastly different from practice of yesterday? How do you motivate lawyers to change their ways, to reorient their visions of how they will practice in the coming decade?

What characteristics of law practice will change to the point of disappearing and what features should be preserved?

If you accept the premise that billing and pricing methods have changed and will change in the future, and that the whole of law practice is subject to reexamination and major evolutionary changes, it is important to ask what existing or past characteristics and features of lawyer-client relationships should be preserved.

My concern is that with emphasis on the bottom line, advancing technology, systematization, consumer demands, transitory relationships, and other impersonal, automated, and sweeping impacts, the legal profession will lose sight of the important justifications for its existence. It is fitting to look to the past and to the present to determine the pillars upon which the profession rests.

The foundation of the profession is that by special training and honed skills lawyers exist to serve clients, to solve legal problems that arise in the relationships of the men and women, the businesses, and the governments of the world. The rule of law presupposes that there are ways other than brute force to regulate the conduct of individuals and to resolve the inevitable differences that characterize human relationships.

Before considering and attempting to predict changes that are likely to occur in both the short and long term, it is imperative to define precisely the functions and characteristics that must and should be preserved throughout the radical processes of change.

At the heart of any law practice is the expertise of the lawyers and those who support them. Expertise, broadly defined, includes a bundle of qualities, including knowledge learned by schooling and by experience; analytical skills; sound judgment; concern for the interests of clients; integrity; loyalty to colleagues and clients; high ethical standards; constancy while being flexible; the ability to judge people and to react appropriately; the ability to evaluate risk; willingness to place the interests of clients above personal gain; mental acuity; perceptiveness; listening and understanding; communication skills, both verbal and written; research capability; ability to strategize; persuasiveness; a demeanor that breeds confidence; intellectual honesty; reliability; acting without conflict of interests; preserving confidentiality; the ability to translate expertise into services that provide a benefit to clients, and other skills that might aid the lawyer in serving clients.

You will note that these are the skills that have characterized outstanding lawyers through past and present generations of clients. Expertise, as defined, should exist in whatever legal environment the lawyer practices, from solo practitioners to megafirms, for both individual and business clients, whether as in-house or outside counsel, whether in private practice or governmental service.

This catalog of skills is essentially a list of individual, human, personal qualities that characterize the essence of lawyering. Many of these skills involve thinking, making judgments, selecting appropriate strategies, and converting substantive knowledge into a work product that meets the needs of clients to their benefit. No matter what the future development of technology is, the ability to think and to reason remain the bedrock of human endeavor. The ultimate valued skill of the lawyer is wisdom, the ability to make right judgments and to employ correctly chosen techniques to reach the goals of the clients. Computers can do wonderful things, but computers cannot think. Expert systems in the final analysis depend on the humans who devised them. Computers are as loyal as the next disk crash. Technology remains a tool, and often an effective tool, but all of the marvels of technology should be recognized as just that, a tool that can be used effectively in providing legal services. But only a tool to be used wisely and well!

In writing this book, I might have chosen to draft in longhand, or by dictating, or by use of a manual typewriter, or by using the word processing capabilities of my computer (which is the case), but each method merely utilizes a tool of choice. The value that is hoped for will depend on the wisdom and applicability of the words, not the means used for organizing words into sentences, paragraphs, or chapters. Lawyers must realize that the solutions provided to clients are more important than the techniques for providing those solutions.

When lawyers join together to practice in private firms or in corporate or governmental law departments, the organization itself generates two additional qualities or potentialities. One is the culture that reflects the composite values of the group. The culture can be either a positive or a negative influence on the ability of the group to serve clients. Cultures often are not planned, but they happen, and whatever the characteristics of the group culture it should be recognized as an integral part of the organization. The second aspect of group practice is the opportunity for synergism, the combination of two or more agencies to achieve an effect greater than that of which each is individually capable. Care should be taken to cultivate the firm culture to be positive in effect and to reap the benefits of synergistic opportunities.

People are the most valuable asset of any legal service provider, and consistent with that, people are the most costly expense in a law practice. Even the solo practitioner normally has support personnel that aid in producing client services. When lawyers come together in firms or in legal departments, the selection, retention, training, motivation, and assignment of people become critical. Lawyers can leverage their personal skills by means of both people and technology, but this in no way diminishes the importance of the composite traits and skills included in the defined term, expertise.

A lawyer practicing alone or lawyers working together in groups develop what has been aptly termed "intellectual capital." As with the term "intellectual property" in substantive law, the definition and boundaries of intellectual capital are difficult to define. There is no doubt, however, that the composite of knowledge and skills, the ability to use those skills and to transform substantive knowledge into a work product that benefits clients, and the bundle of personal relationship skills constitutes one of the most valuable assets of lawyers. Care must be taken to promote, preserve, and use the intellectual capital of the lawyer/lawyers no matter what transformations may occur in future law practice.

My entreaty is to safeguard these essential skills and to maximize the benefits of group practice and changing technology in the turbulence of the coming revolution. The core characteristics and qualities must remain if the legal profession is to continue as a useful, helpful, independent, and serving profession.

Having said all this, now is the time to try to tie together all of what has been written thus far into a glimpse of the future in an attempt to provide a guide for those lawyers who will succeed in the profession in the years ahead. The approach will be to organize the crystal-ball-gazing under six headings that reflect the totality of any legal organization's function. They are as follows:

- **Strategic plan**—A formal or informal determination reflecting a consensus of the objectives of the group based on an evaluation of present and future strengths and weaknesses with steps to be taken to reach those objectives (to know where you want to go).
- **Quality of services**—A broad term that includes all services or work products that the group is able to provide (what the group sells).
- **Billing and pricing**—Considering the type of services provided and the objectives of the firm, the setting of charges to be made (the prices that will be charged).

- **Marketing**—A plan for how the services of the group will be promoted (a sales program).
- **Compensation system**—The method for determining how those who carry out the strategic plan by providing services will be paid for their services (the value of individual contributions to the group).
- **Governance**—The structure for operating and managing the group that is sufficiently strong to ensure the internal consistency of the other five functions (who runs the operation).

Two of these functions, quality of services and billing and pricing, have already been discussed in considerable detail. Discussion of the remaining four, strategic plan, compensation system, marketing, and governance, will follow in chapters 14 through 17. Remember as you read further that it is absolutely essential that these six functions must be *internally consistent* for success. Internal inconsistency may defeat or negatively influence one or more of the other functions.

CHAPTER 14

Strategic Planning—A Road Map

THE BEST STARTING POINT for confronting the changes that are taking place in the legal profession and to chart the course for the future is the discipline of the strategic planning process. When done properly, the current environment will be analyzed, the strengths and weakness evaluated, the goals and objectives set, and the plans for meeting those goals and objectives agreed to by consensus.

The strategic plan is the first and most critical function for lawyers who are thoughtful about how they will approach the future of law practice. Many lawyers seem to black out when this term is used and to resist any formal planning process. Perhaps this is because the regimen of the traditional planning process becomes too bureaucratic if the process becomes more important than the objective.

The type of strategic planning that is needed by law firms in today's changing profession might better be termed *strategic thinking*, a term that in all probability will be more palatable to creative lawyers who have a vision of what their practice should be in the future. This distinction was well described by Professor Henry Mintzberg in his *Harvard Business Review* article "The Fall and Rise of Strategic Planning." Strategic thinking, wrote Mintzberg, involves gathering hard data and then "synthesizing that learning into a vision of the direction that the business should pursue."[1]

A plan is like a road map. If you decide to take a trip, one of the requisites is to decide where you want to go. It makes a lot of difference in planning a trip whether your ultimate destination is a small village in Switzerland or a coral lagoon in Fiji. Once you decide where you want to go, you then can decide how you wish to travel to that destination, what it will cost, who will go with you, how you will make arrangements, what routes are available, how long will it take, and what you wish to do when you arrive.

The process of planning can be simple or complex, written or oral, formal or informal, detailed or general, applicable to a solo practitioner or to a megafirm, flexible or inflexible. The vision for the firm can be expressed in a mission statement that gives direction and inspiration to the firm. Details can be implemented along the way. Often those who refuse to acknowledge the benefits of having a plan are the leaders who provide the vision that others may call a plan.

One puzzlement as to why many lawyers resist strategic planning is that lawyers handling either litigation or transactional matters engage in planning in handling matters for clients. For example, a litigator determines the objectives of the client, learns the facts, researches the law, determines who the witnesses will be and how strong their testimony will be, explores the availability of documentation, anticipates the roadblocks and how to overcome them, considers the contingencies, and maps alternative approaches, all to the end that the outcome will be successful, the fulfillment of the vision.

Because of the enormity of the changes that are taking place, it is doubly important for lawyers to take time now to analyze the impact of the forces that exist or in all probability will exist in the immediate future. If you don't know where you are going, you probably will not get there, it has been said, or you may end up in Fiji when you wanted to go to the Swiss Alps.

The planning exercise in itself should prove helpful, but the real importance for lawyers practicing in a group is the building of a consensus, the buying-in by members of the group that the group goals and means for attaining them are agreed. With strategic *thinking*, as the vision unfolds and the group moves in the direction of that vision, enthusiasm and support should grow as innovative new ideas supportive of the vision are brought into play.

Alternative billing and pricing methods are important aspects of the legal profession, but only one part of the whole. The strategic planning process should consider all aspects of the other five component functions of law practice, for they are interrelated.

The general topics that might be considered in doing strategic planning will be set forth next. Since the readers may be in different practice settings in groups of different sizes, some topics may be of greater importance than others. For example, for a solo practitioner, the compensation system is simple—whatever profit remains belongs to that lawyer, but for lawyers in group practice, total profits (or available funding in the case of government and corporate law departments) must be allocated in some fashion making the compensation system highly relevant. With this admonition, it is suggested that consideration be given to each listed topic, passing quickly over those that do not apply. Each topic should be screened through a sieve that poses the following questions: (1) Is the way things are done now worthy of being preserved? (2) Is there a better way to do this in the future? (3) If you were starting from scratch, how would you do it? Carefully consider the following, regarding it as a suggested checklist, remembering that intuitive thinking should bear some relationship to hard facts:

- **Existing environment.** This involves an analysis of all relevant factors that affect the practice as it is now being conducted: economic, political, demographic, or otherwise. It includes trends that may be emerging and, for the most part, involves external conditions and forces rather than the internal operation of the organization. General economic conditions should be considered, including the position in the economic cycle likely to govern in the future—that is, whether there will be depression or prosperity in the years just ahead.

- **Changes in the profession.** Of particular relevance at this time is the need for awareness that major changes are occurring for the legal profession and that the premises of the past may not be applicable today. For example, the shift from a seller's market in the 1980s to a buyer's market in the 1990s has created a new set of problems to be dealt with. There should be consideration of the extent of client resistance to fees and dissatisfaction with the complexity and delays of the legal process, the impact of increased sophistication of the purchasers of legal services, the requirements for task-based billing, and the insistence on quality of service at reasonable prices. Changing paradigms require different reactions, so the ultimate questions involve the extent to which paradigms that exist or are likely to exist in the future require new methods and new solutions.
- **Competition.** In the broadest sense, with whom does the group compete for clients, funding, or support? What amount of legal work is available in the marketplace? Are competitors becoming more active, aggressive, or competent, and are new competitors entering the market? Included would be the impact of an increasing number of lawyers in the profession, the effect of nonlawyer competition from other providers, and the relative ability of your group to compete based on either a declining or increasing capability. For corporate or governmental law departments, is the area of operation losing or gaining in relative importance and support, and is the organization for which services are provided vibrant and expanding or stagnating and contracting? Consider also which practice areas are expanding or contracting relative to the need or demand of clients for services in that practice area.
- **Strengths and weaknesses.** Looking internally, there should be careful evaluation of the strengths and weaknesses of the lawyer, firm, or department to determine which strengths can be utilized or improved and which weaknesses can either be corrected or areas of weakness abandoned. This involves practice areas and the level of available expertise, the extent to which these fit the emerging trends in the profession, and the foreseeable needs of existing or potential clients.
- **Internally vs. externally competitive.** Some firms are internally competitive, a collection of practitioners who essentially are solos operating under one roof, even though they may be partners. The way files are handled and lawyers compensated in such firms will differ from that in externally competitive, or team-oriented, firms. The philosophy of an externally competitive firm is that as the firm as an entity succeeds, the members of the firm will prosper. Either approach can be successful as long as the firm knows which type it is.

  In today's world and the world of the future for law firms, the externally vs. internally competitive decision is critical. With the emphasis on quality and value demanded by clients, varied contributions by the lawyers to the firm are required, not all of which will result in immediate revenue. Yet some of those contributions will be essential for the long-term success of the firm. As lawyers move away from hourly billing, the intangible contributions that add value for the clients and the firm are of special importance. One of the vices of hourly billing is the way that billable hours have permeated the fabric and culture of the firm. Production, hours billed, realization, and reliance on short-term revenue-producing contributions are to a major extent the result of hourly billing, making firms internally competitive even though they may have proclaimed that they are externally competitive. A fair compensation system in an externally competitive firm must recognize all contributions to the firm. The lateral movement and cherry picking that have characterized the recent past place emphasis on how many clients a lawyer will bring to the new firm. In an externally competitive firm, clients are "firm clients" and do not "belong" to any one lawyer.

- **Services provided.** This examination involves not only what services are provided but also how those services are delivered. It is more than work product in the sense of documents or tangible services. Key to planning is to decide what services the firm intends to generate for clients. For example, a firm can decide to specialize for a boutique practice or can plan to provide full services with a wide range of services.
- **Technology and systems.** Depending on the type of services the firm intends to provide, systems and technology can be utilized. The extent and type of systems and technology need to be determined, the skills possessed in designing or using the systems evaluated, and the extent of investment in capital and time specified. In today's conditions some firms have invested heavily in technology with a vision of transforming the ways in which legal services will be produced. This capital investment in dollars, training time, and cultural change is calculated to produce dividends in the future.
- **Level of commitment.** Throughout the planning process, agreement is necessary on the relative priority to be given to each aspect, including commitment of time, effort, and money at each level of priority. Some tasks may be prior in total importance, others prior in point of time—that is, certain steps need to be taken before related steps can be undertaken.
- **Competence in hiring, retention, and training.** To carry out a plan, the firm will need to engage the services of those with requisite capabilities, provide an environment that attracts and sustains a stable work force, and supply a training cadre that will ensure the ongoing effectiveness of all personnel, lawyers, and staff.
- **Client base—existing and future.** One of the most critical planning issues is an examination of who the present and future (or desired) clients are and the legal needs of those individuals and businesses. This review should include the type of clients, revenues derived from those clients, practice areas involved, and likelihood that there will be a continuing need for services by those clients in the range of services provided by the firm. If there are targeted future clients, the foresee-

able legal requirements of those clients should be anticipated and planned for.

- **Leveraging.** Leveraging involves increasing the capabilities of individual lawyers by using other lawyers, legal assistants, staff members, and technology. Some practice areas permit leveraging to a greater extent than others. In terms of the value curve, unique and experiential services require personal involvement of an expert lawyer, so less leveraging is possible. On the other hand, for commodity services, systems and technology can be used, as can the services of less skilled individuals. Related is the question of determining the optimum size of the firm.
- **Culture.** Groups of people working together consciously or unconsciously develop traits that characterize the group. The planning process should include an honest evaluation of dominant characteristics. For example, if the firm is composed primarily of individuals who work long hours and are high producers, the culture will differ from that of a firm or group that regulates the number of hours worked, participates in community or pro bono activities, or recognizes vacations, sabbaticals, or shorter work hours. The plan as developed should take into account the personal work habits of the persons involved and set goals consistent with those traits.
- **Billing methods and pricing.** After an analysis of the types of services that will be furnished, it is important to consider which method of billing would be most appropriate. Are there defined services that could be billed for a fixed fee, contingent fee opportunities, or some hybrid approaches that would be acceptable to clients? Do the strength of the competition and your level of expertise suggest the level of pricing (as distinguished from billing method)? Consider the effect of pricing policies on whether the objectives of the firm will be promoted and achieved. Can billing methods be used as a marketing ploy? Included in this is an analysis of the effect of different methods and levels of pricing on firm profitability.

  For example, here are the key steps needed to successfully implement alternative billing methods:

  1. Educate lawyers regarding the client's needs and problems.
  2. Have a lawyer or section of the law firm prepare a list of the client's projects that may be susceptible to standardization.
  3. Analyze the law firm's costs to produce the legal services for the particular project on five occasions to focus lawyers' efforts on improving strategy and identifying solutions for other inefficiencies.
  4. Develop standard forms, software systems, and internal procedures to produce a standardized package for each project.
  5. Accumulate a list of all internal costs, and price the package in excess of the cost to produce.
  6. Develop a prototype project to present to the client, such as a fixed fee program to handle market-sized commercial real estate loans for financial institutions.
  7. Develop an engagement letter that sets parameters for the package and also discusses exception pricing.[2]

- **Marketing.** Marketing efforts done without being a part of the strategic planning process will be less effective in that the objectives of the firm and the direction of marketing may be at odds. Those responsible for marketing should also be involved in the planning project to ensure internal consistency. Part of the plan should be to set the level of marketing and to provide appropriate funding. The details of the marketing plan can be separately set forth and managed once the parameters for marketing have been agreed.
- **Compensation system.** The critical issue is whether the compensation system will promote the goals of the firm by rewarding those who contributed to achieving those goals. Compensation is both a reward and a motivator. How will contributions to the firm that do not result in immediate billable services be recognized, and how can firm members achieve a feeling that they have been treated fairly in compensation systems? Inherent in this consideration is who makes the compensation decisions and how those people are chosen. What fringe benefits will be provided, and what retirement program will exist? Tied in with these considerations are agreements for buy-in and buy-out for partners entering or leaving the firm. Affecting the amount of profits to be distributed as compensation is the issue of how much capital will be required to operate the firm and the effect of capital contribution requirements on the take-home pay of the partners. Closely related is the anticipated length of the partnership track. The demography of the firm will influence the choice of compensation systems and should be considered as part of the planning process. There will be more about compensation systems that reward and motivate in the next chapter.
- **Optimum firm size.** Consensus should be reached on the approximate size of the firm that is desired and planned for. The decisions made will affect logistics, recruiting policies, and capital required. Policy as to lateral hiring should be considered, including the effect on firm culture.
- **Form of governance.** While there are choices of the form of governance, it is imperative that governance be sufficiently centralized to ensure the internal consistency of the six functions or components. However, unless there is consensus on the form of management, personal relationships will suffer. One person–one vote; concentration in one managing partner; a strong (or weak) management committee; ultimate control; availability of competent managers; committee structure; recognition of contributions to management with appropriate compensation—all of these need to be considered. Currently, the effect of the movement towards a more horizontal form of organization should be anticipated, as well as the impact of technology; telecommuting; access to information; part-time work; entrepreneurial attitudes; voting methods including supermajorities—these are some of the considerations affecting a determination of an effective governance format.

There may be other considerations in your own situation that should receive attention in your thinking and planning process. From the foregoing, you can conclude that a wide range of topics should be considered in order to end up with an integrated, comprehensive plan for the future. As to the length of the planning cycle, you can be either long-term or short-term or both, depending on your preference. However, the rapidly changing environment suggests that planning for longer than three to five years will be difficult, unless you are alert to the need for periodic reviews and adjustments to meet changed conditions.

From total quality management came the concept of "benchmarking," that is, devising ways to measure the progress being made. Setting specific, measurable goals makes it possible to gauge progress. Benchmarking can include not only obvious measurable results, but with some ingenuity it is now possible to use benchmarking to measure intangible achievements or results.

The secondary effects of strategic planning include providing specific targeted goals that should motivate individual performance, concentrating the resources and efforts of the firm, and creating change on a positive, proactive basis.

NOTES

1. Henry Mintzberg, "The Fall and Rise of Strategic Planning," *Harvard Business Review* (January/February 1994): 107.
2. Based on materials prepared by Shelby R. Rogers published in *Counselor's Computer and Management Report* 5, no. 1 (Chicago: Section of Law Practice Management, American Bar Association, Summer 1994).

CHAPTER 15

Compensation and Evaluation Systems—Rewarding and Motivating

THE COMPENSATION SYSTEM OF a firm should provide a means for rewarding those who have contributed value to the firm and motivate the members to do those things that promote the goals set forth in the strategic plan. If the method used for determining compensation is not consistent with the other component functions, there will be negative consequences.

If quality, value, and the innovative use of technology are the watchwords, it is critical that lawyers be compensated in ways that promote those goals. In the minds of clients, neither "quality" nor "value" relates necessarily to the number of hours spent by the lawyer in providing legal services. Yet firms committed to these new approaches to law practice should recognize that to achieve quality and to deliver value there must be a substantial investment of lawyer time. This signals a movement away from income statement thinking where the current month's bottom line is the measure of success. Rather, the firm's valid objective should be to increase its true balance sheet.

The balance sheet approach has been suggested by David Maister and others to recognize that traditional law firm balance sheets showing only hard assets such as furniture and furnishings, cash such as bank deposits, and credits such as work in progress and accounts receivable do not reflect the true value of the firm. That value also includes the composite skills, expertise, wisdom, knowledge, integrity, training, experience, and reputation of the lawyers, the competence and experience of staff and all others who contribute to the work product of the firm, and a loyal client base. In addition, a firm develops systems, problem-solving skills, shared knowledge, and judgment, all of which are part of the intellectual capital of the firm.

In the era of hourly billing, where recorded time came to be the basis for billing and unbilled billable hours the measure of the inventory of the firm, billable hours infiltrated the stated or unstated criteria for compensation systems of the firms, with scant or lesser recognition of the value of "nonbillable hours" invested in firm management, training, mentoring, marketing, community and professional activities, and the like.

A recent survey confirms that fees collected are the dominant criterion for lawyer compensation. The Altman Weil Pensa *1993 Survey of Compensation Systems in Private Law Firms* tabulates the results of 412 carefully edited responses. Fourteen formal compensation factors were listed in surveying the compensation philosophies of the responding law firms, which ranged in size from two to more than one hundred lawyers. These factors included fees collected; business origination; hours recorded; client responsibility; case responsibility; firm management; legal expertise; fees billed; seniority with firm; cooperativeness; relative ownership percentage; professional involvement; community involvement; and seniority since bar admission.

On a scale of zero ("not considered") to five ("critical"), fees collected ranked first for firms with 2 to 19 lawyers, 20 to 49 lawyers, and 50 to 99 lawyers (whether measured by mean or median). For firms of 100 or more lawyers, fees collected (median) ranked equally with business origination, hours recorded, client responsibility, and fees billed and second only to business origination based on mean measurement. This survey result confirms the working thesis that fees collected have dominated the compensation systems of law firms of all sizes.

To foster the closer client relationships that inhere in the theories of total quality management and alternative billing methods, as well as in the emerging concept of "partnering," it will be essential for firms to invest substantial amounts of time and effort in what will not be immediately realizable in terms of billable hours and short-term revenue. Time spent cultivating and implementing these concepts must be regarded as investments in the future or additions to the true balance sheet. This is the compelling reason why thought should be given now to appropriate changes in compensation system philosophies.

A perfect compensation system (which in the real world does not of course exist) would directly reward the efforts of those who contribute to making the strategic plan of the firm a living reality. Redesigning the compensation system will be difficult for at least two reasons. First, production of fees is a strong influence in existing systems, and, second, efforts to strengthen the firm's balance sheet will not be the same either within the firm or from firm to firm, nor will those contributions be of equal value.

Part of the problem is that while fees collected or hours recorded are easily quantifiable, legal expertise, delivery skills, and the fostering and maintenance of close client relationships deal more with intangible contributions that are inherent in concepts of value, quality, and partnering, yet are not easily measured.

Assuming that the firm in its strategic planning has determined to concentrate on improving the quality of its services to implement its strategic plan, that commitment to provide total quality service requires the expenditure of a substantial amount of the firm's resources and the time of lawyers and staff within the firm. Lawyers who have generated billable hours will be called upon to play varying roles in the process, hours that will not be immediately billable but that will ensure the future success and survival of the firm in the longer term. Unless those contributions are recognized and valued for purposes of compensation, the project is likely to fail.

The pivotal question is how best to modify the compensation system to recognize the varying contributions of the lawyers to the firm. This challenge will apply irrespective of the existing compensation philosophies of the firm, whether prospective or retrospective, whether formula or nonformula, whether units, percentages, or points.

Many firms have evolved written criteria for compensation awards. Typically, these list the numerous factors that the firm deems important and are set up to apply across the board to all partners in the firm. Other firms have weighted the compensation factors to reflect the relative importance to the firm of each of the criteria. Firms with weighted criteria often will change the weighting to reflect what is deemed most important at that point in the history of the firm. For example, in one year where available law work is plentiful, production will be stressed. At another time when volume of work has declined, the emphasis might be on client development or marketing.

There are two major problems with this approach. The first is that, notwithstanding the written criteria for compensation, in actuality different or even unwritten criteria are given disproportionate emphasis. To illustrate, the written criteria may state that seniority shall not be a major factor, yet in practice, seniority may be heavily recognized when the compensation decisions are made. The second problem is that written criteria intended to apply to all partners means that all people will be measured by the same yardstick, yet their contributions to the firm will vary in kind and amount.

The mind-set of most firms in making compensation decisions is to rely heavily on production (hours worked, hours billed, fees billed, or fees collected) as reflected by the honor paid to the billable hour. These firms tend to be number oriented. The recognition of contributions that are the result of nonbillable hours, such as serving as the managing partner, or as a member of the management or executive committee, is often done by granting credits reflected in either hours or dollars that the firm agrees to consider as if they were "billable." Firms using this system often set a maximum limit on the credit that will be given. Typically, the dollar/hour credit is at the same hourly rate as the lawyer would have charged if doing client work. This is predicated on the assumption that but for the nonbillable work the lawyer would have filled those hours with billable client work. It fails to recognize that there may be no correlation between the value of lawyering skills to the client and the value of managerial skills to the firm. It also assumes that internal management, systems development, rainmaking, and application of technology are, for the most part, part-time functions and that most persons engaged in these activities will practice law in the sense of providing direct services to clients.

So how can we devise a method that will motivate lawyers to contribute to the long-term value of the firm? How do you reward those lawyers based on benefits conferred or value rather than on hours spent?

These considerations make it necessary for law firms to have a paradigm shift, to adopt new rules for the compensation game, to adopt a new set of values for compensating lawyers.

In his book *Future Edge*[1] Joel Arthur Barker defines "paradigm" as follows:

> A paradigm is a set of rules and regulations (written or unwritten) that does two things: (1) it establishes or defines boundaries; and (2) it tells you how to behave inside the boundaries in order to be successful.

Barker points out that a paradigm can help you solve many problems within the limits of that paradigm, but that same paradigm can get in the way of solving other problems you would like to solve.

The *existing* paradigm for law firms is that production and collection of fees is the dominant factor to be recognized in determining compensation. The question that then arises is whether this is what the firm wants or needs.

Translated, this means that the lawyer who attracts the best clients, works the most hours on client business, and bills the most is regarded as the most productive lawyer and, therefore, is entitled to the most compensation. This is consistent with the income statement thinking that prevails in many, if not most, law firms. While these contributions undoubtedly will remain important, the problem remains of finding ways to compensate for other less measurable contributions to the long-term success of the organization.

The *new* paradigm to which law firms should consider shifting is that for long-term survival and success, a firm's compensation system must recognize and reward the diverse contributions made to the firm by its lawyers.

Translated, this means that fee collections are important, but so also are planning, managing, supervising, delegating, developing manual and technological systems and procedures, improving quality, recruiting, mentoring, marketing, team-playing, participating in community and professional affairs, and a whole host of activities that go to make up a successful legal organization.

This holistic approach recognizes that the whole is made up of parts, but the parts are different in kind, size, and importance. Each must be recognized as a contribution to be rewarded with the further recognition that different people have different skills that are valuable to the firm, but not identical or necessarily of equal value.

Perhaps it may appear that we are headed in our discussion towards a compensation system that only a large law firm would consider. On the contrary, the shifting of the paradigm and the principles that will follow apply to firms of all sizes, even to a solo practitioner practicing with a legal assistant and secretarial personnel.

In crafting a compensation system under the new paradigm it may be useful to borrow from or at least consider how compensation systems of businesses other than private law firms are designed and work effectively.

For example, take a manufacturing company, say one that manufactures automobiles. An auto company has owners, as does a law firm. Typically, there will be a top management that controls the day-to-day operation of the company. General policies are adopted by a governing board, but the details of management are handled by others. Skilled designers plan for the next new models of cars. Machinists and toolmakers ready the plant for production, utilizing appropriate technology. Financial people have calculated the cost of production and determined the pricing. Once the new models are in production, various workers fabricate the cars, their efforts having been monitored by quality control experts. In the meantime, sales and promotion employees have begun the marketing program. Dealers handle the direct sales to customers and are equipped to provide proper servicing following delivery to the customer. During the process the law department has handled any legal matters that arose in the conduct of the business.

The automobile that rolled off the assembly line and ended up in the driveway of the ultimate purchaser was the product of many people using numerous and different skills. So many skills and people were involved in the finished product that it is difficult to state categorically which was the most important. In such a chain of production, the pay scale or compensation will differ according to skill levels, but each contribution is rewarded, as each is indispensable.

The second comparison may be a bit closer to life in a private law firm. Consider the compensation systems typically employed in a corporate law department. Like private law firms, law departments have a client or clients. The client may be the corporation itself, but in many instances the law department is called on to serve various component units of the company, so it can be said that each division or unit requiring legal services is the client and each must be satisfied with those services.

The size of corporate law departments varies from one lawyer to hundreds of lawyers, depending on the corporation, its needs, and its own table of organization. A small law department may have only two levels of supervision and a simple structure, while larger departments may have several levels of supervision. Working units within the department may be specialized and have different reporting chains or may be assigned to specific operating units of the corporation. The job designations of people employed in the law department typically would involve all or some of the following, depending on the complexity of the organization.

The chief legal officer heads the corporate legal function for the parent company. In complex law departments there may be a deputy chief legal officer who shares law department-wide management responsibility with, and reports to, the chief legal officer. A division or group general counsel may report to either the chief legal officer or deputy chief and may have responsibility for the departmental budget and employment. This person may supervise subordinate lawyer-managers. A managing lawyer exercises management supervision over several salaried lawyers, including responsibility to effectively recommend promotion or retention. This person usually heads a group of lawyers organized along lines of legal specialization or company components. The managing lawyer may also perform legal work.

A high-level specialist is an experienced specialist capable of dealing with members of senior management on legal problems in his or her area of expertise. Typically this person may work with other lawyers or train less experienced lawyers, but normally is not in a supervisory relationship. The job designation of lawyer includes all other lawyers, who may assist in training, are expected to perform direct legal services of either a generalized or a specialized nature, and report to a managing lawyer. Other typical employment categories in a law department include recent law school graduates, paralegal assistants, and a legal administrator. The latter may be responsible for budgeting, controlling, salary administration, personnel review, purchasing, internal systems, and nonprofessional personnel supervision. In addition, there will be requisite secretarial or staff employees.

The structure of a law department as just described, while hierarchical, illustrates the manner in which law departments may manage the business of the department and perform direct substantive legal services for one or more "clients," that is, the corporation itself or components or subdivisions thereof.

As in the case of the automobile manufacturing company, the levels of compensation in the law department for the various job positions will vary depending on a variety of factors, with reward given in proportion to skills, performance, and the relative value of the individual's contribution to the company.

Too often the criteria for compensation within a law firm or law department are not clearly defined, articulated, or understood. A properly designed compensation system can become a motivational tool if there is a *consistent relationship* between the *value of the contribution* by an individual and the *reward or compensation* that results.

If a lawyer or staff person shows initiative and acts innovatively in providing value or quality to clients, but is criticized or not supported for having done so, that individual will doubt the organization's commitment to empowerment. Similarly, if those actions are not suitably rewarded under the organization's compensation system, management should not be surprised if that individual loses motivation and slips back into the attitude of entitlement. Likewise, if nonperformers receive the same compensation as those who have performed exceptionally well in doing all that the group has determined is important, management should not be surprised when the superstars return to a level of mediocrity or move to another organization where the value of their contributions will be recognized and rewarded.

Performance competence, the ability to translate expertise, knowledge, and experience into services that bring value to the client, are timely delivered, and priced reasonably in relation to the value of those services to the client, should be the objective of every lawyer and every law firm. Recognizing that responsibility, expertise, and productivity are more important than hours spent is the first step towards a major reorientation of both billing and compensation systems. In the process of analyzing what is truly important, the key step lies in recognizing that individual practitioners who add value to their clients will be the lawyers most sought after by clients who want to receive value and by law firms who will benefit most by having value-giving lawyers within their firms. With the acknowledgment that adding value is paramount, there will inevitably be an awareness that "time spent" should not be the major determinant for fee setting or for compensating lawyers.

Let's go back in time a bit to see problems that lawyers wanted to solve and the shifting of paradigms that helped to solve one or more problems, but at a later point left problems that could not be solved within the parameters of the initial paradigm.

The Problem: Lawyers wanted to produce written words faster and more efficiently than could be produced by manual typewriters that required retyping when errors were made in original typing or when changes needed to be made in the text.

The shift in paradigms (paradigm A) was to change from manual typewriters to electronic typewriters with memory features that permitted easy correction, duplication, and storage of the materials and greater speed than could be produced manually, later known as word processing. The result was increased speed and efficiency with a reduction in the human time required for a given project.

Another problem that lawyers wanted to solve was how to store and retrieve data more effectively than by the use of manual systems (paradigm B). This problem existed initially in the accounting aspects of law practice and later in the storage and retrieval of substantive information. The shifting of the paradigm was to change from manual hand-posted accounting, individually typed statements for services rendered, and manual indexing systems for the retrieval of information from documents and records. The solution was to use computers, which was more efficient, faster, and reduced the human time required.

At this stage word processing was done by stand-alone word processing units that could produce words, and computers (usually mainframes or minicomputers) that could produce figures.

The next problem to be solved was to eliminate having two separate types of technology (word processing units and computers used primarily for accounting purposes) combined into one piece of equipment (paradigm C). The merging of the two came in the form of the personal computer, which could manipulate both words and numbers. The resulting use of PCs reduced the human time required for a given project.

These three illustrative paradigms involve problems that were ultimately solved by the use of technology, and in each illustration the quality of the product was improved, efficiency was greater, the product could be produced more quickly, and there was a reduction in the human time required for a given function or assignment.

However, problems that lawyers need to solve are not limited to those that can be solved by a paradigm shift to a new technology. Keep in mind that the end result of the shift to paradigms A, B, and C was that less human time was required.

But the goal is to meet the needs of clients. Add to these trends another problem of lawyers, that of modifying the adversarial relationship between in-house legal departments and outside law firms. "Partnering," the emerging solution to this problem, has as its foundation the concept that the separate skills of inside and outside counsel should be used harmoniously to meet the legal needs of the employing corporations. Thus the paradigm shift is that all legal talents of inside and outside counsel should be used in concert for the resolution of clients' problems.

Life is not a single paradigm but many different paradigms for dealing with many different problems. The usefulness of paradigm analysis is that when the rules and regulations of one paradigm leave problems that cannot be solved within that paradigm, there must be a shift in paradigms to provide a new way of thinking, a new set of boundaries, a new set of rules and regulations that will permit solution of the previously unsolved problems.

In shifting to alternative billing methods, in implementing the principles of managing for quality, and in developing the close client relationship of partnering, significant amounts of time, energy, and skill will be required by members of the law firm. There will be a diversion away from billable hours in the short term, and an investment in the future of the firm. Those who contribute value to the firm in the transition period need to be rewarded by a compensation system that recognizes the value of these nonbillable contributions.

• • •

How does the firm make the transition in its compensation system to reward these valuable contributions to the long-term success of the firm?

First, the firm should have a clear vision of where it wants to go and agreement on how it will reach those goals. This is best accomplished by a strategic plan supported by a consensus of the owners of the firm and endorsed by all lawyers and staff. The consensus involves a commitment.

Second, the firm needs to dissect its operation to determine what activities and contributions are essential if the strategic plan is to be successfully carried out. This can be accomplished by having each participating lawyer respond to a questionnaire designed to recognize the important and needed contributions to the firm that will not be immediately billable. An example of such a questionnaire is set forth in Exhibit 15-1, but with the admonition that it should be customized to fit the needs of the specific firm.

EXHIBIT 15-1: Recognition and Comparative Valuation of Nonbillable Contributions to the Law Firm

You are requested to indicate your recognition and valuation of *each of the contributions* by marking with an *X* in the appropriate column. Leaving a line unmarked or marking it with an *0* will be interpreted as meaning that you do not recognize that contribution as either meaningful or valuable to the firm. If you feel that the question is not applicable to your firm, you can mark it *N/A*. PLEASE COMPLETE EVERY LINE.

The left column lists contributions that may be regarded as essential and valuable to the firm. You can identify other contributions in the Comments section at the end of the questionnaire.

Column A should be marked if you feel that the listed contribution is something *all lawyers* should contribute by reason of being a lawyer in the firm and that there should be no special recognition and valuation for purposes of additional compensation.

Column B should be marked if you feel that the listed contribution should be given some recognition and *minor additional compensation* given to the contributing lawyer.

Column C should be marked if you feel that the listed contribution should be given significant recognition and *significant additional compensation* (major) to the contributing lawyer.

If you wish to explain or qualify your response, use the Comments Section at the end, referring to the response by line number.

CONTRIBUTION TO THE FIRM	A (None)	B (Minor)	C (Major)
1. Recruitment of new lawyers			
a. Member of recruitment and hiring committee			
b. Chair of recruitment and hiring committee			
c. In-office interviewing of screened candidates			
2. Training of lawyers			
a. Incidental to occasional contact			
b. As practice area/department manager			
c. As part of regular contact			
3. Firm management			
a. Managing partner/shareholder			
b. Executive/management committee member			
c. Chair, compensation committee			
d. Compensation committee member			
e. Attending meetings of partners/shareholders			
f. Chair, other major firm committees (please specify which committees) ______________________________			
g. Committee member (not chair)			

(continued on next page)

EXHIBIT 15-1 (continued)

CONTRIBUTION TO THE FIRM	A (None)	B (Minor)	C (Major)
3. Firm management (continued)			
h. Chair of department			
i. Practice area manager			
j. Manager of branch office			
k. Chair, marketing committee			
l. Member, marketing committee			
m. Supervising other lawyers			
4. Participating in firm activities			
a. Attending firm retreats			
b. Attending firm social events			
c. Attending recruiting functions			
d. Contributing to firm newsletter			
5. Educational activities			
a. Attending in-house continuing legal education (CLE)			
b. Presenting in-house CLE			
c. Attending outside CLE			
d. Presenting outside CLE			
e. Writing books and articles			
f. Mentoring			
6. Professional activities			
a. Chair of bar association committee			
b. Member of bar association committee			
c. Officer in bar association			
d. Chair/officer of professional society			
e. Member of professional society			
7. Community/civic/church/fraternal organizations			
a. Member of organization			
b. Position of responsibility in organization such as chair, president, etc.			
c. Doing pro bono legal work			

(continued on next page)

EXHIBIT 15-1 (continued)

CONTRIBUTION TO THE FIRM	A (None)	B (Minor)	C (Major)
8. Marketing and rainmaking			
a. Bringing in new clients			
b. Maintaining existing clients			
c. Cross-selling			
d. Team marketing			
e. Group marketing			
f. Client visits and audits			
9. Systems/technology development			
a. Developing in-house systems for processing work			
b. Developing or maintaining in-house systems utilizing technology			
c. Participating in quality councils under total quality management program			
d. Generating original thoughts, projects, and programs that are useful to the firm			
10. Daily management of individual practice			
a. Managing personal lawyer workload, organizing daily schedule			
b. Delegating work to others, where possible			
c. Meeting mandatory CLE requirements			
d. Contributing work products to brief/forms bank			
e. Responding promptly to requests from firm management			
f. Promptly returning phone calls			
g. Being a team player			
h. Assisting other lawyers in emergencies			
11. Individual financial management			
a. Recording time on daily basis			
b. Preparing and reviewing billings			
c. Reviewing accounts receivable and following up on collections			
d. Reading firm financial statements and reports			

(continued on next page)

EXHIBIT 15-1 (continued)

Comments (and any other nonbillable contributions that should be evaluated):

The responses in column A will show which contributions each partner in the firm is expected to make as part of that partner's basic compensation from the firm. The column A contributions then become part of the written job description of each partner. They also become criteria for the admission of new partners when the partner criteria are compared to the professional qualifications of each prospective partner.

The responses in column B should be fewer in number than the column A responses and more numerous than the column C responses. While every partner will be expected to make column A contributions, column B responses will require a detailed analysis of available talent in the firm to determine which partner(s) should be placed in a position of authority. Not all of the contributions in the column B category will be of equal value to the firm, so some ranking or gradations may be appropriate. Once this is done, some dollar recognition will be required to motivate the individual to contribute in the desired fashion. Part and parcel of this process is the need to recognize that the time and effort required to carry out the assigned functions may reduce productive billable hours. This requires the firm to make a value judgment weighing short-term loss of billable hours against the long-term value of needed contributions.

The responses to column C need to be analyzed in similar fashion, as these contributions should reflect the consensus on the major needs of the firm. Once again, the talents available within the firm should be canvassed, followed by a careful selection of the persons best suited to make these important contributions to the soundness of the organization. In all probability, the time and effort required to make the column C contributions will be greater than for the column B contributions. Hence the reward should be greater as a reflection of the perceived value of those benefits.

For firms that have traditionally used percentages, units, points, or a formula to determine compensation, it has been difficult in the past to determine how to compute the value of the contributions of those lawyers with managerial responsibilities (if, indeed, there was any recognition of those contributions).

As mentioned earlier, the traditional assumption that the value of a manager's services to the firm equated with the normal hourly billing rate for client work of that individual may not be valid. All of these complications can be easily solved by regarding those with column B or column C responsibilities as being *salaried employees* of the firm with a fixed salary agreed in advance. For purposes of compensation decisions, these "salaries" can be treated as part of overhead as a cost of operating the firm. If a nonlawyer administrator is paid a salary for administrative services, a full-time managing partner can also be salaried. If a part-time associate or part-time staff person can be paid a salary commensurate with part-time services, a part-time manager can be compensated appropriately. The same approach can be used for any given task or assignment that the firm deems important, such as rainmaking, research, systems designs, technology applications, or training.

This exercise does not deal with the contributions made by the partners in the performance of their professional activities (distinct from internal managerial or other duties) in terms of responsibilities assumed, expertise, productivity, experience, stability, stature, and other attributes of a skilled practitioner. Whatever the compensation system normally used by the firm, that system should relate to valuing the contributions made by partners resulting from service to *clients*. The analysis of nonbillable contributions as suggested here deals with valuing the contributions made by partners in providing services to the *firm*.

The shifting compensation paradigm thus involves accepting and affirming that for long-term survival and success a firm's compensation system must recognize and reward the diverse contributions made to the firm by its lawyers.[2] Billable hours will affect short-term profits; nonbillable contributions will determine the future of the firm.

Within the parameters of that compensation paradigm, it will be appropriate for the firm to go through the analysis process at periodic intervals, since the needs of the firm will change from year to year. As those needs change, the value of the different contributions may change. Fine-tuning should be an ongoing process.

For purposes of compensating the professional skills and contributions to the firm, firms will be well advised to establish written criteria for setting compensation levels. These criteria, whether weighted or not, act as general guidelines to advise the partners of the standards by which their performance will be judged when it is time to make compensation decisions. But those criteria should also be used by the members of the compensation committee (or whoever makes decisions on compensation) as reminders of the standards they are responsible for applying. The advantage of having written criteria is that there first must be agreement on the rules of the compensation game (which involves adoption by a consensus and hopefully acceptance and ultimately commitment). The drawback or limitation of firm-wide criteria is that all lawyers are measured by the same yardstick. It should be recognized that professional skills, expertise, client acceptance, and other attributes vary from person to person and that a deficiency in meeting a single criterion may be offset by strength in another. General criteria for determining partner compensation might include these seven key factors:

Chargeable time and productivity. The lawyer's productivity in terms of client hours worked and recorded, as well as time devoted to firm administration, client development, and screening of potential new matters. Include as an element of this factor evaluation of the productive use of these hours.

Professional ability and responsibility. The professional competence of the lawyer together with his/her willingness and effectiveness to accept and carry out the primary coordinating responsibility for larger, more complex cases involving the efforts of several lawyers.

Business generation and perpetuation. The lawyer's effort and ability to generate new clients, as well as the ability to expand business from existing clients and maintain proper relationships with clients of the firm.

Profitability. Fees charged and collected from clients compared with the fair value of the time that the lawyer and those working under his/her direction devote to client work. Proper fee and billing arrangements with clients and proper effort to collect fees due to the firm.

Administrative and training responsibilities. The lawyer's participation and involvement in management of the firm or departments. Willingness to take on and effectively discharge administrative assignments. Participation in effectively training associates and paralegals.

Cooperation. Working with other lawyers and administrative staff for the best overall benefit of the firm. Adherence to established policies and procedures. Implementation of management decisions as appropriate.

Professional and community activities. The overall effort and effectiveness of the lawyer in maintaining professional competence and image at a high level by attending seminars and other educational programs, by writing and speaking about legal topics, and by participating in bar activities. Also take into consideration any special involvement in community activities and trade or professional associations that enhance the image of the firm.

More precise measurement of the value of a lawyer's professional contribution can be achieved if the firm adopts the practice of having each lawyer annually adopt an individual business plan. An individual business plan consists of much more than getting and maintaining clients. In this approach, each lawyer proposes what he or she will accomplish in the period just ahead. It may be production; it may be to learn new skills; it may be to target and capture designated new clients. Each lawyer and the firm management come to an agreement on the game plan for the coming year. Negotiations incident to agreement on the individual business plan can direct the efforts towards specific targets that, if accomplished, will benefit the firm. For example, assume that the firm wishes to develop competence in a new practice area and that doing so will require a period of education, skills development, and client cultivation. In the short run little revenue will be generated, so the individuals undertaking this project should not be penalized during the transition period. If the new practice area proves to be financially successful, the firm, as a whole, will benefit.

When it comes time to determine compensation, in addition to the general compensation criteria, the individual business plan provides an additional and more customized measuring stick. The question then becomes to what extent that specific lawyer accomplished the stated goals of his or her individual business plan. Interestingly, it has been suggested that one of the factors to be considered in making compensation decisions is client satisfaction.[3] When a file closes, a client survey would ask the degree of client satisfaction, and the response would be factored into the compensation decision.

In recent years there has been a trend away from limiting the lawyers in the organization to being either a partner or an associate. Non-equity partners, senior associates, of counsel, permanent associates, contract lawyers, and part-time lawyers are some of the new categories. This trend suggests that the internal structure of law firms may be moving in the direction of the typical corporate or governmental law department model. It also suggests that not all lawyers working for a firm need to aspire to or be considered for partnership status. In the future, being a partner/shareholder or owner of the firm may be restricted to those individuals who are entrepreneurs and who excel in some special way that contributes major value to the firm.

There are numerous opportunities for innovation in designing compensation systems in this new world. Albert L. Moses has suggested that where one or more lawyers within the firm take the time and have the skills to develop a system (such as document assembly) that other lawyers in the firm will use to produce a product, the value of that system should be recognized. Moses stated:

> The lawyers who contributed that system have made a contribution to the firm's intellectual capital, and when that intellectual capital produces a return for the firm the contributors should be rewarded.

> A compensation system might involve a credit to the producer of the system each time the system is used by anyone in the firm. Another compensation method might involve establishing the value of a proposed system and crediting the creator of the system with its value when it is completed, just as other lawyers produce value for the firm in the form of client fees. The important thing is for the firm to provide the motivation for lawyers to produce and use systems.[4]

If the law firm is incorporated, the concept of a "salary" is easier to accept. Using the corporate model, compensation in the form of a salary can be set prospectively. If differs from the traditional draw of partners, which is an advance against future partnership distributions. If profits and individual contributions to value justify payment of additional amounts, these can be distributed retrospectively as a bonus. Partnerships can follow the same methodology.

Evidence that others are thinking in the terms described in this chapter can be found by reading an article by Robert W. Denney, "Firms Re-evaluate Partner Compensation Systems," published in the May 1, 1995, issue of the *National Law Journal*.[5] Mr. Denney emphasizes the need to strike an appropriate balance between recognizing current performance and long-term contributions. The process of awarding compensation should not only divide last year's profits but also focus the firm's and the partners' attention on the future. This involves a performance-based system and requires a careful evaluation of the total contribution each partner has made. The process should not be solely a numbers-driven process. Mr. Denney deals in some detail with how the evaluation process can be structured, including a discussion of who should make the evaluation. He concurs that if the firm has adopted a planning process in which each partner has established a written set of objectives for the coming year, partners may be evaluated on their performance as compared to their own particular plan.

Whatever the approach is to compensation systems, there is a clear need for the reward system to be consistent with the other five component functions of the firm, but with special attention given to the nonquantifiable contributions made to the long-term success of the firm.

NOTES

1. Joel Arthur Barker, *Future Edge* (New York: William Morrow and Company, Inc., 1992): 32.

2. This idea is not new, but has not often been used by law firms. For example, Avery Cohen, Cleveland, Ohio, and his firm experimented with a compensation system designed to reward nonbillable work. This was reported in Richard C. Reed, "Rewarding Non-Billable Work," *National Law Journal* (January 10, 1983). Under the described approach each partner was initially awarded a number of "shares" and received compensation prospectively based on the number of shares. When firm profits for the year reached \$100 per share, \$5.00 of each share went into a bonus pool (increasing to \$14.50 per share when profits per share reach \$125.00). The bonus pool was distributed using a point system, with each partner having a potential maximum of 180 points. The schedules of potential points were as follows:

Table No. 1	**Maximum Points**
1. Billable hours by lawyer doing the work	25
2. Dollars received in excess of per-share distribution for billable hours by working lawyer	30
3. Effective rate for working lawyer	10
4. Reducing inventory of unbilled hours	3
5. Fees billed by responsible lawyer	12
6. Fees collected by responsible lawyer	13
7. Realization rate by responsible lawyer	8
8. Credit for origination outside of responsible lawyer	9
Subtotal	110

Table No. 2	**Maximum Points**
1. Administration	20
2. Community involvement and business development	25
3. Technical competence and continuing legal education, including speaking engagements, in-house education, and other contributions to the firm	15
4. Team play and associate utilization	10
Subtotal	70
TOTAL	180

The calculations for table 1 criteria could be computer generated. Table 2 points were subjectively determined by the compensation committee. After preliminary computations were done, the awards were reviewed for overall fairness. Compensation from shares is prospective; bonus compensation is retrospective.

3. 1995 National Compensation Survey, *Canadian Lawyer* (June 1995): 30.

4. Albert L. Moses, "Warning! Fixed Fees Ahead (Engage All Systems)," *Law Practice Management* (March 1995): 60.

5. Robert W. Denney, "Firms Reevaluate Partner Compensation Systems," *National Law Journal* (May 1, 1995): B12.

CHAPTER 16

Marketing—Selling Your Services

WHETHER THERE IS an aggressive or a passive approach to obtaining clients, a successful firm must sell its services. Even before it was fashionable in law firms to use the term "marketing," lawyers developed their practices and attracted their clients in a variety of ways. A lot of the new ways to do so are really variations of the old ways, except for advertising of legal services and rates, which used to be viewed with distaste but now is condoned.

Too often firms engage in what they believe is marketing but are disappointed with the results. In many instances the person in charge of marketing is not part of management and works without an intimate knowledge of the strategic plan and the specific levels of quality and expertise possessed by the lawyers in the firm.

To maximize results in carrying out the strategic plan, the marketing plan must fit hand in glove with the strategic objectives of the organization. The first objective of marketing is to do those things that will move the firm towards its strategic goals.

The second objective of marketing is to promote the sale of the services that the lawyer or the firm produces, exploiting the strengths with an awareness of the needs of clients or potential clients for those specific services. If the quality level of the firm's services is not up to the standards of the firm clients, marketing efforts may be futile. It is difficult to sell a poor product.

The third objective of marketing relates to billing and pricing. If a good work product is priced too high, marketing efforts will be handicapped because of the inability to compete with other providers.

Thus, for marketing to be successful, the firm must know what services it wishes to sell, have an acceptable quality level, and ensure that billing methods and pricing levels reflect the true value of those services.

Traditionally, lawyers thought that if they did good work, clients would come to them. To a certain extent, this was true because of the then-existing ethical constraints on promotion, and even more true in the seller's market of the 1980s. Such is not the case now. The oversupply of lawyers, the economic downturn, increased competition, and the more sophisticated demands of clients make marketing essential.

Having an appropriate pricing policy in connection with marketing is essential and basic, but it is not the whole story. The choice of billing method and pricing techniques can be used affirmatively as a marketing ploy. For example, if you are the first to offer fixed fee billing for a commodity service, you can use that as a selling tool in marketing. Or you can talk about and promote the idea that the firm is willing to share risks with the client, if you are willing to devise that type of billing method. If you can provide predictability as to what the fee will be, sell predictability. If you are strong on technology and systems, sell the idea that the firm can produce services at a lower cost with a resultant lower fee. If you can differentiate your services by providing some extras, sell that type of service. If you have broken away from straight hourly billing, sell results or events, not hours.

Once again we see the importance of internal consistency. The marketing function is inextricably tied to the other component functions.

The ultimate purpose of marketing is to keep and add clients. The way that a law firm bills for its legal services will either promote or detract from the success of the marketing efforts.[1] Price is determined in the marketplace as an expression of value or worth. Value connotes a benefit, and because the client is the purchaser of legal services, he or she must receive some benefit so that value may result. Not only must there be "actual value" of the services provided, but there must be perceived value. To the extent that marketing efforts can convey that the charges for legal services will be an investment in something of value rather than an expense, marketing efforts will be a success.

Marketing is a process of communicating. The lawyer must communicate to the client what services can be, are being, and have been provided. The client must communicate what problems are to be solved, what goals the client would like to achieve, and how success will be measured.

Marketing suggests differentiation, and differentiation enhances the perception of value. Differentiation is how the services of the firm, even though essentially the same as the services provided by its competitors, can be set apart in the mind of the client. If the client perceives that the firm's services are in some respects better or different, the firm will benefit by being able to bill for a greater amount or by having increased volume, or both.

For example, firms may differentiate by:

- Providing a better-looking work product.
- Being readily available.
- Evidencing a caring attitude toward the client.
- Always being timely in performance.
- Being friendly, concerned, and courteous.
- Communicating well with the client.

Even a small thing that evidences consideration for clients can be enough to differentiate your services. The little extras can slide the services up on the value curve where price is less sensitive and profit margins are greater.

In the evolving competitive world, marketing efforts must become even more ingenious and imaginative. Clients now pick specific lawyers or practice areas rather than firms as a whole. Marketing efforts, therefore, must be particularized to promote the specific talents or expertise that clients are seeking. Since clients are concerned with churning of lawyers on a given matter, marketing can include a detailed proposal of exactly which lawyers will be assigned for the representation.

In earlier chapters the customizing of billing and pricing methods was emphasized as a current trend. For the same reasons, marketing efforts increasingly will need to be customized and tailored for each presentation or approach.

Marketing can be part of a circular process. Assume that in doing strategic planning the firm decides to develop a new practice area. Having set this objective, the firm must develop expertise in the new area. To do so and as part of the carrying out of the strategic plan, the firm hires new people with expertise in that practice area or develops skills in-house, by writing, speaking, researching, or training. Once the level of expertise is reached, marketing can emphasize the very activities used to develop the expertise as reasons why the firm should be hired. With successful marketing, new business in the desired practice area becomes a reality, thereby achieving the strategic goal or objective.

We can conclude that marketing should emphasize the strengths of the lawyer or firm, promote the attainment of strategic goals, be fine-tuned to sell specific skills and to meet the specific needs of clients and, overall, be internally consistent with the other five component functions of the firm.

All the marketing in the world will produce nothing if improper billing and pricing methods are used. If the charge for services does not fairly measure the value to the client and results in a significant overcharge, the client will not return, nor will that client recommend the firm to other potential clients. If the price is too low and thus does not produce a profit for the lawyer or law firm, the business may have to fold.

Market in ways that will enhance client trust and build confidence in the firm. High-quality services give you something to sell; equitable billing and pricing practices that fairly measure value will enable you to compete; a fine-tuned marketing program will help to bring in new clients and hold on to the old ones. All three functions are essential parts of implementing a changeover to the modern operation of a successful legal operation.

NOTE

1. Portions of the following materials were first presented at the Second International Conference on Marketing Legal Services in 1990 in San Francisco and appeared in revised form as chapter 12, "New Billing Strategies and Marketing," in the book *The ABA Guide to Legal Marketing* (Chicago: Section of Law Practice Management, American Bar Association, 1995). This book contains much valuable information on various aspects of marketing.

CHAPTER 17

Governance—Controlling and Leading the Practice

TO ELABORATE ON the comments about governance in chapter 14, law firms choose diverse organizational structures for the management of their practice. This diversity reflects the culture and preferences of the individual firms. The size of the firm has a lot to do with how a firm is governed. In a four-partner firm, for example, all partners most likely would be involved with a majority of the decisions, although one partner may be more concerned with day-to-day administrative decisions.

As firms increase in size, it normally is necessary to have delegated authority for management since it becomes impractical to involve all partners in management. In that situation, it is characteristic to have the partners, as partners, retain the right to approve major decisions of the firm such as mergers, dissolution, hiring of associates, major borrowing, or expenditures beyond routine amounts. In my mind, once a firm has twenty or more lawyers, some concentration of management functions should occur.

Whether a firm chooses to be democratic and collegial with decision-making on a one partner–one vote basis, or chooses to concentrate authority in a managing partner or management committee, depends on the firm's preferences to a considerable extent. While there are traditional management schemes, arrangements vary considerably from firm to firm.

One influencing factor is the demography of the firm. Where there are major differences in seniority, expertise, and client attraction among the partners, the dominant lawyer often is the ultimate manager. Another influencing factor is the management skills available within the firm. Some firms have lawyers who like to manage and are willing, if not eager, to spend time on firm management. Others firms, lacking people with outstanding management experience or skills, tend either to manage by committee or to rotate individuals into the position of managing partner for a three-year "sentence" (in those firms where nobody really wants the job).

In many situations, unfortunately, obtaining a position in management is primarily a move aimed at power and control. Many who ascend to management roles do so without particular regard to whether they have either the time or the skills necessary. One often sees the lawyers with the most seniority, legal expertise, or ability to attract and hold clients going into management of the firm. Being an outstanding lawyer does not automatically make that person an ideal manager.

In other situations, having to take a management role in the firm is regarded as a drag, a burden, and an intrusion on the time and energy of a lawyer who would really rather be serving clients. The result is often a lack of enthusiasm, lowered priorities given to managing, and an unwillingness to learn and perfect managerial skills.

In coordinating the six essential functions of the firm, governance is the umbrella that covers the other five functions, strategic planning, quality of services, billing and pricing, marketing, and the compensation system. It is my opinion that the firm will be happiest if the members adopt whatever system of governance best fits their individual preferences and the history and culture of the firm. One major proviso should, however, be observed.

That overriding requirement is that whatever system of governance is adopted, it must be sufficiently strong and centralized to ensure the internal consistency of the other five component functions. Heavy emphasis has been placed on internal consistency. If all essential elements of the operation are not coordinated and internally consistent, there will be mixed results. Poor quality of service, improper billing and pricing, uncoordinated marketing, and failure to compensate lawyers for doing those things the firm deems important to carry out the strategic plan can result from a governance system that fails to control, lead, coordinate, and manage the components.

These generalizations about governance are sound. Allowing the firm to choose whatever governance system it prefers should produce a happier situation than if you try to force adoption of one of several traditional forms of governance. This is subject to the requirement that whatever method of governance is adopted, it must promote the interests of the members of the organization and provide the requisite authority to control the firm's total operations.

The issue remains, however, of whether the demands of the coming decade can be met unless the governing authority has certain needed skills to adapt to the new and different ways of practicing law and to meet the new and different requirements of clients.

In the coming era in the legal profession firm management must have vision, understanding of the outside forces influencing the demand for legal services, flexibility, a willingness to change, an intimate awareness of how technology can be used to promote efficiency, and a commitment to providing outstanding service to clients. As economic demands for lower prices and improved quality of product will become more insistent, managers should be chosen for their ability to produce legal services on a cost-effective basis. It will not be enough to continue to manage in the old ways. Leaders and managers must be paradigm shifters, able to induce all people in the firm to think creatively about *how* the firm operates and how clients can be better served.

Lateral movement in the profession characterized by cherry picking, mergers for the wrong reasons, the up-or-out policy that wastes maturing skills and talents for purposes of leveraging, and inattention to the quality of life of firm members have resulted in the reduced stability of legal organizations. Management in the future must focus on finding ways to strengthen the firm as an entity to preserve and increase the intellectual capital of the firm. One of the vices of the emphasis on billable hours as a measure of worth to the firm is that it conflicts with the management approach that recognizes the importance of training, mentoring, development of systems, adaptation of technology, and long-term client development to ensure the survival of the firm in the years ahead. Short-term profits achieved at the expense of long-term investment can affect the ability of the firm to meet the new demands of the future.

In a competitive market it is important for management to know the cost of doing business. This suggests that management needs to have sufficient financial skills to understand and foster adequate cost-accounting practices that can provide a sound basis for billing and pricing policies.

In the final analysis, in deciding upon the appropriate form of governance the format for governing may be less important than the ability to obtain and fully use managers who have the characteristics and skills just described. It involves a holistic approach to firm governance, emphasizing the organic or functional relation between parts and wholes. The zany, crazy, wild ride through the seller's market of the 1980s with heavy reliance on billable hours was a much more atomistic approach.

However, the role of the managing partner is changing. In 1992 and 1994 there was a survey of law firm managing partners and chief executive officers.[1] Participants in both years came from firms of all sizes, ranging from firms with fewer than 40 lawyers to one with 176 or more lawyers. This survey provided the first benchmarking data available on the role of the managing partner in today's environment. In both 1992 and 1994, 73 percent of the respondents were from law firms with 75 or more lawyers, where the managing partner role is likely to be well defined and at a maturing stage. Significant finds in the survey regarding the changing roles of managing partners include the following:

- On average the managing partner has been with the firm twenty years, of which he or she will have spent an average of seventeen years as a partner/shareholder.
- 86 percent of the managing partners are elected by either the partnership or the executive/management committee.
- Managing partners are carrying an increased role in both management of the firm and development and management of client business. Their role in the actual practice of law has decreased significantly. For example:
  - — Managing partners' median billable hours *decreased* from 1,000 in 1992 to 812 in 1994.

— Their average fees generated decreased from $246,000 in 1992 to $226,000 in 1994.

— There has been an increase of eight percentage points in time spent by managing partners on managerial matters.

The allocation of time/responsibilities of managing partners was allocated as follows:

	1992	1994
Managerial matters	47%	55%
Marketing	13%	15%
Practicing law	40%	30%

These trends point to the increasing importance of having sufficient time available for the management of the firm, whatever the form of governance, and the high level of managerial competence necessary to lead the firm.

In summary, choose the form of governance that fits your culture and preferences, but always keep in mind the qualities, skills, and characteristics of innovative, imaginative, visionary management necessary for success. Governance sets the rules for how the game is to be played. In some firms it appears that every partner sets his or her own rules, a luxury that can no longer be tolerated. To tie together the other functions of the firm, it is essential that there be some sort of governing structure strong enough to assure that each of these functions can be achieved. More than that, the structure must be acceptable to, and have the affirmative support of, all the individuals in the firm. Governance then becomes the control mechanism by which the goals of the firm are fulfilled. It shouldn't just happen: governance needs to be planned and coordinated.[2]

NOTES

1. *Survey of Law Firm Managing Partners and Chief Executive Officers* (Newtown Square, Pennsylvania: Altman Weil Pensa, Inc., 1992 and 1994).

2. Richard C. Reed, "The Changing Law Practice Environment: New Problems Need New Solutions," *Law Practice Management* (March 1991).

CHAPTER 18

Technology—The Revolutionary Force

THE RELENTLESS PRESSURE for change in law practice is economic. The revolutionary force enabling change is technology and the willingness and ability of lawyers to use technology in finding new and better ways to serve clients.

The law itself is an evolving, constantly changing process, so it is not surprising that the practice of law also evolves. Consider the changes that have occurred in the past three decades, but more dramatically, in the last decade with the use of technology. The repercussions of technology on society in general have affected the daily life of the citizens of the world.

The use of technology in law practice in earlier forms was to automate methods and practices that hitherto had been done manually, hoping that technology would improve and make more efficient work processes that had been fairly well stabilized for generations of law firms. As I write I have at my desk *Webster's New World Dictionary of Computer Terms, Fifth Edition (1994)*, a 624-page dictionary of more than 7,000 computer terms. Most of these words did not even exist ten years ago, at least not in any common usage. For computer-literate individuals this is almost a new global language spoken by the informed. Even words that had an established meaning have been adapted by computerese and given different meanings. Take the word *global*, for example. It used to mean just "worldwide," but now in the language of computers it may mean "pertaining to a variable whose name is accessible by a main program and all its subroutines."

We refer to "generations" of technology, whether applied to word processing or to computers. With the rapidity of change, a generation may mean only the time it takes to develop a new software program or computer chip. Orwell's *1984* has come and gone. Toffler's *Future Shock* and his predictions for the ten years that followed publication have come and gone. Yet the pace of technological change accelerates and shows no signs of abating.

While the pressure to change the way that law is practiced may be economic—the quest for more effective legal services at a reasonable price—the means for change will undoubtedly be a combination of two factors: the ongoing development of technology and the ability of far-sighted individuals to use that emerging technology in meaningful ways. The thesaurus listing for the word *impetus* includes "catalyst," "force," "motivation," "spark," and "stimulus." You can frame your thinking in any of these terms as you envision the future of the practice of law.

If the business of lawyering is to solve client problems, information is a resource, management of information is a skill, and technology is a tool, superimposed upon which are the ultimate judgment, skill, expertise, knowledge, and integrity of the lawyer. This definition could have described law practice fifty, one hundred, or two hundred years ago except for the accelerating force of technology that is revolutionizing law practice today but was virtually nonexistent in earlier years.

Back in the Dark Ages when I commenced law practice in 1948, the only technology in our law office involved manual typewriters, a hand-cranked adding machine, and a switch that would bring a Western Union messenger to pick up urgent telegrams. Law books and yellow pads were our major tools.

Senior lawyers will recall the advent of electric typewriters; wet-process copy machines; early computerization, usually through service bureaus; paper-tape word processing machines; electronic dictation machines on drums that had to be shaved, followed by records and then electronic tapes; telephones where Central said "Number, please"; mag card typewriters; ink-jet printers in centralized word processing centers; in-house mainframe computers in air-conditioned rooms; telecopiers that transmitted one page at a time with an attendant standing by; the first personal computers that only a few knew how to use.

As I write this chapter on my 286 personal computer—soon to become a planter because it is no longer compatible with my 486 laptop—I recall an article in this morning's paper reporting that Intel has completed design of a P-6 chip that will nearly triple the speed of the Pentium chip, which was nearly five times faster than the first model of the 486 chip. Reading further, I was told that Intel has packed a silicone chip about the size of a postage stamp with six million transistors. By the time you read this, this P-6 chip may have become obsolete.

The dramatic developments of technology in the past decade make the early evolutionary changes of the 1950s, 1960s, 1970s, and 1980s seem like baby steps, even to people who tried to keep abreast of new developments in those years.

The *evolution* of technology of the past decades has now changed to the *revolution* caused by technology, a revolution that will irrevocably change the way law is practiced, the relationships with clients, the structure of law firms, methods of billing and pricing, and the personal lives of lawyers.

Progressive law firms and lawyers have moved increasingly during the past decade to the use of technology in the production of legal services. Substantial sums have been invested in communications equipment, hardware, software, the creation of technology-based systems, and the training of personnel, including the firm's lawyers. Effectively used, technology should produce a better-quality product and increase timeliness in the delivery of services. Keep in mind, however, that one of the key advantages of technology is to reduce the human time required to produce the services. The reduction in time expended has been concurrent with an accelerating change in the pace of law practice and the pace of living.

The use of technology in law practice may be merely an extension of manual systems, but increasingly technology is being used to reengineer legal processes to create new and better ways to accomplish a desired result. The earlier changes in technology related primarily to the improvement of old ways of doing things. Now emerging technology promises to be the keystone to revolutionary changes in law practice, with all the related fallout effects. Technology as a mind-boggling tool must be accompanied by changed paradigms, flexibility, creativeness, innovation, and a continuing, anticipatory awareness of the needs of clients. Firms that have developed a high technological level know that the reasons for using technology are

1. To improve quality of product and quality control.
2. To improve timeliness.
3. To improve cost effectiveness.
4. To leverage the intellectual and physical capacities of a lawyer.
5. To increase the ability to delegate.
6. To reduce the human time required to produce legal services.

The reduction of human time required to perform a given task also reduces the number of billable hours. Hourly billers see this as a disadvantage, since time is their predominant measure of value. As mentioned earlier, this is called the productivity paradox. If you continue to bill by the hour, the more you invest in and use technology and the more you reduce the human time required, the less you earn.

Ronald W. Staudt and Rosemary Shiels summarized the situation well in their article "The End of the Beginning: The Computerization of the Practice of Law in Large Firms":

> Our data suggests that we are approaching the end of the beginning of law office automation. Technology with the capacity to make remarkable changes in law practice is now in place in large firms.
>
> Law firm economics is pushing for change in the form of new efficiencies. Value billing puts inside and outside counsel on the same side in seeking time reductions and quality improvements. And the same computing and communications technology that are proliferating in law firms will affect legal education.[1]

Now to be more specific.

Joseph L. Kashi, a solo practitioner in Soldotna, Alaska, wrote a thought-provoking article, "Technology and Economics Are Changing How You Practice Law," which appeared in 1994 in *Law Practice Management*.[2] With his consent an edited version of portions of his article follows:

Constant Change Is Forced upon Us by Technology Itself

Technology is like an arms race. Because it makes early adapters more efficient and competitive, their opposite numbers must adapt as well to avoid losing too many clients or too many cases. Emerging nonlawyer competitors will use technology to penetrate the legal market more easily and compete with established firms for routine transactional and documentation services. Business clients are automating rapidly and expect the same level of sophistication from their attorneys as they do from their own companies.

Technology Is Reducing the Number of Lawyers Needed for Existing High-Quality Business

As of 1990, there were about 655,000 lawyers and 5.7 million businesses in the United States—about one lawyer for every nine businesses, large or small. The million-lawyer society is not too far away. Clients will demand more value as competition among lawyers becomes more apparent. Some large litigation projects are already bid for a flat fee rather than an hourly rate, placing a premium on automation, efficiency, and lower profit margins.

A recent article in *Forbes ASAP* documented how DuPont Corporation used advanced wide area networking (WAN) technology to standardize, share, and consistently use its bank of proven defense motions and litigation data common to each type of product litigation, and then to shed most of its several hundred outside defense firms. DuPont then instituted software controls, comparing each firm's success rates and detailed billings, acquiring a very firm handle on billing. Electronic mail among defense counsel across the country enables them to quickly share strategies, tips, and comments about any expert witnesses. Because WAN technology forces all defense counsel to use the same data and proven brief banks across the country, success rates have risen and total defense costs have dramatically decreased. Is it any wonder that vigorous law firm downsizing is so prevalent?

Many of the shed lawyers will become small firm or solo practitioners, competing for much of the same middle-class business at which technically sophisticated nonlawyer competitors now aim. Many sophisticated users, such as banks and title companies, already produce much of their own transaction documentation, using powerful document assembly programs devised solely for them.

Prepackaged legal forms programs will encourage the rise of do-it-yourself users and paraprofessional legal documentation clinics for the middle class.

As the quality of routine documentation improves through the use of standardized document assembly programs, high-quality clients will shop around for the best deals, if they do not produce the work in-house. Consumer programs already on the market will tempt individuals to prepare legal documentation like wills, powers of lawyer, and real estate transactions on their own, just as they now do with IRS returns.

Neural net legal advice programs will be mass-marketed. Neural programs that actually guide a person's analysis of the factual "symptoms" and recommend generally correct approaches to a potential legal problem are undoubtedly on the way.

Technology Quickens the Pace of Law Practice

Businesses and consumers are becoming used to faster results and are *demanding it from their lawyers*. Clients have become accustomed to quick transactions—faxes, electronic mail, and overnight delivery—and in getting something done now. *They are demanding this same speed from their lawyers*. New information technology is the principal factor causing our working pace to accelerate continually. In fact, even times that should be restful have become less so, as technology now allows us to work at home in the evenings, work at the beach, and get our E-mail from every airline seat, car, and phone booth.

Technology Will Increase Our Personal Stress and Malpractice Risk

Our now-constant companion the fax machine has, by itself, sharply increased the speed of legal practice. Instead of opposing counsel mailing you a letter, with an average delivery and response cycle of a week or more, a letter is often faxed, received, and answered within an hour or less. There is less time for thoughtful decision-making, bouncing ideas off your colleagues, and later insight.

As the pace of practice increases, we tend to make snap judgments, with little time available for reflection. As the result, the quality of the resulting decisions suffers. We will be forced increasingly into a kind of very fast-paced, higher-volume summary practice that puts us at higher risk of burnout, stress, incivility, and malpractice.

Coping with Technology's Challenges

Technology is forcing law firms to change into radically different, flexible entities that respond quickly to market and technological changes. A firm's organizational structure is probably the most important single determinant of whether it will prosper in the turbulent years to come. Future law firms must adopt a more flexible and democratic horizontal structure that facilitates sharing critical information.

Basically, firms must learn how to use information technology to make necessary information quickly available to whoever needs it. Computer and communication technologies are changing how we practice law. All lawyers, particularly small firm and solo practitioners, will be forced to become technically literate, because of both competitive pressures and ethical requirements that we use all available means to further client matters entrusted to us. As we struggle to implement these new technologies, we will find that whom we

> employ, how we organize our law firms, and the very economics of practicing law will be far different from what young lawyers imagined it would be. Only the technically literate will prosper.

Staudt and Shiels reported the results of surveys made over the years by the Chicago-Kent College of Law Center for Law and Computers. In the 1993 survey, the respondent large firms reported an average of 162 lawyers (minimum 70 lawyers; maximum 638). In the 1980s, computers were used primarily for back office operations (accounting, timekeeping, and payroll) with word processing centers for long document preparation also in vogue. By 1993 most specialties reported that at least 75 percent of their lawyers used computers. It is interesting that lawyer use of computers was virtually the same in various practice areas, namely, tax lawyers 75 percent, litigation lawyers 76 percent, corporate lawyers 76 percent, real estate lawyers 76 percent, and trust/estate lawyers 75 percent.

As faster and more-powerful personal computers became available, 81 percent of the lawyers moved to the faster models. Laptops became popular by 1993. The survey reported the widespread use of local area and wide area networks and electronic mail, ultimately moving to use of the Internet. By 1993, 76 percent of the firms used a document management or archival storage system that helps create, store, and retrieve files in every practice area throughout the firm. Also reported was the increased use of integrated automated document assembly programs.

Here are some quotes from the Staudt and Shiels article:[3]

> Motivation to use these new tools arises out of the need to provide more efficient services to clients who demand more for their legal expenditures. Technology can make change possible, but economics will make change inevitable.

• • •

> At its most fundamental level, value billing requires that lawyers justify their fees not by measuring the number of hours the work took to complete but by specifying the benefits to the client provided by the work done.

• • •

> Technology would replace leverage, ushering in a new age and a new paradigm.

It appears that lawyers are increasingly using CD-ROM technology in daily practice. Graphics-interface techniques have been improved and are easier to use. Software for lawyers is becoming easier to use. The mouse makes it easier for nontyping lawyers to use personal computers. Lawyers, even senior lawyers, increasingly understand and accept the importance of becoming computer literate.[4]

It is not only lawyers that are moving towards the increased use of technology. Court administrators and court rules are moving the courts into computerized case management. By October 1995 all bankruptcy courts had computerized docketing. Bankruptcy notices go out electronically. Electronic filing is starting to be an option in some courts. On-line access to court data is increasing. Court by telephone, video trials, voice mail, and electronic case management are here or are coming.

On top of all of the other advances in technology, now comes the Internet, a sprawling, unregulated, evolving web that offers new possibilities and uses whose impact on law practice is yet to be clearly defined. Electronic mail and research appear to be its early uses. Will it be useful for marketing legal services? Some law firms seem to think so, as evidenced by their postings. Will the Internet reduce the need for lawyers when a potential client can pose a question, receive free responses, and make a personal judgment without ever having retained a lawyer? Already there have been instances where an individual had received a settlement offer for a personal injury claim and solicited comments on whether the offer should be accepted.

The best explanation of the Internet that I know of is in the 1995 book by G. Burgess Allison, *The Lawyer's Guide to the Internet*.[5] The vastness of the possibilities boggles the mind. The jury is still out on how lawyers will use the Internet and, perhaps more important, on whether clients will use the Internet to bolster or to diminish the role of the legal profession. Undoubtedly the ingenuity of lawyers in this regard will be the determinant.

The creativity of individuals in the legal profession may result in applications and uses of technology that no one imagined were possible. History may repeat itself. When the mag card word processor came into use, the operators devised uses and techniques that went far beyond the scope of what IBM had contemplated. Where such creativity exists, the opportunities for meaningful improvement in producing legal services increase geometrically.

The pyramid structure of law firms in the 1980s resulted from the benefits of leveraging through hourly billing timekeepers and the abundance of legal work available. In today's market, the pyramids will flatten, and leveraging by people will be reduced. The true opportunity for leveraging in the legal world of today and tomorrow will come from the application of technology. Leveraging, as used in this paragraph, is the ability to expand and use the composite skills, expertise, and intellectual capacity of a lawyer beyond what that one person alone could produce. One nail-maker alone could hammer out one nail at a time at the forge, but the inventor of a nail-making machine could produce a huge number of nails whenever the machine was turned on, even without the inventor present to flip the switch.

A survey of 200 lawyers at 116 of the nation's largest law firms on the impact of technology reported that almost 90 percent of the respondents felt that with the use of technology in their practice the competitive edge had increased, almost 90 percent felt quality of work had increased, almost 60 percent felt morale had improved, and 40 percent felt profitability had increased. Approximately 20 percent felt operating costs had increased while a like number felt operating costs had decreased.[6]

Despite the impact that changing technology will have on the way law is practiced, the economics of the relationships between lawyers and their clients, the compensation systems of law firms, the quality of life inside and outside law firms, the pricing of legal services, the pace of lawyering and life in general, the structure of law firms, the marketing of lawyers, and the ethics and attitudes of the profession, it should always be remembered that technology in all of its forms, existing or to come, is but a tool, a means to carry out the ultimate purpose of the legal system.

We should always remember that technology does not make judgments, create expertise, display judgment, develop and sustain client loyalties, understand people and how humans interact, build and maintain morale, develop strategy, or exercise the ultimate judgment of a legal adviser, counselor, or trial advocate. As lawyers respond to the forces of change, it is important to remember that human relationships, not computer chips and modems, are the heart of the legal profession.

NOTES

1. Ronald W. Staudt and Rosemary Shiels, "The End of the Beginning: The Computerization of the Practice of Law in Large Firms," *Technology* (1994).

2. Joseph L. Kashi, "Technology and Economics Are Changing How You Practice Law," *Law Practice Management* (November/December 1994): 44.

3. See endnote 1.

4. For an excellent primer, read: Carol Woodbury, *Becoming Computer-Literate* (Chicago: Section of Law Practice Management, American Bar Association, 1995).

5. G. Burgess Allison, *The Lawyer's Guide to the Internet* (Chicago: Section of Law Practice Management, American Bar Association, 1995).

6. *National Law Journal* (June 5, 1995): A5 (reporting a survey by Pitney Bowes Management Services).

CHAPTER 19

Designing for the Future: Vision, Change, and Reaction

WHERE DO WE GO FROM HERE? To this point in this book there have been testimonials with real-life examples that alternative billing works. The extent of the movement has been quantified by surveys. Special topics have been discussed in a more than passing manner. The importance of consistency of the six component functions of any legal organization has been stressed repeatedly. The key point has been made that billing and pricing are just one part of the emerging new world of law practice. More than 75 percent of the respondents to the 1995 Altman Weil Pensa survey believe that the use of alternative billing methods will increase.

If you remember only one thing from your reading, remember the four key words that should be used to measure every step you take and should serve as the framework for your decisions and your goals for the future:

QUALITY — VALUE — TECHNOLOGY — INFORMATION

Quality in the sense of the total services rendered; value as the extent of benefits conferred; technology as a tool to increase efficiency and to lead to new ways to serve clients; information as a major resource to be managed and used.

If you can remember more, retain these words: VISION, FLEXIBILITY, CHANGE, CULTURE, STRUCTURE, INTELLECTUAL LEVERAGING, and ADAPTABILITY.

Remember that the ultimate business of law practice is to SOLVE or PREVENT CLIENT PROBLEMS and that the critical objectives are quality of service and value *as perceived by the clients*.

What will it take to succeed in the next decade? The requisites are to achieve quality and to give value. Many different approaches, with many different labels, have been proposed to accomplish these goals.

One of the most widely used is total quality management (TQM), which focuses on the needs of clients and preaches the doctrine that the quest for improvement is never-ending. TQM gave us the discipline of benchmarking and the notion that even intangible services or processes could be measured so that progress could be monitored. TQM gave us empowerment, suggesting that everyone in the chain of providing service should be given the latitude to do what is necessary to meet customer needs.

One writer called this attention to the customer "outrageous service."[1] It is when someone in your organization goes way beyond the call of duty or normal expectations to serve the customer. To give a personal example, once when I was shopping at Nordstrom's department store in Seattle I asked a clerk on the first floor for a specific item. She replied that the item was not in her department but could be found on the second floor in a different department. She then left her counter, walked with me to the escalator, rode to the second floor with me, and went to a specific rack of clothing to show me the merchandise I wanted to locate. That was outrageous service. Another example is the service I got from the manufacturers of Zippo lighters, who guarantee free repairs for the life of the lighter. Once when I sent in a customized lighter to have a hinge repaired they called to say they did not have such a case available to them, but if I would send them my signature they would engrave it on another case before returning the repaired lighter to me. That was outrageous service. Take from the total quality management doctrine whatever you feel helps to improve the quality of your service.

One of the concepts of total quality management is that each person or entity involved in producing a work product is regarded as a "supplier," a term that includes legal services provided to a client. There are internal "customers" within a law firm. For example, an associate producing a brief or research memorandum for a senior partner is providing a product for a customer, the senior partner. If the brief is late or is poorly done, the associate has failed the customer. A mailroom clerk in preparing and posting mail for a secretary must promptly and correctly complete the task so as not to fail the secretary, the customer, who has prepared the documents and left them for mailing.

As TQM faded into the background, pundits began to talk about business process reengineering (BPR). Where TQM deals with continuous incremental improvement of existing processes within an organization, BPR suggests that every aspect of business operations should be redesigned from scratch, often referred to as "starting with a blank piece of paper."[2]

Michael Hammer, with James Champy, published a book in 1993, *Reengineering the Corporation*, subtitled *Forget What You Know About How Business Should Work—Most of It Is Wrong*. The approach dealt primarily with process, contending that most problems of a business are caused not by people but by process.

As applied to a law firm or legal department, a sound reengineering program focuses on four key components of change: (1) process and procedures, (2) people and culture, (3) organization and structure, and (4) systems and technology. Inherent in this doctrine is to view every aspect of the organization without preconceived notions, to "start with a blank page" and to ask whether the process, people, organization, and system being examined is necessary and whether there is a better, new way to do things. A reengineering process unearths the fact that cost problems usually reside in inefficiencies of process, not inadequacies of people.

Reengineering differs from total quality management in several respects. Reengineering requires reinvention of a major process; quality refines existing processes. Reengineering aims for major improvement; quality deals with incremental improvement. Reengineering is driven from the top, quality from the bottom up with the commitment of top management. Reengineering suggests innovative use of information technology; quality does not depend on technology.[3]

As with total quality management, take from the principles of business process reengineering whatever features help you the most to improve the quality of the services you provide. The ultimate lesson to be learned from reengineering is that in a changing world it is important to think in new terms, new goals, new ways of doing things to meet the new demands of clients. When you improve a process with TQM you do not necessarily ask whether the process you are improving is necessary. When you use computers to do what you used to do manually, only do it faster, cheaper, or better, you ordinarily do not ask whether the process itself is necessary or the best way that the task could be accomplished. Borrow from TQM, borrow from BPR, but work towards improved quality of service.

In thinking about reengineering, I hope you recall the materials in chapter 12 about new paradigms. As with business process reengineering, a shift in paradigms is analogous to the blank sheet of paper. The boundaries are not yet defined (the size of the paper), nor are the rules established. Nothing is written on that paper that limits you or requires conformity to some past ideas. Using a bit of history of billing for legal services as an example, when lawyers began to keep time records and to bill by the hour in order to make more money, the paradigm was adopted that lawyers are in the business of selling time. It followed that the more time you recorded and the more people you had recording their time, the more time you had to sell. In maximizing the hours, lawyers worked to the limits of physical endurance and had to forgo some of the other, more pleasurable aspects of human life. Consistent with this paradigm is that inefficiencies produced profit by requiring more time to be spent. Inconsistent with this hourly billing paradigm were considerations of value or benefit to clients. It was only when hours had expanded to the maximum, and hourly rates reached the level where clients would no longer pay, that it was necessary for lawyers to switch to a new paradigm emphasizing benefits, efficiency, results, and the interests of clients as the rules of the game. The hourly billing paradigm broke down when the productivity paradox created by technology and the economic pressures from clients caused by the business recession forced lawyers to consider alternate approaches to how law should be practiced and how clients should be charged for legal services.

Think about this. When you bill by the hour there are finite limits on the number of hours a lawyer can work, a limit on the number of persons working on a given matter, and an upward limit on the dollars per billable hour that clients will pay. When you bill for value, there is no limit to the value to the client. Billing for value holds the prospect of lower cost to the client on the one hand and the possibility of increased profitability on the other.

Whether you call it TQM, BPR, paradigm shifting, or some other label relating to quality, *it is absolutely certain that the pressures for quality and value will continue.*

The reengineering approach should not be limited to processes and procedures but should be the framework and philosophy for examining people and culture, organization and structure, and systems and technology in law firms and legal departments. You can also reengineer relationships, such as the emerging doctrine of partnering.

DuPont has made major changes in the operation of its legal department.[4] Among other moves it reduced the number of outside law firms from over three hundred to approximately thirty-one firms. Those firms share research, briefs, and work product with other firms representing DuPont in a collaborative effort with the DuPont legal department. This partnering relationship among providers of services to DuPont is creating some synergism and is leading to opportunities for the DuPont networking firms to provide services on non-DuPont matters.[5] This is in addition to the benefits of a closer, long-term, mutually beneficial relationship with the DuPont legal department.

Fred H. Bartlit Jr., an outstanding Chicago trial lawyer, has written significantly of the changes in law practice. He left a large firm to form a small group designed to deliver more efficient legal services through technology and the adoption of nontraditional billing arrangements. He speaks of the pressure of economics and the changes that have occurred in the legal marketplace. He suggests that winning at the right price, rather than at all costs, will guide corporate law departments. He believes that discovery as practiced with hourly billing rewards "thoroughness" rather than "effectiveness at trial" and suggests that lawyers in the future must be better tuned to the cost/benefit approach to decision-making. He argues that systems must be developed that leverage experience, quality, and efficiency and contends that experienced lawyers, working efficiently, can produce better results at a lower cost.[6] He envisions a change from the pyramid structure of law firms toward a diamond-shaped structure.

Several writers have suggested that the expanding, multitiered pyramidal structure of law firms will change. One of the major complaints against hourly billing was that inexperienced lawyers were getting their training and experience at the expense of the client, as the services of these young lawyers were charged out at rates that exceeded the value of their contribution. To maintain the leveraging, associates had to be replaced with a new crop of inexperienced lawyers. The upward pressure continued to the point that the now matured and experienced associates either had to be made partners or be terminated under the "up-or-out" policy. One legal department, in an attempt to avoid paying for the cost of training young lawyers, has refused to have an associate with less than three years' experience work on a case for that corporation. In another instance, a law firm negotiated a representation agreement that made no charge to the client for work done by associates with less than three years' experience.

The diamond-shaped structure of law firms has the senior/owner lawyers at the top of the diamond and relatively fewer, inexperienced lawyers at the bottom, with the big bulge of the diamond consisting of experienced lawyers with capabilities and experience levels that meet the needs of the client.

If this comes about, where will new lawyers get their training? Will it be at the expense of the law firms, who must absorb training costs as part of overhead? Will law schools be called upon to change their traditional approach and provide experience and practical training? Will the answer be an articling system such as that used in Canada where a law graduate works for a year in a law office at a nominal salary before being called to the bar?

Private law firms, law departments, and clients are turning more and more to a cost/benefits analysis mode. With greater predictability on what the legal fee will be, clients will be enabled to weigh costs against benefits in deciding whether to litigate or to settle. With more accurate information on the cost of doing business, law firms can judge with more precision the cost and benefits of expanding, branching, deleting, or adding practice areas and acquiring expensive technology.

This use of cost-benefit analysis differs significantly from what happens with straight hourly billing, where all the cost goes to the client and all the benefit goes to the lawyer, who gets paid whether he/she wins or loses, settles well or poorly, achieves the client's goals or falls short.

The most significant element of reengineering that can carry over to all aspects of your practice is the challenge to wipe the slate clean and try new approaches. This becomes an attitude and a philosophy that influences the culture of the organization. It dispels inertia. It eliminates from the firm's vocabulary the phrase "This is the way we've always done it." In my forty-one years of law practice, I observed that our firm collectively was the happiest when we were trying something new.

Doing something new can be both proactive and reactive. Being proactive is anticipating what will occur. Being reactive is responding to changes that have been forced upon you by your clients, the general economy, or your competitors. The pendulum swings, requiring adjustment periodically. Just a few years ago, as some firms grew exponentially and the merger mania was predicated on the notion that it was necessary to be a full-service firm to survive, the demise of the small and medium-size firms was predicted. In today's environment, however, law business is being assigned to talented individual lawyers or practice groups irrespective of firm size. Being relatively smaller, being able to provide more personalized services to clients, and practicing outside major metropolitan areas where overhead is lower are now regarded as advantageous. With the benefits of technology, solo practitioners and small firms are better able to compete with the large firms in many instances.

The January 1995 issue of the *American Bar Association Journal* carried an interesting article, "Small Firms Big Clients," that described many small firms that represent major national clients. According to the article, to obtain such clients it is necessary to have aggressive plans for client development, leveraged prior law practice experiences and contacts, capped expenses, and specialty niche skills.[7]

Another swing of the pendulum in recent years was the change made by some of the major corporations to substantially reduce the number of outside firms handling the work of the corporations. Presumably, the earlier use of a large number of outside firms was thought to foster competition and to reduce legal expense. The current trend of looking to fewer firms is based on the sharing of knowledge and skills of inside and outside counsel, the development of a deeper knowledge of the business of the client, and the perceived mutual benefits of long-term relationships.

One of the pitfalls in writing a book of this nature is making the assumption that all law firms and all clients are alike. Though they share many basic similarities, there are significant differences that pose different problems and justify different approaches. Not all law firms work for large, multinational clients. A lawyer practicing in a small community primarily with individual clients is in an arena vastly different from that of an international megafirm providing legal services to international megaclients. In some instances leadership in change comes from the large firm, but often it is the solo or small-firm practitioner who pioneers and is the more progressive. It is my considered opinion, however, that notwithstanding the differences, there are basic principles that apply and trends that must be recognized throughout the profession. Among these basics are the quest for quality and the need to deliver value.

Earlier we talked about the movement towards a diamond-shaped structure. It is a little difficult for a two-lawyer firm to build a diamond structure! One of the irresistible trends, however, in an era of cost consciousness, is that administrative levels in the firm structure that do not produce value need to be trimmed. A forecast many have made is that even in pyramidal firms there will be a flattening of the pyramid. One of the benefits an individual lawyer derives from rising within the pyramid is access to information. Where there is an integrated computerized operation, the collective information base (about clients, intellectual capital, internal financial information) is accessible by each lawyer. This alone suggests a flattening of the pyramid.

The danger to be avoided lies in preserving old organizational structures that do not add value and do not relate to current conditions. Inertia should be overcome by the reengineering philosophy. For example, at one time letters were commonly produced by a lawyer dictating to a shorthand secretary; then by dictating to a machine to be transcribed; then to a centralized word processing center; then by secretaries or administrative assistants using decentralized word processors or computers; and now by lawyers with personal computers on their desks or on their laps wherever they may be located. With each change, adjustments in structure should have been made.

Much of this book is related to value, how to create it, how to sell it, and how to charge for it. Billing by the hour may not completely disappear, but it is a reasonable prediction that *straight hourly billing*, that is, the uncontrolled running of the meter, will be greatly diminished within the foreseeable future. Clients do not want to buy hours; they want to buy results.

F. Leary Davis, a professor at Campbell University School of Law, wrote a thought-provoking article published in the *Campbell Law Review* in 1994 entitled, "Back to the Future: The Buyer's Market and the Need for Law Firm Leadership, Creativity, and Innovation."[8] Over the years Professor Davis, an "out of the box" thinker, has made perceptive observations about the state of the legal profession. In this law review article he traces how the legal market and legal profession have changed in the transition from a buyer's to a seller's market and back again over the past forty years: "The dominant cultural change in the seller's market was the advent of the billable hour, followed by the 'tyranny of the time sheet' during the transition back to a buyer's market." After examining the factors influencing the legal profession in the transition to a buyer's market, he sees three stages or waves. The first wave brought incremental tactical adjustments to the net income per partner formula. The second wave involved attempts to change the method of billing without changing the product. The genesis of the third wave was symbolized by the total quality management movement, particularly its client-centeredness and its call for changes in law firm culture.

In the following paragraphs from his article Professor Davis summarizes the focus on clients that characterizes the third wave:

> The thinking of lawyers has evolved from a focus on their needs in the first wave, through a rethinking of what they do and how they charge for it in the second wave, to a focus on the needs of clients in the third wave. Clients insist on this focus. When clients bargain for fixed, contingent, or percentage fees in a buyer's market, they are quite explicit about what they are and are not paying for. They are not paying for time, at least not in the sense of billable hours, or minutes or multiples of minutes. They desire certain events to occur, and they consider themselves to be paying for those events. The events may be closings of transactions or trials of cases, or they may be decisions—decisions that lead clients to pursue or refrain from certain courses of actions. Clients use lawyers to make these events happen because they lack the requisite information and skills to make the events happen by themselves or, if they possess the requisite knowledge or skill, because it remains economically efficient to utilize lawyers.
>
> Lawyers, then, help clients make and implement plans they cannot make, or find it economically inefficient to make and implement, by themselves. By thinking of lawyers' work in the contexts of planning and leadership, one can develop frameworks for reinvention of the profession. Leaders focus resources to create desirable opportunities.

Leaders, lawyers, and other planners use seven categories of resources in making and implementing plans. They are time, talent, commitment, capital, facilities, information, and positioning. . . .*

As clients make and implement their plans, they are most concerned about the timeliness and the quality of the events that lawyers help them facilitate. So value is a function of time and quality in the delivery of legal services. In any representation of clients' plans we can expect time to be inversely proportional and quality to be directly proportional to the quantity of the six planning resources other than time and to the harmony of their interplay.

The concept can be illustrated by depicting the resource of time as a frame in which the other resources are displayed.

TIME		
CAPITAL	TALENT	INFORMATION
FACILITIES	COMMITMENT	POSITIONING

The more of the other resources a firm possesses and the better coordinated their utilization, the smaller the time frame required for the firm's lawyers to cause events to occur for clients.

---

* 1. TIME. Time as a resource can be neither created nor destroyed. It merely provides a context or frame within which one can cause a series of events to occur. If it is not utilized for that purpose, the particular frame is gone forever. Time cannot be transferred from one person to another, but by working on projects together individuals can create large numbers of events as teams.

2. TALENT. Talent is the ability to do. It consists of knowledge and skill, plus the personal attributes that allow one to translate one's knowledge and skill into competent representation. Talent can be created. The more it is used, the more it grows. If talent is not used it will atrophy.

3. COMMITMENT. Commitment is what causes people to use their talent. Like talent, commitment must be utilized or it will disappear. But unlike talent, even when commitment is utilized it will deteriorate if its utilization is not reinforced at least intermittently by some positive response.

4. CASH AND OTHER CONSUMABLE OBJECTS. Cash can be traded for other resources or wasted. Either way, once it is used, it is gone, just as are stationery, envelopes, and other consumable supplies for which cash might be exchanged.

5. FACILITIES AND OTHER NONCONSUMABLE OBJECTS. To implement plans, one needs housing and hardware. If a firm aggregates individuals to build resources of time and talent, the firm must house them and have equipment with which they can work.

6. INFORMATION. Information used to be considered a subset of talent. Today information can be separated easily from personality, whether on computer disk, substantive system, or otherwise. Information can be leveraged. If it is marshalled into a substantive or procedural system, it can cause a series of events to occur in much less time than a talented individual without ordered information can make them occur. Information other lawyers do not have is very valuable, particularly in the form of a system. Information tends to become less valuable as others acquire and systematize it.

7. POSITIONING. Positioning is other people's perception of what one can do, not necessarily what one can in fact do. Creating this perception has a lot to do with trustworthiness and with integrity, the idea that one will do what one says one will do, and that if for any reason one is unable to do what one says, one will inform others so that they may protect themselves. Positioning relates to the ability of lawyers in firms to approach, be listened to, and to be believed by other lawyers, judges, potential witnesses, and the parties to proceedings and transactions.

Readily apparent characteristics of the seven resources are narrated in the footnote. It is useful to think about other aspects of their interplay. For instance, while specialized information is the resource around which the profession is built, information in the sense of raw data is not valuable in itself. It is the processing of information that makes it valuable. Both the speed and the quality of information processing within a firm are dependent upon the firm's facilities and the talent of its personnel. They are what translate information into decision-events. The conversion of information into work products will allow lawyers to remain both professionals and capitalists even if their ability to leverage associates' time disappears. As capitalists and as professionals, lawyers should remain aware that information loses value as it becomes readily available in the marketplace, that information-based experiential services can quickly become commodity services, and that the continuous creation of new information is necessary to retain positioning on the value curve.

The importance of positioning cannot be overemphasized. It is what motivates clients to come to lawyers for the differentiated and more expensive legal services that fall into the experiential and unique categories on the value curve. As the perception of others, positioning represents what people *think* a lawyer will do based upon preconceived ideas before the lawyer is retained. But thereafter the perception of the client is informed by experience. There exists a feedback loop between talent and positioning, and the perception of clients will be strengthened or weakened depending upon the lawyer's application of talent both in the rendering of legal services and in communicating with the client about the representation. In turn, the utilization of talent for those ends will depend upon the lawyer's commitment and the information and information-processing facilities available to the lawyer.

Commitment is the resource that is most imperiled in a billable hour culture that encourages lawyers to work physically taxing hours to meet unreasonable billable hour goals. At one level the billable hour culture is adverse to commitment to the goals of the client; it penalizes efficiency. The less time a lawyer takes to cause events for the client within the culture, the less money the lawyer makes. At a second level the billable hour culture encourages and even rewards overcommitment. Firms need many clients and cases to be assured their lawyers can work and charge for long hours. Yet the overcommitted lawyer becomes committed to no one. No single client is able to access the talent of the overcommitted lawyer, except at the expense of other clients. Information that would ordinarily be accessible to the lawyer becomes inaccessible because of cognitive distress and competing demands and distractions. The brief period of relation that falls between incubation and illumination phases of the creative process is unavailable to the lawyer when the truly creative solution is needed by the client. Finally, if lawyers are overcommitted they cannot do for clients what they have said they will do; as a result they lose their trustworthiness and their positioning.

Because of the interrelationships of planning resources, focusing them to create desirable opportunities is often complex. These interrelationships may be most readily apparent in small and midsized

> firms. Such firms certainly find it easier than do megafirms quickly to focus resources to solve problems and take advantage of opportunities. It is in these firms that we should expect to observe the first of the Third Wave innovations.

Professor Davis concludes with the thought that with tools unavailable in earlier years and with appropriate use of the seven planning resources lawyers have the potential to make more high-quality events occur for their clients in less time, and in the process of creating value for clients, to nurture the justice values that brought most lawyers to the profession in the first place.

Reinventing the corporation is a process that some major corporations have undertaken. An article by GE's Jack Welch entitled "A Master Class in Radical Change" in the December 13, 1993, issue of *Fortune* states

> At any business, the revolutionary process starts with an analysis of the business environment and the recognition that radical change is the organization's best response to the challenges it faces. That first stage is turbulent, marked by conflict, denial, and resistance. Next, leaders and employees begin to create a shared vision of what their company should become and turn their attention outward, to customers and competitors. In the final phase, the company creates systems for compensation and appraisal that enforce the new values and help reshape corporate culture. Ideally, the process never ends.[9]

In dealing with processes, flowcharts are useful to analyze how things are done now and how they might be accomplished using some other method. Old notions tend to disappear during the analytical exercise. For example, delegation has been preached as a management philosophy. With process engineering, too many "handoffs" are considered a sign of inefficiency, a flag that there is wasteful and redundant effort going on. It is important to note, however, that efficiency does not mean adding people or technology to make a system go faster, it means looking at an entire legal process and removing every obstacle (people, procedures, tasks) that wastes time and does not contribute specific value to the end result. Ideally, the result of a reengineering program should be a dramatic improvement in the cost of doing business. This means more efficient delivery of services internally and externally, lower service cost, greater productive capacity, and satisfied clients.

Whenever a task can be systematized or broken down into a series of minisystems it will be economical to do so. Whenever a system can be performed through the use of technology, that will further reduce the amount of human time required to accomplish the task and create the event or decision that clients want. Technology becomes the tool for improving quality, timeliness, and value. The system, manual or technological, then becomes an addition to the intellectual capital of the firm, the composite of the firm's knowledge, expertise, and skill.

The May/June issue of *Legal Management* contained two articles about the impact of technology "as an enabler" in the movement towards quality of services. *Using Technology to Help Implement Quality Management*[10] uses the billing process as an example of how technology can reduce the steps and improve the efficiency of that process. *Law Firm Re-Engineering Picks Up Speed with Technology's Help*[11] suggests that reengineering focuses on identifying the value-added and non-value-added aspects of a business process and eliminating the latter, and that reengineering can be divided into two categories, big "R" and small "r" reengineering. Big "R" reengineering reinvents the entire organization. Small "r" reengineering applies reengineering concepts to a pilot process or a single business process. The authors point out that automating a process should not be confused with reengineering a process. Making a process go faster differs from creating a better process. While technology may improve the efficiency of a given process, technology can create opportunities for improvement when new capabilities of technology open the door.

Examining the legal profession in 1995 to determine whether there is any consensus on how the profession is evolving and adjusting uncovers apparent contradictions. There is evidence of upheaval and major changes that are taking place and considerable searching for right answers. Some multinational firms have closed their foreign offices, yet others are expanding or are merging or becoming affiliated with firms in countries other than the United States. There is some indication that non–United States firms are moving in various ways into the U.S. domestic market.

In May 1995 *Of Counsel* released the results of its annual survey of the nation's seven hundred largest firms, which range in number of lawyers employed from 1,703 to 52.[12] The reporting group involved over 100,000 partners, associates, and counsel. This survey based on 1994 figures showed an overall growth of 2.1 percent, in contrast to 1 percent growth in 1993 and virtually no growth in 1992. The summary reports that the greater growth was in the larger firms included in the survey. Three reasons for the growth were given: improvement in the economy, the resurgence of complex, multitask new work that could not be handled by previously reduced staffs, and the end of the downsizing that had begun in 1991.

With respect to prior downsizing, the economic benefits from more efficient operations resulting from earlier corrective action influenced the survey results. Mergers were not as frequent, but acquisitions by cherry picking existed, including the absorption of lawyers from firms that dissolved or split. Altered demands by practice areas resulted from changes in the general economy. While it is difficult to generalize from the survey results, it is a fair statement that the changes reflect a search for correct answers and attempts to adjust to changing demands for legal services. While the survey reports average billable hours, it does not deal with billing methods or the revenues produced by various billing methods.

Mergers continue to occur, some firms being convinced that it is critical to be a full-service firm with national coverage. On the other hand, there have been spin-offs of individuals or practice groups from large firms into smaller, specialized firms. At this moment these are first-generation firms; it remains to be seen whether they will remain in that posture once the dominant lawyers who fostered the move retire or move onward and whether these smaller, specialized firms will yield to the temptation to expand in size and in the number of practice areas. "Boutique" often connotes "small," but today's boutique firm, in the sense of being a specialized firm with a single practice area, may practice nationally and be of substantial size.

In the quest for reduced costs, corporate counsel are looking for legal talent in smaller firms and, in many instances, firms located in nonmetropolitan areas. Some corporations have dissolved their legal departments and outsourced the functions.

There is sound evidence that nonlawyer organizations are staffing to compete with law firms in substantive areas previously the domain of law firms. Gary R. Garrett and Ward Bower wrote a thought-provoking white paper in 1995, "A Competitive Analysis of the Complex Litigation Services Market: Implications for Larger Law Firms,"[13] in which they observed:

> It is fairly clear that most of the Big 6, some regional accounting firms, law firm boutiques, and consultancies are actively seeking legal work in the litigation area at the expense of larger law firms.

• • •

> Litigators in private firms need to understand that clients, particularly in-house counsel, are very receptive to alternatives to traditional pricing of services and skeptical of large-firm management capabilities in general. There is no need to prove this point. Corporations are outsourcing litigation, partnering, creating consortiums to build task-based billing models, using bill auditing firms, soliciting competitive bids, mandating price reductions, selecting alternative providers, and narrowing their panels of law firms. In point of fact, most large law firms are viewed by consumers and many lawyers as inefficient and too costly.

Garrett and Bower document the specific steps taken by nonlawyer organizations to position themselves throughout the world, expending heavy funds to invade the traditional practice areas of lawyers. They postulate that law firms are, in the main, in a state of denial as relates to this new marketplace and that bar associations clearly have not gotten the message.

It is not just the larger firms that are threatened by new economic forces. Solo and small firms proliferate as new law graduates enter the market or established firms downsize or reduce the opportunities for partnership status. The partnership track has been extended, and many firms have developed a two-tiered partnership or permanent associate approach.[14]

Long-established firms have gone out of business when they were unable to adjust to new challenges, were debt-ridden, or had failed to provide for management succession. When firms are not prospering, internal conflicts and dissension rise to the surface.

In this setting of contradictory approaches to the buyer's market there are some confirmatory empirical data and also some surprises, as reflected by the 1995 Altman Weil Pensa Survey of Law Firm Economics, which is based on 1994 data drawn from 618 law firms.[15] Based on their 1994 receipts and disbursements, law firms appeared to blend increased receipts with better management practices to produce greater firm income per lawyer. Law firm gross receipts in 1994 were up 6.2 percent over 1993, while expenses per lawyer rose only 3.5 percent over the same period. Average income for law firms, per lawyer, reflected an improved 8.5 percent over 1993 performance.

Median billable hours dropped for partners, associates, and paralegals in 1994. However, with partners having 25 to 29 years of experience, the average number of hours billed held steady at 1,619. Five-year associate billable hours also remained essentially flat at 1,854 hours, up less than 1 percent from 1993. In 1994 hourly rates and realization rates increased. Lawyer compensation increased, the median compensation for all partners being up 5.4 percent to $168,000. Compensation for lawyers with 25 to 29 years of experience, however, rose only 1 percent over 1993.

The survey also indicated that senior lawyers in private law firms lagged behind their counterparts in corporate legal departments. In both 1993 and 1994 the median cash compensation of chief legal officers employed in industry surpassed the level of compensation of 25-to-29-year partner/shareholders in private practice by 7.7 percent.

In researching the law and by reason of their training, lawyers must look to the past; in carrying out the vision of the firm and in its management, the lawyer/manager must look to the future. With the challenges and unknowns of the future, successful lawyer/managers should have the following strengths and abilities:

- To project a **VISION** of the firm;
- To have **FLEXIBILITY** to consider new approaches;
- To adapt to **CHANGE** and to make changes occur;
- To effect a change in the **CULTURE** of the organization;
- To adopt the most effective **STRUCTURE** for the firm;
- To achieve **INTELLECTUAL LEVERAGING** of the firm's intellectual capital; and
- To have **ADAPTABILITY** to adjust to new situations.

All of these qualities inhere where a leader, a managing partner, the firm as a whole, a practice group, or one lonely lawyer as a voice in the firm wilderness is willing to take some risks and bring about change. The November 5, 1994, issue of *The Economist* in defending reengineering states it well:

> Reengineering is the mechanism for creating strengths in operating processes, which can then be exploited in many ways. Reengineering can be used to provide cost advantages or improved customer service, thereby defending an existing market; it can enable penetration of new markets for existing products; and it can provide entry into entirely new businesses, either by turning internal processes into revenue-generating services or by identifying new applications for the

> same skills. Companies would do well not to ignore reengineering, lest they find themselves staring down the barrel of a competitor's superior processes; and critics would do well to make sure they understand reengineering before they condemn it.[16]

Until a firm ceases to use hourly billing, the employment of systems for delivering substantive legal services is counterproductive, at least from the profitability standpoint. Once a firm is being paid for a service and not for the time it takes to deliver it, a systematic approach becomes the best way to ensure that the service can be accomplished at a profit. Fixed fees cause amazing things to happen: lawyers and their staffs find ingenious ways to improve efficiency and often come to realize that perhaps the old way was filled with time-consuming tasks that contributed to a firm's profits but did little to advance or add value to the matter being handled for the client. Simply put, firms will not begin to find ways to improve efficiency unless and until they have entered into alternative billing arrangements with their clients.

When law firms combine a systems approach to practice with nonhourly billing and process engineering, there are opportunities to improve the profit margin on legal services and to reduce the cost to clients. When this happens, firms will be enabled to increase the quality of their substantive legal services, provide a better return on the firm's work, and make it more likely that the firm will obtain even greater amounts of business, since the price for the services will actually decrease.[17]

Penultimately, here are four diverse, intellectually challenging notions for your consideration while you ponder the total impact of the major topics discussed thus far:

1. Geoffrey C. Hazard wrote an interesting article, "Size Creates Tension: Large-Firm Practice Can Threaten Professionalism," published in November 1994.[18] Because large firms must have a bureaucratic form of governance, the essence of professionalism (the exercise of professional judgment) rests with the senior lawyers and must be made on the basis of facts and legal research done by junior lawyers. Similarly, the junior lawyers are deprived of the opportunity to exercise professional judgment by being limited to working on preliminary or specialized aspects of the representation. As the result, senior lawyers are frustrated by a system that does not permit their developing the factual and legal research upon which to make the ultimate judgment; junior lawyers are frustrated by not being able to be involved with the total process of client representation.

2. Bullivant, Houser, Bailey, a medium-sized firm in the Pacific Northwest, undertook a program to meet the demands of clients for reduced costs, being able to see value, having greater involvement in making decisions during the litigation process, and sharing critical information.[19] The key was found in using technology and in devising ways to force decisions on critical issues earlier in the litigation process. Four core services forms are used: (a) evaluation form, (b) strategy form, (c) settle-

ment form, and (d) budget form. All forms are updated as consensus is reached with the client during the litigation process. All relevant information is stored electronically, with full access by the lawyers and the client. Client involvement, early analysis, considerations of cost, and full communication are the results. Is this a model for the future?

3. Is there another lawyering skill developing that will be indispensable in future law practice? In an article discussing the computer laboratory that Mark Hellman helped develop at the John Marshall Law School in Chicago, "Survival of the Techno-Savvy,"[20] David P. Vandagriff contends that when a lawyer presents a client's case during a video hearing, the ability to "think on-line"—to rapidly organize graphics and reference materials to display on the court's computer screen—will be just as vital as thinking on one's feet is in the courtroom.

4. The February 11, 1995, issue of *The Economist* has an article, "Technology and Unemployment: A World Without Jobs?"[21] that traces major technological inventions over the years that caused many people to lose their jobs. The article poses the question whether service industries such as lawyering will change so much by using technology that lawyers will no longer be needed. Making things more efficient may reduce jobs; making *new* things (or providing *new* services) using technology may have the effect of increasing employment.

The challenge that I pose after reading *The Economist* is whether the legal profession, using new methods and new technology, will be able to create new services at a reasonable cost to vastly expand the market for legal services to the large segments of the population who are now essentially unserved. How radical is my crystal ball?

While the future is hard to predict, one certainty is that law practice will change radically to meet the needs of clients. Some things will remain constant, namely, the importance of mutual trust and satisfaction in lawyer-client relationships. Where there is trust that lawyers are working in the interests of their clients, there will be loyal clients. With loyalty there will be mutually beneficial long-term relationships. With trust—mutually felt—many good things can happen. With trust, clients will be satisfied that they have received value. Where value has been conveyed, there will be long-term satisfaction. Clients must be happy with their lawyers; lawyers will be more motivated to provide quality services when they feel there are loyal and satisfied clients. In mutually beneficial relationships, favorable changes will be more apt to take place, including the movement towards more equitable billing practices.

Revolutionary changes in the legal profession are happening now. It is not possible to predict with certainty what changes will take place, but two certainties exist. Clients will demand quality services, and the billing and pricing method must reflect value. Remember that 79.5 percent of the 1995 survey firms expect the use of alternative billing methods to increase!

Are you ready?

NOTES

1. Janet Fox, "Want to Be Outrageous?," *Amtrak Express* (May/June 1994).

2. Ira D. Moskatel and Susan Resnick-West, "Starting with a Blank Sheet of Paper: Reengineering Law Practice," *Law Practice Management* (May/June 1994): 30.

3. Theodore B. Kinni, "A Reengineering Primer," *Quality Digest* (January 1994).

4. Mike France, "Reengineer Your Lawyers," *Forbes ASAP.*

5. Daniel B. Mahoney, "The Revolt: Where It's Leading," *Revolutionizing Litigation Management* (Washington, D.C.: Business Development Associates, Inc., March 1995).

6. Fred H. Bartlit Jr., "The Revolt: Why and How It Began," *Revolutionizing Litigation Management* (Washington, D.C.: Business Development Associates, Inc., March 1995).

7. "Small Firms Big Clients," *American Bar Association Journal* (January 1995): 48.

8. F. Leary Davis, "Back to the Future: The Buyer's Market and the Need for Law Firm Leadership, Creativity, and Innovation," *Campbell Law Review* 16, no. 2 (Buies Creek, North Carolina: Campbell University School of Law, Spring 1994). Professor Davis has generously permitted use of any or all of the materials contained in his law review article, whether by direct quotation, paraphrase, or abridgment.

9. Jack F. Welch, "A Master Class in Radical Change," *Fortune* (December 13, 1993): 82.

10. Louise H. Booth and M. Catherine Stevens, "Using Technology to Help Implement Quality Management," *Legal Management* (Association of Legal Administrators, May/June 1995): 85.

11. Lisa Rasmussen Smith and John M. Kuttler, "Law Firm Reengineering Picks Up Speed with Technology's Help," *Legal Management* (Association of Legal Administrators, May/June 1995): 97.

12. Larry Smith, editor in chief, *Of Counsel* 14, nos. 9 & 10 (Aspen Law & Business, a division of Aspen Publishers, Inc., May 1995).

13. Gary R. Garrett and Ward Bower, "A Competitive Analysis of the Complex Litigation Services Market: Implications for Larger Law Firms," Altman Weil Pensa, 1995 (a privately distributed paper).

14. Thom Weidlich, "No-Share Partners on Rise: Nearly Half of Big Firms Have a Non-Equity Track," *National Law Journal* (October 25, 1993): 1.

15. *1995 Survey of Law Firm Economics* (Newtown Square, Pennsylvania: Altman Weil Pensa, Inc.).

16. *The Economist* (Nov. 5, 1994): 70.

17. James Wilber, "Increasing the Profitability of Legal Services through Reengineering," *Report to Legal Management* 21, no. 8 (Newtown Square, Pennsylvania: Altman Weil Pensa Publications, Inc., May 1995).

18. Geoffrey C. Hazard, "Size Creates Tension: Large-Firm Practice Can Threaten Professionalism," *National Law Journal* (Nov. 21, 1994): A21.

19. Cynthia Lavoie, "A Seattle Law Firm Uses Technology to Improve Client Satisfaction," *Legal Management* (Association of Legal Administrators, March/April 1994).

20. David P. Vandagriff, "Survival of the Techno-Savvy: Electronic Communication for Lawyers Will Be Vital in a Computerized Future," *American Bar Association Journal* (March 1995): 84.

21. "Technology and Unemployment: A World without Jobs?" *The Economist* (February 11, 1995): 21.

UNIFORM TASK-BASED MANAGEMENT SYSTEM

Litigation Code Set

April 7, 1995
Final Draft

THIS DOCUMENT CONTAINS the Litigation Code Set and related definitions developed by a tripartite initiative of the American Bar Association Section of Litigation, the American Corporate Counsel Association, and a sponsoring group of major corporate law departments and law firms.

Table of Contents

Overview

The Uniform Task-Based Management System is a budgeting and billing system designed to provide clients and law firms with meaningful cost information on legal services. The first major area of legal work addressed by the System is litigation. This document presents the Litigation Code Set and definitions developed by a tripartite effort of the American Bar Association Section of Litigation, the American Corporate Counsel Association, and a group of major corporate clients and law firms coordinated and supported by Price Waterhouse LLP. The System enables lawyers to budget and bill by litigation task, aiding client and counsel in understanding, managing and conducting litigations. It is intended to cover all contested matters, including judicial litigation, binding arbitration and regulatory/administrative proceedings.

The goals of the Litigation Code Set are to:

1. Enable client and counsel to plan and maintain an efficient and effective litigation.
2. Facilitate effective communication of the tasks and costs of litigation and any variations from the expected or the norm.
3. Provide each client and law firm with a means to individually understand and compare the cost of litigation, for greater efficiency and as a foundation for use of alternative billing arrangements.
4. Harmonize the various task-based efforts to ease widespread adoption of a simple, concise and flexible task-based management approach.

The Litigation Code Set is grouped into five basic phases or aspects of a litigation, plus expenses:

- Case assessment, Development and Administration
- Pre-Trial Pleadings and Motions
- Discovery
- Trial Preparation and Trial
- Appeal.

Each phase consists of a number of tasks, such as Written Discovery, Document Production and Depositions. All work associated with a task should be included in that category. For example, Depositions (L330) encompasses all time spent on depositions including deposition notices and subpoenas, deposition scheduling and logistics, planning for and preparing to take the depositions and any deposition summaries. The intent is to provide a true picture of the labor cost of each task. (Out-of-pocket expenses, such as witness fees and transcripts, are treated under Expenses.)

For each billing period, the time charges by attorney or other professional are recorded by task. Expenses are similarly tracked. The System also allows for accumulation of the time charges and expenses, providing a comparison at a glance of the cost of each phase and each task for the month, for a specified budget period, and cumulatively for the litigation.

For those desiring, a budget can be prepared for each phase, and within that, each task for the whole case and/or by quarter. The monthly bills would then compare that month's bill and the cumulative total with the budget.

The System also provides a long form for those wishing to capture the task-based work by specific activity. The activity identifies how the work is being performed (e.g., communicating in firm, researching, drafting, and reviewing). For this purpose, any or all of eleven activities can be used with any or all of the tasks of the System.

The intention of the Litigation Code Set is to minimize multiple interpretation and options for coding time. It is recognized that not all litigation work will fit neatly in a particular category. Work can overlap tasks, categories may be imprecise, or time may be expended on the truly unusual. Please try to categorize the work to its primary purpose. Definitions are provided for guidance. Where uncertainty envelopes substantial or repeating work, it is best for client and counsel to agree in advance on the category to be used.

Following the Litigation Code Set is additional information about the history and background of this initiative, and the guiding principles and assumptions that informed the development of the Litigation Code Set. It is important to understand the considerations that went into the development of consensus around a single standard.

Litigation Code Set

L100 *Case Assessment, Development and Administration*

- L110 Fact Investigation/Development
- L120 Analysis/Strategy
- L130 Experts/Consultants
- L140 Document/File Management
- L150 Budgeting
- L160 Settlement/Non-Binding ADR
- L190 Other Case Assessment, Development and Administration

L200 *Pre-Trial Pleadings and Motions*

- L210 Pleadings
- L220 Preliminary Injunctions/Provisional Remedies
- L230 Court Mandated Conferences
- L240 Dispositive Motions
- L250 Other Written Motions and Submissions
- L260 Class Action Certification and Notice

L300 *Discovery*

- L310 Written Discovery
- L320 Document Production
- L330 Depositions
- L340 Expert Discovery
- L350 Discovery Motions
- L390 Other Discovery

L400 *Trial Preparation and Trial*

- L410 Fact Witnesses
- L420 Expert Witnesses
- L430 Written Motions and Submissions
- L440 Other Trial Preparation and Support
- L450 Trial and Hearing Attendance
- L460 Post-Trial Motions and Submissions
- L470 Enforcement

L500 *Appeal*

- L510 Appellate Motions and Submissions
- L520 Appellate Briefs
- L530 Oral Argument

A100 *Activities*

- A101 Plan and prepare for
- A102 Research
- A103 Draft/revise
- A104 Review/analyze
- A105 Communicate (in firm)
- A106 Communicate (with client)
- A107 Communicate (other outside counsel)
- A108 Communicate (other external)
- A109 Appear for/attend
- A110 Manage data/files
- A111 Other

E100 *Expenses*

- E101 Copying
- E102 Outside printing
- E103 Word processing
- E104 Facsimile
- E105 Telephone
- E106 Online non-legal research
- E107 Online legal research
- E108 Delivery services/messenger
- E109 Postage
- E110 Ground transportation
- E111 Airfare
- E112 Hotel
- E113 Meals
- E114 Court fees
- E115 Subpoena fees
- E116 Witness fees
- E117 Deposition transcripts
- E118 Trial transcripts
- E119 Trial exhibits
- E120 Litigation support vendors
- E121 Experts
- E122 Private
- E123 Arbitrators/mediators
- E124 Local counsel
- E125 Other professionals
- E126 Other

Litigation Code Set: Sample Budget Format

Case: ______________________________

Month From Inception: ______________________________

Budget Period: ______________________________

Month into Budget Period: ______________________________

Current Billings	For Budget Period		From Inception	
	Budget	Bills to Date	Budget	Bills to Date

L100 *Case Assessment, Development and Administration*

- L110 Fact Investigation/Development
- L120 Analysis/Strategy
- L130 Experts/Consultants
- L140 Document/File Management
- L150 Budgeting
- L160 Settlement/Non-Binding ADR
- L190 Other Case Assessment, Development and Administration

L200 *Pre-Trial Pleadings and Motions*

- L210 Pleadings
- L220 Preliminary Injunctions/Provisional Remedies
- L230 Court Mandated Conferences
- L240 Dispositive Motions
- L250 Other Written Motions and Submissions
- L260 Class Action Certification and Notice

L300 *Discovery*

- L310 Written Discovery
- L320 Document Production
- L330 Depositions
- L340 Expert Discovery
- L350 Discovery Motions
- L390 Other Discovery

L400 *Trail Preparation and Trial*

- L410 Fact Witnesses
- L420 Expert Witnesses
- L430 Written Motions and Submissions
- L440 Other Trial Preparation and Support
- L450 Trial and Hearing Attendance
- L460 Post-Trial Motions and Submissions
- L470 Enforcement

L500 *Appeal*

- L510 Appellate Motions and Submissions
- L520 Appellate Briefs
- L530 Oral Argument

L600 *Expenses (Itemize)*

TOTAL

Litigation Code Definitions

The Litigation Code Set is intended for use in all adversarial matters including litigation, binding arbitrations, and regulatory/administrative proceedings. The following definitions elaborate on the intended scope of each phase and task and should guide attorneys in coding time.

L100 Case Assessment, Development and Administration. Focuses on the cases as a whole, the "forest" rather than the "trees."

L110 Fact Investigation/Development. All actions to investigate and understand the facts of a matter. Covers interviews of client personnel and potential witnesses, review of documents to learn the facts of the case (but not for document production, L320), work with an investigator, and all related communications and correspondence.

L120 Analysis/Strategy. The thinking, strategizing, and planning for a case, including discussions, writing, and meetings on case strategy. Also includes initial legal research for case assessment purposes and legal research for developing a basic case strategy. Most legal research will be under the primary task for which the research is conducted, such as research for a summary judgment motion (L240). Once concrete trial preparation begins, use L440 for trial strategy and planning.

L130 Experts/Consultants. Identifying and interviewing experts and consultants (testifying or non-testifying), working with them, and developing expert reports. Does not include preparing for expert depositions (L340) or trial (L420).

L140 Document/File Management. A narrowly defined task that comprises only the processes of creating and populating document and other databases or filing systems. Includes the planning, design, and overall management of this process. Work of outside vendors in building litigation support databases should be an Expense.

L150 Budgeting. Covers developing, negotiating, and revising the budget for a matter.

L160 Settlement/Non-Binding ADR. All activities directed specifically to settlement. Encompasses planning for and participating in settlement discussions, conferences, and hearings and implementing a settlement. Covers pursuing and participating in mediation and other non-binding Alternative Dispute Resolution (ADR) procedures. Also includes pre-litigation demand letters and ensuing discussions.

L190 Other Case Assessment, Development and Administration. Time not attributable to any other overall task. Specific use in a given matter often may be pre-determined jointly by the client and law firm.

L200 Pre-Trial Pleadings and Motions. Covers all pleadings and all pretrial motions and procedures other than discovery.

L210 Pleadings. Developing (researching, drafting, editing, filing) and reviewing complaints, answers, counter-claims and third party complaints. Also embraces motions directed at pleadings such as motions to dismiss, motions to strike, and jurisdictional motions.

L220 Preliminary Injunctions/Provisional Remedies. Developing and discussing strategy for these remedies, preparing motions, affidavits and briefs, reviewing opponent's papers, preparing for and attending court hearings, preparing witnesses for the hearing, and effectuating the remedy.

L230 Court Mandated Conferences. Preparing for and attending hearings and conferences required by court order or procedural rules (including Rule 16 sessions) other than settlement conferences (L160).

L240 Dispositive Motions. Developing and discussing strategy for or opposing motions for judgment on the pleadings and motions for complete or partial summary judgment, preparing papers, reviewing opponent's papers, defensive motions (e.g., motion to strike affidavit testimony, Rule 56(f) motion), and preparing for and attending the hearing.

L250 Other Written Motions/Submissions. Developing, responding to, and arguing all motions other than dispositive (L240), pleadings (L210), and discovery (L350), such as motions to consolidate, to bifurcate, to remand, to stay, to compel arbitration, for MDL treatment and for change of venue.

L260 Class Action Certification and Notice. Proceedings unique to class action litigation and derivative suits such as class certification and notice.

L300 Discovery. Includes all work pertaining to discovery according to court or agency rules.

L310 Written Discovery. Developing, responding to, objecting to, and negotiating interrogatories and requests to admit. Includes mandatory meet-and-confer sessions. Also covers mandatory written disclosures as under Rule 26(a).

L320 Document Production. Developing, responding to, objecting to, and negotiating document requests, including the mandatory meet-and-confer sessions to resolve objections. Includes identifying documents for production, reviewing documents for privilege, effecting production, and preparing requested privilege lists. (While a general review of documents produced by other parties falls under this task, coding and entering produced documents into a data base is Task L140 and reviewing documents primarily to understand the facts is Task L110.)

L330 Depositions. All work concerning depositions, including determining the deponents and the timing and sequence of depositions, preparing deposition notices and subpoenas, communicating with opposing or other party's counsel on scheduling and logistics, planning for and preparing to take the depositions, discussing deposition strategy, preparing witnesses, reviewing documents for deposition preparation, attending depositions, and drafting any deposition summaries.

L340 Expert Discovery. Same as L330, but for expert witnesses.

L350 Discovery Motions. Developing, responding to, and arguing all motions that arise out of the discovery process. Includes the protective order process.

L390 Other Discovery. Less frequently used forms of discovery, such as medical examinations and on-site inspections.

L400 Trial Preparation and Trial. Commences when lawyer and client determine that trial is sufficiently likely and imminent so that the process of actually preparing for trial begins. It continues through the trial and post-trial proceedings in the trial court. Once trial begins, lawyers who appear in court presumptively should bill their court time to L450 Trial and Hearing Attendance. Litigation work outside the courtroom during this phase (e.g., evenings, weekends and the time of other attorneys and support personnel), should continue to be classified using other L400 Tasks.

L410 Fact Witnesses. Preparing for examination and cross-examination of non-expert witnesses.

L420 Expert Witnesses. Preparing for examination and cross-examination of expert witnesses.

L430 Written Motions/Submissions. Developing, responding to and arguing written motions during preparation for trial and trial, such as motions in limine and motions to strike proposed evidence. Also includes developing other written pre-trial and trial filings, such as jury instructions, witness lists, proposed findings of fact and conclusions of law, and trial briefs.

L440 Other Trial Preparation and Support. All other time spent in preparing for and supporting a trial, including developing overall trial strategy, preparing opening and closing arguments, establishing an off-site support office, identifying documents for use at trial, preparing demonstrative materials, etc.

L450 Trial and Hearing Attendance. Appearing at trial, at hearings and at courtmandated conferences, including the pre-trial conferences to prepare for trial. For scheduling conferences that are denominated as "Pre-Trial Conferences," but not directed toward conduct of the trial, use Task L230.

L460 Post-Trial Motions and Submissions. Developing, responding to and arguing all post-verdict matters in the trial court, such as motions for new trial or j.n.o.v. for stay pending appeal, bills of costs, and requests for attorney's fees.

L470 Enforcement. All work performed in enforcing and collecting judgments and asserting or addressing defenses thereto.

L500 Appeal. Covers all work on appeal or before a reviewing body.

L510 Appellate Motions and Submissions. Developing, responding to and arguing motions and other filings before a reviewing body, such as motions and other filings for stay pending appeal.

L520 Appellate Briefs. Preparing and reviewing appellate briefs.

L530 Oral Argument. Preparing for and arguing an appeal before a reviewing body.

Initiative Background, Definitions, Principles, and Assumptions

A. The Need

Emerging trends in the relationships between law firms and their corporate clients have led to a need for standardization in the categories used by law firms to plan, budget, and bill for their services. In the past few years several initiatives to develop standard categories have been announced and have made important contributions to the visibility of this issue. However, none seems to have progressed to the point of being widely accepted in the industry.

In the past year, Price Waterhouse LLP has coordinated an industry initiative—led by fifty corporate law departments and law firms—to build off these earlier efforts and establish these standards. From the beginning planning stages, this initiative has been open to various industry groups, including the American Bar Association Section of Litigation, the American Corporate Counsel Association, and the West Coast Bank Group. Shortly after the first kick-off meeting, an agreement was reached to work jointly toward developing a standard approach.

Until the past decade, law firm billing was relatively straightforward. Firms billed their clients in greater or lesser detail, typically providing in-depth narrative descriptions of the tasks and processes underlying their hourly charges. In issuing bills and providing the underlying detail, each firm followed its own approach. In recent years, however, law departments have become more focused in requesting additional billing information of their outside law firms, or asking that billing data be presented in specific formats. In some instances companies have wanted to analyze their costs along various dimensions to provide benchmarks for the more systematic evaluation of legal costs. In others, there has been a desire to develop a database of costs on discrete legal activities. Most of these efforts have been part of an overriding effort to manage corporate legal expenses more effectively by considering inside/outside mix, comparative performance by attorneys and firms of discrete activities, and other aspects of cost.

As a consequence of these trends, many law firms' administrative organizations are faced with the challenge of complying with a broad range of specialized billing requirements—each unique to one client. This situation already poses a substantial burden to a number of firms. As law departments expand their use of "task-based billing" and broaden their efforts to manage outside legal costs more effectively, firms face the prospect of overwhelming complexity as they strive to comply with the various requests of dozens of clients. Ultimately, law departments will be burdened by different law firm coding structures and billing systems.

Aside from "need" narrowly defined, there are significant benefits to both law firms and law departments in terms of administrative simplicity and cost reduction to be gained from standardization. In addition, the development of standard billing categories will permit introduction of billing based on Electronic Data Interchange (EDI). This technology is already widely employed in other areas of commercial activity. By linking the suppliers and consumers of legal services, EDI offers the prospect of "paperless billing" and a new level of administrative and cost efficiency.

The need, therefore, is for a uniform set of billing and task categories—detailed describers of legal work that would be acceptable to both law departments and firms, and that could prevail across American industry, financial services, and commerce. Analogous to the role of standards in other industries and functions, standard billing categories would make it possible for law firms to standardize their billing systems and for corporate law departments to work with their law firms in a far more efficient manner than prevails today.

B. Definitions

Following is a glossary of terms that will be helpful in understanding the Litigation Code Set.

1. **Coding set/coding scheme.** A list of alphanumeric codes and corresponding terms and definitions that describe the universe of legal work in a given area.
2. **Field.** A specific, defined category of information that is entered into an information management system or database.
3. **Area of law.** A label describing a discrete area of legal practice or specialization. Examples include real estate, intellectual property, and environmental. The group envisions that each department and firm would define these as appropriate.
4. **Matter type.** This designation describes or categorizes a specific legal services project for purposes of analysis and reporting. In most cases, matter types are more detailed than areas of law though for some specialized areas of law there may not be a more detailed listing of matter types. For example, a litigation case might be categorized as an antitrust, environmental, international trade, etc. matter.
5. **Phase.** This is the highest level category in the coding hierarchy. For litigation, examples are preliminary case assessment and discovery. Phases represent collections of tasks and activities that occur largely in a sequence during the course of a case or matter. Typically, timekeepers will enter time at the task level, but phase-level time entry will also be permitted. This might be useful in smaller cases in which task-level detail is not needed.
6. **Task.** This represents more detail under the phase level in the coding hierarchy. All tasks roll up to a phase. Tasks are intended to capture tangible work product produced or business results achieved. Tasks (or phases) are one of two fields to be recorded by timekeepers.
7. **Activity.** This is a code intended to describe how work is accomplished (e.g., communicating, drafting). Activities represent the second field to be recorded (optionally) by timekeepers.

C. Principles

The following list of guiding principles has informed the development of the Litigation Code Set. These principles emerged throughout a number of meetings held during 1994 and early 1995 and discussions of the various options under consideration.

1. **Support of business objectives and processes.** A primary, recurring consideration has been to focus on the purposes and uses of standardized coding. A number of business objectives and administrative processes that should be supported by the coding scheme were identified. These include planning and budgeting, time entry, status monitoring and reporting, bill preparation, electronic transmission of bills and payments, bill review and analysis, development

of alternative financial arrangements, and practice and profitability analysis. Consistently, the group returned to the question: How are we going to use the data to be tracked?

2. **Simplicity.** The Litigation Code Set must be simple and straightforward to ensure widespread use. This includes limiting the total number of codes to a manageable level. The team consistently returned to this fundamental principle as it explored a wide range of alternatives, which frequently suggested more detailed coding schemes than we developed.

3. **Ease of use.** In practice, the Litigation Code Set should be easy for attorneys and other staff to use. The codes should be intuitive and capture an attorney's logical work processes.

4. **Suitability for all size offices.** Currently-available technology will be an important asset in the efficient implementation of the coding scheme. Still, the group has assumed that not all law offices will have technology solutions at their disposal to facilitate the capture and analysis of time. For the coding scheme to be used widely, law offices and attorneys must be able to use the codes in a manual fashion.

5. **Avoidance of multiple interpretation.** A primary concern with some existing code sets is the multitude of ways in which a single time entry can be coded, depending on individual interpretation. The codes should minimize opportunity for multiple interpretation.

6. **Flexibility to track both tasks and activities.** Some team members value the ability to analyze work according to categories of activity (e.g., communication, drafting) in addition to task (e.g., deposition). Others emphasize the importance of tracking and analyzing the level of effort expended to complete tangible work product, segments of a case, or defined business objectives. For this group, simply using task codes is sufficient. As an option for those seeking activity detail, the System permits firms and departments to code activities separately from tasks.

D. Assumptions

Following is a list of assumptions that guided the development of the Litigation Code Set. These assumptions were drawn from discussions during past team meetings.

1. **The fundamental coding structure has two fields: tasks (embedded within phases) and activities.** Whereas task codes track time associated with tangible work product accomplished (e.g., motion, deposition), activity codes describe how the work was performed (e.g., communicating, drafting). Not every law office will wish to use activity codes, but the coding scheme is flexible to accommodate those who value activity analysis. The team discussed the desirability of coding at a lower level below task. In the interest of simplicity, though, this additional detail may be captured using narrative rather than adding more levels. This experience was borne out by those team members with direct experience coding time.

2. **Narrative time entries will be retained.** The Litigation Code Set does not envision the elimination of narrative descriptions of time entries. However, the need for this level of detail may be reduced in

smaller, less complex cases with successful adoption and implementation of the coding scheme.

3. For purposes of tracking and analysis, a matter type code distinguishes among various types of matters. A matter type designation can be used to distinguish among various types of litigation and to identify alternative dispute resolution matters.
4. The Litigation Code Set focuses on meeting the requirements of most matters. The Litigation Code Set has been designed to be suitable for use with most matters. However, there may exist cases of such size, complexity, or other unique characteristics that the codes are not sufficiently detailed. The objective was to develop a code set for the vast majority of cases and to provide a framework in which more detailed codes can be developed for extraordinary cases.

CORPORATE SPONSORS

American Airlines, Inc.
BellSouth Corporation
Chase Manhattan Bank, N.A.
Chrysler Corporation
Cigna Corporation
Citicorp/Citibank N.A.
Coca-Cola Company
Dow Chemical Company
DuPont Company
Eastman Kodak Company
Metropolitan Life Insurance Company
NationsBank Corporation
Niagara Mohawk Power Corporation
NYNEX Corporation
The Pacific Telesis Group
Pfizer Inc.
Philip Morris Companies Inc.
Prudential Insurance Company of America
TRW Inc.
Viacom International Inc.
Westinghouse Electric Corporation

LAW FIRM SPONSORS

Abelman, Frayne & Schwab
Adams, Duque & Hazeltine
Arnold & Porter
Cravath, Swaine & Moore
Crowell & Moring
Goodwin, Procter & Hoar
Heller Ehrman White & McAuliffe
Hunton & Williams
Jones, Day, Reavis & Pogue
Kenyon & Kenyon
King & Spalding
McCutchen, Doyle, Brown & Enersen
McMillan Binch
Milbank, Tweed, Hadley & McCloy
Nixon, Hargrave, Devans & Doyle
O'Melveny & Myers
Paul, Weiss, Rifkind, Wharton & Garrison
Peterson & Ross
Pillsbury Madison & Sutro
Reed Smith Shaw & McClay
Sedgwick, Detert, Moran & Arnold
Shearman & Sterling
Sidley & Austin
Skadden, Arps, Slate, Meagher & Flom
Weil, Gotshal & Manges
White & Case
Wilmer, Cutler & Pickering

LIAISONS FROM OTHER GROUPS

American Bar Association (ABA) Liaisons

J. Michael Hemmer, Covington & Burling
Richard Alpert, Digital Equipment Corporation
Robert D. Fram, Heller Ehrman White & McAuliffe*
Julie Welborn, Liberty Mutual Insurance Company
Raymond L. Ocampo, Jr., Oracle Corporation

American Corporate Counsel Association (ACCA) Liaisons

Charles H. Goodman, Independent Consultant
Richard Mulroy, Mutual Life Insurance Company of New York*
Mark Goodwin, Overnite Transportation Company

West Coast Banks Group Liaison

Michael T. Connell, Bank of California

*Also Steering Committee

Index

Selected Books from . . . THE SECTION OF LAW PRACTICE MANAGEMENT

ABA Guide to International Business Negotiations. A guide to the general, legal, and cultural issues that arise during international negotiations.

ABA Guide to Legal Marketing. A collection of new and innovative marketing ideas and strategies for lawyers and firms.

Becoming Computer Literate. A guide to computer basics for lawyers and other legal professionals.

Breaking Traditions. A guide to progressive, flexible, and sensible work alternatives for lawyers who want to balance the demands of the legal profession with other commitments. Model policy for childbirth and parenting leave is included.

Changing Jobs, 2nd Ed. A handbook designed to help lawyers make changes in their professional careers. Includes career planning advice from nearly fifty experts.

Compensation Plans for Law Firms, 2nd Ed. This second edition discusses the basics for a fair and simple compensation system for partners, of counsel, associates, paralegals, and staff.

Do-It-Yourself Public Relations. A hands-on guide for lawyers with public relations ideas, sample letters, and forms. The book comes with a diskette that includes model letters to the press that have paid off in news stories and media attention.

Finding the Right Lawyer. A guide that answers the questions people need to ask when searching for legal counsel. It includes a glossary of legal specialties and the ten questions you should ask a lawyer before hiring.

Flying Solo: A Survival Guide for the Solo Lawyer, 2nd Ed. An updated and expanded guide to the problems and issues unique to the solo practitioner.

Getting Started: Basics for a Successful Law Firm. A book that addresses a variety of issues on forming partnerships for the practice of law. It also includes a model partnership agreement on diskette.

How to Draft Bills Clients Rush to Pay. A collection of techniques for drafting bills that project honesty, competence, fairness, and value and how to draft an inviting statement.

How to Start and Build a Law Practice, 3rd Ed. Jay Foonberg's classic guide has been updated and expanded. Included are more than ten new chapters on marketing, financing, automation, practicing from home, and ethics and professional responsibility.

Introduction to Desktop Publishing. A concise guide to learning the essential elements, techniques, and advantages of desktop publishing.

Law Office Staff Manual for Solos and Small Firms. A book to help solo and small firm practitioners set up their own law office staff manuals. It includes a diskette containing the text of the manual. The diskette is in WordPerfect 5.1 and ASCII formats.

Lawyer's Guide to the Internet. A no-nonsense guide to what the Internet is (and isn't), how it applies to the legal profession, and the different ways it can—and should—be used.

Leveraging with Legal Assistants. Reviews the changes that have led to increased use of legal assistants and the need to enlarge their role further. Learn specific ways in which a legal assistant can handle a substantial portion of traditional lawyer work.

LOCATE, 1995–96. Co-published with the Association of Legal Administrators. It includes about 140 vendors, 300–400 different software products, and totally revamped listings that will make it easy for you to find the right software.

Microsoft® Word for Windows® in One Hour for Lawyers. This book includes special tips for users of Windows 95. It contains four easy lessons—timed at fifteen minutes each—that will help lawyers prepare, save, and edit a basic document.

Results-Oriented Financial Management. A Guide to Successful Law Firm Financial Performance. How to manage "the numbers," from setting rates and computing billable hours to calculating net income and preparing the budget. Over thirty charts and statements to help you prepare reports.

Through the Client's Eyes: New Approaches to Get Clients to Hire You Again and Again. Includes an overview of client relations and sample letters, surveys, and self-assessment questions to gauge your client relations acumen.

TQM in Action: One Firm's Journey Toward Quality and Excellence. A guide to implementing the principles of Total Quality Management in your law firm.

Win-Win Billing Strategies. Represents the first comprehensive analysis of what constitutes "value," and how to bill for it. You'll learn how to initiate and implement different billing methods that make sense for you and your client.

Winning with Computers, Part 1. Addresses virtually every aspect of the use of computers in litigation. You'll get an overview of products available and tips on how to put them to good use. For the beginning and advanced computer user.

Winning with Computers, Part 2. Expands on the ways you can use computers to manage the routine and not-so-routine aspects of your trial practice. Learn how to apply general purpose software and even how to have fun with your computer.

Women Rainmakers' 101+ Best Marketing Tips. A collection of over 130 marketing tips suggested by women rainmakers throughout the country. Includes tips on image, networking, public relations, and advertising.

WordPerfect® 6.1 for Windows® in One Hour for Lawyers. This is a crash course in the most popular word processing software package used by lawyers. In four lessons, you'll learn the basic steps for getting a simple job done.

WordPerfect® Shortcuts for Lawyers: Learning Merge and Macros in One Hour. A fast-track guide to two of WordPerfect's more advanced functions: merge and macros. Includes four lessons designed to take fifteen minutes each.

Order Form

Qty	Title	LPM Price	Regular Price	Total
_______	ABA Guide to International Business Negotiations (511-0331)	$ 74.95	$ 84.95	$_______
_______	ABA Guide to Legal Marketing (511-0341)	69.95	79.95	$_______
_______	Becoming Computer Literate (511-0342)	32.95	39.95	$_______
_______	Breaking Traditions (511-0320)	64.95	74.95	$_______
_______	Changing Jobs, 2nd Ed. (511-0334)	49.95	59.95	$_______
_______	Compensation Plans for Law Firms, 2nd Ed. (511-0353)	69.95	79.95	$_______
_______	Do-It-Yourself Public Relations (511-0352)	69.95	79.95	$_______
_______	Finding the Right Lawyer (511-0339)	19.95	19.95	$_______
_______	Flying Solo, 2nd Ed. (511-0328)	59.95	69.95	$_______
_______	Getting Started (511-0363)	64.95	74.95	$_______
_______	How to Draft Bills Clients Rush to Pay (511-0344)	39.95	49.95	$_______
_______	How to Start and Build a Law Practice, 3rd Ed. (511-0293)	32.95	39.95	$_______
_______	Introduction to Desktop Publishing (511-0357)	19.95	29.95	$_______
_______	Law Office Staff Manual for Solos and Small Firms (511-0361)	49.95	59.95	$_______
_______	Lawyer's Guide to the Internet (511-0343)	24.95	29.95	$_______
_______	Leveraging with Legal Assistants (511-0322)	59.95	69.95	$_______
_______	LOCATE 1995–96 (511-0359)	65.00	75.00	$_______
_______	Microsoft® Word for Windows® in One Hour (511-0358)	19.95	29.95	$_______
_______	Results-Oriented Financial Management (511-0319)	44.95	54.95	$_______
_______	Through the Client's Eyes (511-0337)	69.95	79.95	$_______
_______	TQM in Action (511-0323)	59.95	69.95	$_______
_______	Win-Win Billing Strategies (511-0304)	89.95	99.95	$_______
_______	Winning with Computers, Part 1 (511-0294)	89.95	99.95	$_______
_______	Winning with Computers, Part 2 (511-0315)	59.95	69.95	$_______
_______	Winning with Computers, Parts 1 & 2 (511-0316)	124.90	144.90	$_______
_______	Women Rainmakers' 101+ Best Marketing Tips (511-0336)	14.95	19.95	$_______
_______	WordPerfect® 6.1 for Windows® in One Hour for Lawyers (511-0354)	19.95	29.95	$_______
_______	WordPerfect® Shortcuts for Lawyers (511-0329)	14.95	19.95	$_______

*HANDLING
$ 2.00–$9.99 . . . . $2.00
10.00–24.99 . . . . $3.95
25.00–49.99 . . . . $4.95
50.00 + ... $5.95

**TAX
DC residents add 5.75%
IL residents add 8.75%
MD residents add 5%

SUBTOTAL: $_______
*HANDLING: $_______
**TAX: $_______

TOTAL: $_______

PAYMENT
☐ Check enclosed (Payable to the ABA) ☐ Bill Me
☐ Visa ☐ MasterCard ☐ American Express Account Number: _______-_______-_______-_______

Exp. Date: _______ Signature _______________

Name _______________

Firm _______________

Address _______________

City _______________ State _______________ ZIP _______________

Phone number _______________

Mail to: ABA, Publication Orders, P.O. Box 10892, Chicago, IL 60610-0892

Phone: (312) 988-5522
Email: abasvcctr@attmail.com
Fax: (312) 988-5568
World Wide Web: http//www.abanet.org/lpm/catalog

BOOK

THE SECTION OF LAW PRACTICE MANAGEMENT

CUSTOMER COMMENT FORM

ABA

Title of Book:______________________________

We've tried to make this publication as useful, accurate, and readable as possible. Please take 5 munutes to tell us if we succeeded. Your comments and suggestions will help us improve our publications. Thank you!

1. How did you acquire this publication:

- ☐ by mail order
- ☐ at a meeting/convention
- ☐ as a gift
- ☐ by phone order
- ☐ at a bookstore
- ☐ don't know
- ☐ other: (describe)______________________________

Please rate this publication as follows:

	Excellent	Good	Fair	Poor	Not Applicable
Readability: Was the book easy to read and understand?	☐	☐	☐	☐	☐
Examples/Cases: Were they helpful, practical? Were there enough?	☐	☐	☐	☐	☐
Content: Did the book meet your expectations? Did it cover the subject adequately?	☐	☐	☐	☐	☐
Organization and clarity: Was the sequence of text logical? Was it easy to find what you wanted to know?	☐	☐	☐	☐	☐
Illustrations/forms/checklists: Were they clear and useful? Were there enough?	☐	☐	☐	☐	☐
Physical attractiveness: What did you think of the appearance of the publication (typesetting, printing, etc.)?	☐	☐	☐	☐	☐

Would you recommend this book to another attorney/administrator? ☐ Yes ☐ No

How could this publication be improved? What else would you like to see in it?

____

Do you have other comments or suggestions?______________________________

Name______________________________

Firm/Company______________________________

Address______________________________

City/State/ZIP______________________________ Phone______________________________

Firm Size______________________________ Area of specialization______________________________

We appreciate your time and help.

Fold

NO POSTAGE
NECESSARY
IF MAILED
IN THE
UNITED STATES

BUSINESS REPLY MAIL

FIRST CLASS PERMIT NO. 16471 CHICAGO, ILLINOIS

POSTAGE WILL BE PAID BY ADDRESSEE

AMERICAN BAR ASSOCIATION
PPM, 8TH FLOOR
750 N. LAKE SHORE DRIVE
CHICAGO, ILLINOIS 60611-9851

Fold